# Interpreting the World

Kant's philosophy of history and politics

Kant's philosophy of history and politics was made possible by his radical delimitation of the power of human reason. In this study, James Booth seeks to demonstrate the nature and relation of Kant's two revolutions in thought. The first and negative one showed the limits of reason; the second, positive one, which grew out of the first, showed the ability of reason to read purposiveness back into nature and to create moral law.

This book sets the resulting philosophy of history and politics against the background of Kant's moral theory and epistemology, and more generally the critical tradition that guides modern philosophy. In Kant, as in so much philosophy since his time, the spontaneity of human reason becomes the only light beckoning and guiding us, stripped as we are of all other resources by the critical approach to knowledge.

The analysis presented here reveals a Kantian philosophy of history and politics which, far from being a precursor of that developed later by Hegel and Marx, is profoundly sceptical of history and of historical optimism. Booth thus places Kant's political philosophy much closer to classical liberalism than to German idealism.

This book will be of interest to Kant scholars, students of political philosophy, and those concerned with the evolution of liberalism and of competing conceptions of man and society.

JAMES BOOTH is a professor in the Department of Political Science at Duke University in Durham, North Carolina.

WILLIAM JAMES BOOTH

# Interpreting the World:
# Kant's philosophy of
# history and politics

UNIVERSITY OF TORONTO PRESS
Toronto Buffalo London

© University of Toronto Press 1986
Toronto Buffalo London
Printed in Canada

ISBN 0-8020-2577-3

**Canadian Cataloguing in Publication Data**

Booth, William James.
  Interpreting the world
  Includes bibliographical references and index.
  ISBN 0-8020-2577-3
  1. Kant, Immanuel, 1724–1804.
  2. Kant, Immanuel, 1724–1804 — Knowledge, Theory of.
  3. History — Philosophy.  I. Title.
  B2798.B66 1985     193     C85-099603-1

To my parents

# Contents

# Preface

KANT AND MODERNITY

The work that follows is an essay on Immanuel Kant's philosophy of history and politics. Kant was born in Königsberg, East Prussia, in 1724 and died there some 79 years later. My concern here is not with him, but with the ideas to which his name is attached. These ideas have to do above all with the radical delimiting of what can be known, with the critique of traditional metaphysics and theology, with the negative autonomy that results from that critique, and, lastly, with the need to find new standards by which to direct our conduct in a world stripped of the old signposts.

The whole of the modern period might be said to be encompassed by that cluster of ideas. Forming the core of Kant's 'Copernican revolution,' they extend beyond the 79 years of his life and the works that he produced during those years. They are coterminous with modernity, and to illustrate what is meant by this I wish to make a somewhat free use of a passage from Hegel's *Philosophy of History*.

Hegel wrote that the Christian world had once believed in a transcendent God, embodied in the person of Christ. The Crusaders had then gone to Jerusalem in search of his body, but they discovered the tomb empty; they were searching, Hegel concludes, for what could not be found. Men then turned to the exploration of their own world, to the discovery of America and the revival of the Greek and Roman humanist texts.[1]

Hegel intended these remarks on the Crusades to describe a moment in the evolution of Christianity and its conception of the infinite. However, I would like to use this passage as a metaphor for a certain strand – the dominant one, perhaps – in modern philosophy and political philosophy. For want of a better term, we might call it the 'critical current,' which had as one of its central purposes the piercing of the pretensions of past philosophy, the setting of strict limits on the realm of the knowable, and the turn, in some cases joyous, from the speculative heavens to the mundane world of possible experience.

Kant, Hume, Wittgenstein, and much of contemporary Anglo-American philosophy belong, in their very different ways, to this current, as do Machiavelli, Hobbes, and Marx. To use Hegel's image, they have voyaged to Jerusalem (the history of metaphysics and theology) and found it for the most part empty. Chastened, and with a new sense of the worth of the mundane, they set out to discover the human things.

Hegel described this revolution, this turn from the heavens to the world, in the most positive of terms. It may, he wrote, 'be compared with that blush of dawn, which ... first betokens the return of a bright and glorious day.'[2] This description was later taken up by one of Hegel's most profound students, Karl Marx and given economic and political flesh and blood, and an agenda for action. Marx thought that the critique of philosophy and religion, the voyage to Jerusalem's empty tomb, had accomplished much. It had led to a revolution in consciousness, freeing men of their self-incurred illusions. But Marx also held that this revolution was not sufficient, for in place of the old masters of theology and metaphysics, a new one had emerged, the laws of capitalism. Philosophical critique was not adequate to the tasks of the revolution needed to overthrow this new form of the subjugation of man. Hence Marx rejected even the most radical philosophies of his time, the materialism and atheism of Feuerbach and the Young Hegelians, in the name of revolutionary praxis.

Hegel's joyous turn to the discovery of human things, following the voyage to Jerusalem, Marx recast in a markedly Promethean manner. The philosophical critique of religion and metaphysics was for him, but one stage in man's ascent to the mastery of his world. What was required was an extension of criticism from the objects of consciousness to society itself and a program to change the world in accordance with that criticism.

The single most important thread linking Marx's writings is the idea of mastery:[3] of nature, of illusion, of economy and society. The moral indignation that infuses Marx's thought, whether his outrage over life in an Indian village or over child labour in England, arises out of a sense of the subjugation of man, in the one case to the forces of nature and a primitive religion, in the other to the laws of the capitalist market-place.

Similarly, Marx's deep hostility to liberalism emerged from the thought that while liberalism leaves man in control of the political sphere, it subjects him to the rule of religion and capitalism in his private life.[4] Marx is sometimes said to have been largely silent on the nature of a future communist society. Marx's silence is attributed to his contempt for utopian socialism and to his desire to provide an empirical and scientific critique of capitalism. This is not quite so. The essential property of a communist society is already apparent in Marx's critique of capitalism. It is the ideal of mastery, of conscious human control over nature and history (society and economy).

On 16 April 1917, V.I. Lenin arrived at the Finland Station in Petrograd, there to preside over the dénouement of the old order and to found the Soviet regime. A version of Marx's idea of mastery was thereby placed at the centre of the twentieth century's political agenda. The voyage to the Finland Station was short, but the path leading to it was centuries old.

However, the road that leads from the empty tomb to the Finland Station is not the only path from Jerusalem. There is yet a second path. Its origin is, to be sure, the same, but it concludes not in the Promethean vision of mastery over God and nature but in the more modest ideal of a liberal society. Here the 'critical revolution,' the discovery of the empty tomb, is not (in Hegel's words) the beginning of 'a bright and glorious day,' but rather the source of a predicament, a practical and theoretical problem in need of a solution. This is how Alexis de Tocqueville described a somewhat similar revolution: 'Every revolution must shake ancient beliefs, sap authority and cloud shared ideas. So any revolution, to a greater or lesser extent, throws men back on themselves and opens to each man's view an almost limitless empty space.'[5]

It is in those terms that we must understand Kant's critical revolution. Kant grasped the fact that the radical delimiting of what can be known – the assertion that the boundaries of what can be known are coterminous with the range of possible experience – threatened to make the world (including the human world) an incommodious place from a moral point of view. It is part of Kant's greatness that he was one of the principal authors of that critical revolution. And it is a credit to his philosophical courage that he did not retreat from its conclusions, however threatening they were to moral life.

Kant clearly recognized that the critical revolution, the discovery of the empty sepulchre, was not the dawn of a bright new day. The political conclusions that he was led to were not those of the Promethean Marx, but rather something more limited, which nevertheless preserved human dignity. Ernest Gellner's account of Kant is, in this respect, completely accurate: 'Kant did not suppose that we could take with us, when entering the cold cognisable world, *all* our luggage, whole lorry-loads of conceptual furniture. He took the absolute minimum to save our humanity, to make us more than *things*; the rest he spurned ... He was like a refugee from a catastrophe who arrives, nobly carrying but the two or three beings dearest to him.'[6]

Among those things that Kant thought it most necessary to protect were man's moral autonomy and the ideal of a community of persons that reflected and respected that autonomy, namely a liberal regime. Kant's indignation was reserved for man's tendency to sacrifice his moral freedom to the pursuit of his own happiness, as well as for the practice of statesmen to treat their subjects as mere instruments of policy rather than as beings endowed with intrinsic moral worth. For Kant, then, the issue was not whether history could be subjected to the conscious control of men; it was not whether, with still more powerful means of production, man could master nature. Kant was profoundly sceptical of the principles of moral and political judgment to which such a focus could give rise. He saw in that type of judgment a guide for conduct that placed at the centre of our estimation of the worth of actions not the moral quality of the will directing them but their contribution to progress.[7]

The moral and political philosophy that in the end emerges from Kant's analysis centres around three fundamental ideas: the free will, respect for the moral law, and respect for the autonomy of others. Kantian liberalism therefore does not evoke images of Marx's humanizing of nature or of the radical transformation of man. Rather, what it yields is the idea of the quiet dignity of a community of man, an idea that rests on the recognition of the intrinsic worth (autonomy) of each member of that community. That such a theory should awaken the hostility of those with grander designs for mankind is evident in Marx's critique of Kant. Marx contrasted the revolutionary bourgeoisie of France (which 'by means of the most colossal revolution ... ever known, was achieving domination and conquering the Continent of Europe') and England ('revolutionising industry and subjugating India') with German burghers, who 'did not get any further than "good will".'

Kant's idea of the good will, Marx concludes, fully corresponds to the 'impotence, depression and wretchedness of German burghers.'[8] For the philosopher whose political movement promised that 'le monde va changer de base,' Kant's vision of a society based on respect for the autonomy of others was altogether too modest.

Despite the failure of that part of Marx's analysis that Marx himself thought most important, that is, his political economy, Marx's critique of capitalism and liberalism has had a decisive influence on the political agenda of the twentieth century. Mixed with other forces, nationalism, decolonization, and liberal self-doubt, and set walking through the world in 1917, it has shaped the world in which we live. Kant's criticisms of what were to become the underpinnings of Marxism, especially of its conception of man and its philosophy of history, reveal many of Marxism's basic failures. They constitute the outlines of a liberal response to the Promethean humanism of Marx. In that sense, among others, we still have much to learn from Kant.

But Kant is of interest to political philosophers for more than his conribution to that debate. Above all else, Kant set liberal political thought within a wider philosophical project and provided it with a concept of man at odds with the notions of man as primarily a being of avarice and fear that had dominated much of the contractarian tradition of liberalism. Kant may thus have something important to say to those who are dissatisfied with a liberalism that seems to have an empty centre, i.e. no conception of the good life, but rather an indifference to the question of what such a life would be. Kant's political philosophy reveals that beneath the cloak of many colours, as Plato described the democratic regime, there lies a conception of man that grasps the one unequivocally good thing in him, that is to say, his freedom.

The essay that follows is not directly concerned with Kant and Marx, or indeed with Kant and liberal thought. I believe, however, that its conclusions bear on both those topics. But my purpose in this study is more restrictive; it is to return to Kant and to reconstruct from his writings a theory of politics and history faithful to Kant's intention. The next section of this introduction sketches that reconstruction.

OUTLINE OF THE PRESENT STUDY

Heinrich Heine tells us the following story.[9] A group of friends is standing on a road that leads to a certain village. The street lights are not working, and around them all is pitch black. Suddenly, one among them begins to speak, giving the others in the group a long sermon on the 'practical necessity' of lanterns – since without them, we can see nothing. Not a very interesting, or even odd tale, one might say. But what is peculiar is this: the man holding forth on the need for lights has himself broken the lamps on the road over which he and his companions were to travel. And he has destroyed them precisely in order to show how much such illumination is required. He has left the street in darkness so as to prove that a path without light is useless or dangerous. This, Heine says, is just what Kant has done. He has traced a pitiless philosophy (broken old lamps, so to speak) and has then written of the need for lights, if we are to see our way.

Much of this tale is misleading as an account of the relation between Kant's theoretical and practical works. Yet there is a kernel of truth in it, and an essential one. It shows very accurately the predicament, the cause of that predicament, and one of its possible solutions. The dilemma itself is similar to that in which Heine's mythical group of men find themselves – they wish to go somewhere, to do something, but they stand in absoute darkness: their path is not evident to them. This difficulty is practical, but its ultimate cause is the inability to see, to know which direction to take. The critique of past metaphysics and religion has meant the loss of those traditional markers that guided us along the way we are to follow here on earth. And one of the solutions Heine sets out thus: that Kant, feeling sympathy for his servant Lampe (who was deeply shaken by his master's denial of the existence of God), thought to himself 'half good-naturedly, half ironically' that 'old Lampe must have a God, for otherwise the poor man cannot be happy.' So by Kant's 'magic wand,' Lampe was given his God.

Kant's *Critique of Pure Reason* had, as its central purpose, the delimiting of the realm of what can be known. The small 'isle of truth' seemed to exclude ideas of freedom, God, and the immortality of the soul – in short, those ideas of traditional metaphysics, concepts of the greatest practical importance, found no home in this new, critical world. Revelation and natural law became unsuitable as guides, becoming instead unsupported and unsupportable sets of claims about objects to which we have no access. What was left was the firm certainty of a self, a logical self, whose limits (the categories, or the fundamental laws of experience) were at the same time the boundaries of the world. What could not be given in intuition and worked up according to the categories was, for us, nothing, a mere chimera. The ideas of God, freedom, and the soul remained, to be sure, thinkable – mere conceptual possibility, however, falls far short of answering our practical needs.

But this formal or logical self is not the only self; that much is clear from the motto that Kant chose for the *Critique of Pure Reason*, *'De nobis ipsis silemus'* – *'of our own person we do not speak.'* A being different from the kind that we are might find contentment on the little 'isle of truth,' but as worldly beings, we are burdened with needs: to know, to act, to hope, to make our way through this world. And thus we become, Kant says, like mariners lured by false horizons, by the illusory evidence of those distant shores that we seek. This is what Kant calls the dialectic that is natural to man. After the great sceptical revolution of the modern period (embodied, metaphorically, in Descartes's evil genius), we are rather like people standing on what once seemed a sure path to their destination, but is now lost in darkness and can therefore provide no direction.

The problem, then, is a practical one – what ought we to do? And that question, which points to the exercise of our wills, raises the further (and central) difficulty of judgment, of what principles or guiding-threads we should adopt. The sharply limited domain of certain knowledge offers us no answers, and what may have seemed to be adequate solutions have now the appearance of sham answers. The theoretical critique and the practical dilemma are thus shown to be bound to each other. The revolution brought about, in different but related ways by Descartes, Hume, and Kant, clearly has enormous practical implications: for how we think about our place in creation, for how we decide what we ought to do. This predicament parallels, in a certain way, the Hobbesian natural condition. The parallel is not, for reasons which we shall see, with Hobbes's psychology, or the idea of a state of war that arises from it, but rather in the notion of a (human) world without an order or any authority governing its occupants. For Hobbes, the absence of authority referred, on the one side, to the lack of a sovereign in the state of nature but also, on the other side, to the rejection of Aristotelian physics (teleology) and Christian revelation. The result is that men make their own order: the Leviathan – the artificial man and mortal God. Men need to act, to preserve themselves and their felicity, and since the classics have been refuted (nature is not a guide) and so too religion (faith), we must become the artificers of our own earthly kingdom. Science is the answer, not revelation or a purposefully arranged nature.

Something quite like this is at work, now on the level of the theory of knowledge, in Kant as well. And in both cases (Hobbes and Kant) there is a definite link between the theoretical and practical concerns. The difference is that Kant was able to describe (more, to be one of the principal agents of) the real crisis – not the imaginary condition of a war of all against all, or even the genuine though transient calamity of civil strife – and this with such precision that much of the philosophical agenda of the past two centuries was set by the first *Critique*. That real crisis was the tremendous disorientation caused by the sceptical and critical (delimiting) currents of modern philosophy in their attacks on theology and metaphysics. What Weber called the 'disillusionment of the world' was equally a liberation and a problem – a revolution that overthrew the old masters, but left those now made free without a guide.

Thus Kant wrote that 'if there is a science which men need,' it is that which will teach them what their place is in creation, how they are to fulfil that position – in short, 'what one must be in order to be a man' (BZB xx: 45). That such a science is needed points to the fact that our place in the order of things and what we ourselves are are obscure. But the problem is by no means narrowly theoretical: we must 'fulfil' our role in creation, and we have to learn what one must be in order to be (hence a practical imperative) a man. This practical science, this self-knowledge of man (a being who occupies, thanks to the critical revolution, that 'limitless empty space'), is what Kant's work as a whole attempts to provide. In this particular garden of knowledge, self-knowledge, we most certainly are not, to borrow the words of Nietzsche, one of Kant's harshest critics, 'jaded idlers.' Rather, we are needy, practical beings who wish to know what we ourselves are (who are thrown 'back on themselves') because the external guides have disappeared into the critical night, leaving us to find our own path.

The work that follows here is an essay in political philosophy. Every word in it is written with a view to the understanding of Kant's writings on history and politics. This needs to be said because the opening chapters are primarily taken up with a consideration of the more strictly theoretical Kantian arguments. The most obvious justification for this way of proceeding is exegetical: it is a trivial observation to say that little can be understood of any of Kant's writings without a solid foundation in the *Critique of Pure Reason*. Few commentators and (to my knowledge) none successfully have ignored that monumental text in modern philosophy – nor could they have, given the abundance of explicit evidence that the language, concepts, and analytical methods of the first *Critique* spill over on to virtually every page of Kant's other works. The special difficulty in examining Kant's philosophy of politics and history is that its relation to the three great *Critiques* – of pure reason, practical reason, and judgment – is often obscure. One is left, therefore, with the characteristic problem of all interpretation of Kant, but here in an extreme form: namely, the task of erecting out of scattered materials an edifice, the plans for which are themselves equally scattered and uncertain. To interpret Kant – any part of his writings – is to undertake a risky experiment. It is to attempt, in Dieter Henrich's words,[10] an argumentative reconstruction: in brief, to force reluctant texts to disclose their unity and plan. The author of the present work has chosen to disappear, as it were, behind this reconstruction, and thus this essay speaks almost exclusively with Kant's voice. The conceptual edifice that the reader shall see appear is not to be met with as such in Kant's writings. But it has been composed out of his ideas. In that act of composition is to be found the author's argument and whatever modest contribution he may have to make to the study of Kant's political philosophy.

Such are the requirements of exegesis. Much more than that is involved, however, and some of this has already been alluded to in the first pages of this introduction. Kant's political philosophy culminates in the idea of a *Rechtsstaat*, a community of civil persons considered as the authors of the laws that bind them in their public union. Similarly, his moral philosophy ends with the notion of autonomy or self-given law. But the idea of autonomy, whether understood in the moral or political sense, is grounded in a larger theory – in Kant's attempt to draw the outline of that science which, as Kant said, men most need: one that will instruct them as to their place in creation and in what they must do in order to fulfil that place. For Kant, as for much of German Idealism, and for Hobbes and Rousseau (not to mention Plato and Aristotle), thinking about politics inevitably merged with the broader questions of what might be called philosophical anthropology. Kant maintained that arguments concerning autonomy, whether public and political or moral, and those that (often in the guise of the metaphor of a social contract) gave politics a distinctly anthropocentric and artificial (in the literal sense) cast needed to be based upon a more comprehensive science. This Kantian science shows man's autonomy as both the predicament and its solution. We are free in what Kant calls the 'empty space' left to us, on the darkened road of Heine's tale. This we might call the negative side of Kant's Copernican revolution. It shows that we are needy beings, lacking direction in a world which, far from displaying the justice of a wise Creator, seems to reduce man to one creature among many.

There is, however, a second and related side to this revolution. Here our autonomy is reflected not in the mere independence from external guides (an independence that is, at the same time, a predicament) but rather in the capacity we have to give law to ourselves. Through the legislative capacity of reason, human beings become in a practical or moral sense the 'mortal God' – they create in speech (in a priori history) a new world that displays the justice we find wanting in the one given us in experience, or (from the pure moral standpoint) the world is treated as a realm of free agency in which not the laws of God or nature hold sway, but those of practical reason. The small compass of our knowledge of and mastery over nature is not thereby extended but, like those travellers standing in the dark, we can once more find our way, not indeed along a path marked out for us by nature or revelation, but rather on one illuminated by reason alone. History and the idea of law, moral and political, are at the heart of different notions of the self-knowledge of man (to use Collingwood's phrase) – of his place in the order of things and of what he must do so as to fulfil his position here. And they serve (again, in different ways tied to their competing portraits of man) to orient us: to show us what we are, what we ought to do, and what we may hope for.

To conclude, then: what the political philosopher will find in Kant is an attempt to ground practical judgment, both of the moral and political kind, in a theory of the autonomy of human reason. That autonomy is, in turn, shown to be the centrepiece of a peculiarly modern predicament – the disillusionment of the world. It was Kant's particular genius to see the relationship between the modern critique, the sense of loss and need, and autonomy; to take this cluster of concepts and, through the problem of orientation, to show how closely intertwined practical and theoretical questions had become.

The structure of this book can be outlined quite briefly. The first three chapters trace the negative side of Kant's Copernican revloution – the limits of what can be known and the limits of the sort of will that we, as finite worldly beings, possess. Here the connection between the theoretical critique and the problem of orientation (need) is established. Two principal responses to that dilemma are suggested: one thinks into the world the proportion between virtue and reward that it finds lacking in the strictly empirical account of things; the other, the Kantian-Stoic view, does not reinterpret the world according to our needs but rather focuses on the will and the quality of its judgments. Chapter 4 begins with a review of the analysis presented in the earlier chapters and then contrasts Marx's and Kant's concepts of the primacy of the practical – a contrast that concludes with the argument that while for Marx the point was to change and master the world, for Kant the priority of the practical meant the ability (and need) that we have to interpret the world according to our practical (moral, broadly understood) needs. This suggests the positive – the creative, aesthetic, and legislative – sides of Kant's Copernican revolution, a theme that is introduced in chapter 5 by a discussion of the beautiful and sublime views of nature.

The spontaneity of reason can be used to read into nature the purposiveness and wisdom that we wish to see there, to render beautiful what is itself ugly. But nature may be left in all its violent formlessness, and here we are directed to that inner capacity that permits us to resist nature even in her most fearsome exertions. The beautiful and the sublime are, Kant thought, the fundamental ways of viewing nature for practical purposes. They are reflected in the standpoint that we adopt in relation now not to nature, but to human phenomena. Chapters 6 and 7 take up this analysis and apply it to human affairs. Here we find that the human world can be transformed by a sort of artist, the philosophic historian, into a thing of beauty and hope. But this beautiful portrayal proves to be both theoretically inadequate and morally unsuitable – an ultimately implausible tale of a morally repugnant tutelage – and one that, since it locates the source of man's improvement in the cunning of history, offers very little in the way of an answer to the question: what ought I to do? These same human phenomena can also be looked at from the point of view of law alone. What is now important is not hope or consolation, nor evidence that our affairs are purposively arranged, but rather autonomy and respect for persons. No fantastic interpretations of nature or history are needed for this, but only the capacity for self-given law, extended beyond the individual to the community and the respect demanded by that capacity. The concluding chapter draws together the preceding discussion in the form of a commentary on Kant's essay on theory and praxis.

# Acknowledgments

I owe a great debt to Professor Judith N. Shklar, who was unfailingly generous with both advice and encouragement at every stage in the preparation of this book. It was she who insisted that Kant's politics ought to be taken seriously, and that they could be properly understood only against the background of his moral philosophy. I am very grateful to Professor Harvey C. Mansfield jr, from whom I learned of a radically different approach to ethics – that set out in Aristotle's *Nicomachean Ethics*.

I wish also to express my thanks to Professors Stephen Holmes and Susan M. Shell, with whom I spent many valuable and pleasant hours discussing political philosophy. Evelyn Puxley saw this project at its beginning, and I am indebted to her for her advice and counsel throughout its realization.

This book has been published with the help of a grant from the Canadian Federation for the Humanities, using funds provided by the Social Sciences and Humanities Research Council of Canada, and a grant from the Andrew W. Mellon Foundation to University of Toronto Press.

# A note on sources

I apprehend some curious wit may object against me, for proceeding thus far in a Preface, without declaiming, according to the custom against the multitude of writers whereof the whole multitude of writers most reasonably complain.

Jonathan Swift, Preface to *A Tale of a Tub*

## LITERATURE ON KANT

In his *Nicomachean Ethics*, Aristotle wrote that there are two major types of boastfulness: one that we today would call ostentatious display, and the other, which he termed Spartan boastfulness, a contrived and excessive deficiency. Spartan soldiers were said to enter battle lightly armed and barely clothed against enemies well equipped and dressed in elaborately decorated armour. The modesty of the Spartan dress was, in reality, a form of boastfulness, for it said to the enemy that Sparta had such confidence in the prowess of its soldiers that it felt no need for the trappings of its opponents.

The relatively few references to the secondary literature on Kant that I have included in this book are not a scholarly version of Spartan boastfulness. The literature concerning Kant is vast, and much of it is superb. One need mention only the names of Goethe, Schelling, and Fichte, or of Kant's modern commentators, Heidegger, Cassirer, de Vleeschauwer, and Vaihinger, in order to make plain the depth of the tradition of Kant studies. In the English-speaking world, students of Kant are indebted to, among others, N.K. Smith and L.W. Beck, both for their fine traslations of Kant's major works and for their studies of his philosophy.

My own debt to that tradition is great, much greater than might first
appear from the small number of references to it. When I began this
book, however, I did not set out to debate that scholarly literature or
to take issue with current interpretations of Kant. Rather, my thought
was that much recent writing on Kant's philosophy of history did not
do full justice to his arguments. The central error was that Kant's
writings on history were interpreted within the framework of a supposed philosophical nexus composed of Kant, Hegel, and Marx. Here
Kant is read as the author of an essentially optimistic (not to say
utopian) view of history, in which man, guided by the cunning of
nature, progresses from a worse to a better condition. The Kant portrayed here easily fits into a 'school of thought' called 'German Idealism,' in which he finds himself in the warm embrace of Hegel and
Marx. A common question emerging from this line of argument is how
such a philosophy of history, seemingly indifferent to the quality of
men's wills and based on a teleology of the whole of nature, could be
consistent with Kant's moral philosophy and theory of knowledge.

It seemed to me that the best way to determine whether the road to
the Finland Station passed through Königsberg (as Goldmann and Galston come close to suggesting) and whether Kant's philosophy of history is consistent with his critical project was to begin afresh, to return
to Kant himself. The Kant that emerged from that inquiry, the subject
of this book, is not the optimist, not the utopian that he is sometimes
said to have been. On the contrary, the Kant who appears here is
profoundly sceptical, and nowhere more so than in his writings on
history and politics. In a sort of moral Cartesianism, Kant clings to
the idea of a finite but autonomous self, and his critique of the historical
optimist and the revolutionary makers of heavenly kingdoms on earth
flows from that single point. From that same point, the moral agency
in man, is constructed a political philosophy of liberalism, a decent
regime whose guiding principle is not the desire to 'storm the gates of
heaven' but rather to create a community that respects the dignity and
autonomy of its members.

Clearly, the above comments have portrayed the literature on Kant's
historical / political thought in broad (and hence not entirely fair) strokes.
However, I am certain that the reader well versed in Kant and in the
commentaries on his will have little difficulty discerning the differences between the interpretation presented in this book and those to
be found in other works. For the reader less well versed I have, in the
notes, sought to direct him to some competing interpretations of Kant.

Such notes cannot, in and of themselves, do justice to the arguments that they cite; they are intended simply to indicate to the reader where another, different interpretation may be found. Should this same reader wish a critical overview of recent studies on Kant's political thought, he can do no better than chapter 7 of Patrick Riley's excellent text, *Kant's Political Philosophy* (Totowa, NJ: Rowan and Littlefield, 1983). Lastly, for the reader interested in Kant's relation to the most current trends in liberal political philosophy, I would commend Michael J. Sandel's thoughtful and provocative piece, *Liberalism and the Limits of Justice* (Cambridge: Cambridge University Press, 1982).

Ultimately, though, the principle against which this or indeed any text on Kant must be judged is not the fervour with which it does battle with other commentaries, or the number of opponents it is willing to engage, but rather the accuracy of its interpretation / criticism. Thus, while I have included references to other reconstructions of Kant's philosophy of history and politics, I have done so with the certainty that after perusing these various and competing views of Kant (my own included) the reader will be drawn to what is the first and most difficult of his tasks, to the study of the philosopher himself.

WORKS BY KANT

For the sake of simplicity and ease of reference, I have incorporated notes referring to works by Kant in the body of the text, enclosed in parentheses. References to writings by authors other than Kant have been placed in notes at the end of this book.

The Königliche Preussische Akdemie der Wissenschaften in Berlin began publishing Kant's collected works (*Kants Gesammelte Schriften*) in 1902. With one exception noted below, references in this study to Kant's works take the following form: abbreviated title (see list below), volume in Kant's collected works, and page number, and, where available, the corresponding page number of an English translation. Thus, for example, the note 'c3 v: 400 / 248' refers to the *Kritik der Urteilskraft* in volume V, page 400, translated by J. H. Bernard as *Critique of Judgement* (New York: Hafner Press, 1974), page 248. Where no English translation is available, the notes contain only the abbreviated title, the volume in the collected works, and the page number.

The sole exception to the above occurs in notes referring to the *Critique of Pure Reaseon*. In accordance with the accepted scholarly practice, notes citing this work refer to the pagination of the first (A) and / or second (B) editions of the *Critique*, e.g. C1 A36 / B95. Some passages occur in one but not the other of the two editions, and they are cited using the designation of the appropriate edition, e.g. C1A VIII. The A / B pagination can be found in the margins of N.K. Smith's translation of the *Critique of Pure Reason*, and thus the page numbers of that translation are not provided in the notes.

BBM   *Bestimmung des Begriffs einer Menschenrace* (VIII)

BZB   *Bemerkungen zu den Beobachtungen über das Gefühl des Schönen und Erhabenen* (xx)

C1   *Kritik der reinen Vernunft* (III and IV): *Critique of Pure Reason* trans N.K. Smith (New York: St. Martin's Press, 1965)

C2   *Kritik der praktischen Vernunft* (V): *Critique of Practical Reason* trans L.W. Beck (Indianapolis: Library of Liberal Arts, 1977)

C3   *Kritik der Urteilskraft* (V): *Critique of Judgment* trans J.H. Bernard (New York: Hafner Press, 1974)

CB   'Mutmasslicher Anfang der Menschengeschichte' (VIII): 'Conjectural Beginning of Human History' trans Emil L. Fackenheim in L.W. Beck ed *On History* (Indianapolis, Library of Liberal Arts, 1963) 53–68

DV   *Die Metaphysik der Sitten* (Part Two), (VI): *The Doctrine of Virtue* trans M.J. Gregor (New York: Harper Torchbooks, 1965)

END   'Das Ende aller Dinge' (VIII): 'The End of All Things' trans Robert E. Anchor in L.W. Beck ed *On History* (Indianapolis: Library of Liberal Arts, 1963) 69–84

EVT   *Von einem neuerdings erhobenen vornehmen Ton in der Philosophie* (VIII)

FI   *Erste Einleitung in die Kritik der Urteilskraft* (xx): *First Introduction to the Critique of Judgment* trans J. Haden (Indianapolis: Library of Liberal Arts, 1965)

FPT   'Über das Misslingen aller philosophischen Versuche in der Theodizee' (VIII): 'On the Failure of all attempted Philosophical Theodicies' in Michel Despland *Kant on History and Religion* (Montreal: McGill-Queen's University Press, 1973) 283–97

GMM   *Grundlegung zur Metaphysik der Sitten* (IV): *Groundwork of the Metaphysic of Morals* trans H.J. Paton (New York: Harper Torchbooks, 1964)

KEC   *Über eine Entdeckung, nach der alle neue Kritik ... entbehrlich gemacht werden soll* (VIII): *The Kant-Eberhard Controversy* analysis and trans Henry Allison (Baltimore and London: Johns Hopkins University Press, 1973)

LB *Lose Blätter zu den Fortschritten der Metaphysik* (xx)

MAN *Metaphysische Anfangsgründe der Naturwissenschaften* (IV): *Metaphysical Foundations of Natural Science* trans J. Ellington (Indianapolis: Library of Liberal Arts, 1970)

MEJ *Die Metaphysik der Sitten* (Part One) (VI): *The Metaphysical Elements of Justice* trans John Ladd (Indianapolis: Library of Liberal Arts, 1965)

OBS *Beobachtungen über das Gefühl des Schönen und Erhabenen* (II): *Observations on the Feeling of the Beautiful and Sublime* trans J.T. Goldthwait (Berkeley: University of California Press, 1960)

OP *Opus postumum* (XXI)

OQ *Der Streit der Facultäten* (Second Section) (VII): 'An Old Question Raised Again: Is the Human Race Constantly Progessing?' trans Robert E. Anchor in L.W. Beck ed *On History* (Indianapolis: Library of Liberal Arts, 1963) 137–54

PFM *Prolegomena zu einer jeden künftigen Metaphysik* (IV): *Prolegomena to Any Future Metaphysics* trans G. Carus and L.W. Beck (Indianapolis: Library of Liberal Arts, 1950)

PP 'Zum ewigen Frieden' (VIII): 'Perpetual Peace' trans L.W. Beck in L.W. Beck ed *On History* (Indianapolis: Library of Liberal Arts, 1963) 85–135

RH 'Recensionen von I.G. Herders Ideen zur Philosophie der Geschichte der Menschheit' (VIII): 'Reviews of Herder's "Ideas for a Philosophy of the History of Mankind" ' trans Robert E. Anchor in L.W. Beck ed *On History* (Indianapolis: Library of Liberal Arts, 1963) 27–52

RSV *Recension von Schulz's Versuch einer Anleitung zur Sittenlehre* (VIII)

RWL *Die Religion innerhalb der Grenzen der blossen Vernunft* (VI): *Religion within the Limits of Reason Alone* trans T.M. Greene and H.H. Hudson (New York: Harper Torchbooks, 1960)

RZR *Reflexionen zur Rechtsphilosophie* (XIX)

TP 'Über den Gemeinspruch: Das mag in der Theorie richtig sein, taugt aber nicht für die Praxis' (VIII): *On the Old Saw: That May Be Right in Theory But It Won't Work in Practice* trans E.B. Ashton (Philadelphia: University of Pennsylvania Press, 1974)

UGP *Über den Gebrauch teleologischer Principien in der Philosophie* (VIII)

UH 'Idee zu einer allgemeinen Geschichte in weltbürgerlicher Absicht' (VIII) 'Idea for a Universal History from a Cosmopolitan

Point of View' trans L.W. Beck in L.W. Beck ed *On History* (Indianapolis: Library of Liberal Arts, 1963) 11–26

VAT *Verkündigung des nahen Abschlusses eines Tractats zum ewigen Frieden in der Philosophie* (VIII)

VVR *Von den verschiedenen Racen der Menschen* (II)

VZEF *Vorarbeiten zu Zum ewigen Frieden* (XXIII)

VZR *Vorarbeiten zur Rechtslehre* (XXIII)

WIE 'Beantwortung der Frage: Was ist Aufklärung?' (VIII) 'What Is Enlightenment?' trans L.W. Beck in L.W. Beck ed *On History* (Indianapolis: Library of Liberal Arts, 1963) 3–10

WOT 'Was heisst: Sich im Denken orientiren?' (VIII)'What Is Orientation in Thinking?' in *Kant's Critique of Practical Reason and Other Writings on Moral Philosophy* trans L.W. Beck (Chicago: University of Chicago Press, 1949)

# PART ONE

# Kant's negative revolution:
# The limits of reason

# 1

# The limits of knowledge

Those born blind cannot have the least notion of darkness, since they have none of light. The savage knows nothing of poverty, since he has no acquaintance with wealth. The ignorant have no concept of their ignorance, because they have none of knowledge.

Kant, *Critique of Pure Reason*

Kant's Copernican revolution: the phrase is so familiar, the names flow so easily together, that we give hardly any thought to this curious pairing. Yet how strange it is that the philosopher from Königsberg and the great Polish astronomer, separated by centuries and by vastly different intellectual pursuits, should now find themselves keeping such intimate company. We know that their names are forever bound together not because of Kant's enduring, and quite secondary, interest in astronomy but rather because of the first of Kant's four questions: 'What can I know?' The Copernican Kant, then, is to be found in the *Critique of Pure Reason*, not in the *Theory of the Heavens*. But knowing where to find him, we remain uncertain as to who he is. Is the Copernican Kant the author of a theory that makes of reason the form-giver, the near-divine creator of nature, or is he rather the philosopher accused by Nietzsche of having confessed that astronomy diminishes man's importance? We shall not be able to answer this, the first of our questions, until we have returned to the *Critique*. It is to that task that we shall now proceed.

The preface to the first edition of the *Critique of Pure Reason* portrays metaphysics as a once glorious queen, now outcast. Like Ovid's Hecuba, she laments the passing of her great power, of her despotic regime, presided over by 'dogmatists,' which has now given way, under the attack of the 'sceptics' (that 'species of nomads'), to anarchy, weariness, and 'indifferentism.' The weariness caused by this ceaseless combat, a battle forever without issue, will lead, Kant hopes, to a renewal of metaphysics. This renewal will be based upon her lawful claims, established before the tribunal of pure reason, and not upon a reassertion of her old despotic authority (c1 Aviii, x, xii). Kant here presents the *Critique* as an attempt to restore metaphysics to its former exalted position, which will also make its sovereignty constitutional, that is, law-governed and moderate. The limits of the new government, its constitution, will be written in the court of pure reason. And it is Kant who will adjudicate over the unbounded pretensions of the *ancien régime* and the equally immoderate assertions of the anarchists. The *Critique* will then put an end to the Hobbesian state of war (though its sovereign will be limited and not the 'mortal God' of Hobbes's *Leviathan*) and institute an external and lawful peace (c1 A751–2 / B779–80).

The preface to the second edition of the *Critique* offers a rather different account of Kant's project. Here the language of constitutions, of despotism and anarchy, and of tribunals yields to the language of revolution. But this revolution is no mere change of regimes, a new order among old disputants; rather it is analogous to the change that gave order not to a regime but to the heavens themselves. This revolution Kant entitles his 'Copernican Revolution.'

Kant seems to be making two different sorts of claim: on the one hand, that the *Critique* is intended to mark out a middle path between dogmatism and scepticism and, on the other hand, that the critical or transcendental inquiry is more than simply a renewed and moderated metaphysics and that, in fact, it constitutes a revolution in thought similar to Copernicus's revolution in astronomy. How these two types of claim can be made compatible with one another is a problem that we must settle before we can proceed. For what is at issue in this seeming discrepancy is precisely how radical Kant meant his arguments to be: were they to do nothing more than provide a discipline, a collection of rules for any future metaphysics, or were they, in the manner of Copernicus's heliocentric theory of the universe, to demonstrate the true relationship between observer and object, man and nature?

The direction of Kant's argument in his rejection of the sceptical attack upon metaphysics provides us with a key, by means of which we may reconcile these two competing descriptions of the critical philosophy. The sceptics, Kant says, fail to distringuish between accidental and necessary ignorance. While it may well be true that all previous philosophy has been unable to supply adequate proofs for its central propositions, those concerning God, immortality of the soul, and freedom, this failure becomes philosophically significant only if it can be shown that ignorance in regard to these questions is necessary: even if 'we find that all attempts of this sort have hitherto failed ... that proves nothing against the possibility of a better result' (c3 v: 460 / 311). For ignorance to be necessary would mean that the limits of human cognition exclude the possibility of intelligible assertions about such objects. Thus, in order to distinguish necessary from accidental ignorance, an examination of the primary sources and limits of our knowledge is required.

The question of the possibility of metaphysics – and it is just this possibility that is at stake in the debate between the 'dogmatists' and the 'sceptics' – can be answered neither by the grand, but unsupportable claims of the old school nor by the sweeping, and equally unfounded, denials of the sceptics, but only by a critique of pure reason. Transcendental philosophy precedes metaphysics and sets the foundation for it (PFM IV: 279 / 26). It is, to use the current term, a meta-theory, which seeks to show how theory is possible at all: critical philosophy 'includes a philosophical inquiry into the possibility of that sort of knowledge [rational knowledge], but instead of forming a part of such a system, primarily demarcates and examines the very idea of the system' (FI XX: 195 / 3). The *Critique*, far from being itself a metaphysical system, defines the boundaries within which all knowledge and, a fortiori, metaphysics must be contained. And because it describes these limits, those of any knowledge whatsoever, it is at the same time, a theory of all possible experience; thus, in Kantian terms, it also provides an answer to the question: how is nature possible?

What began as a dispute between sceptics and dogmatists and seemed to require little more than a tribunal to judge their respective claims is now seen to have a deeper import. To settle the problem of metaphysics, an investigation of the most fundamental type is required, into the possibility and boundaries of knowledge and experience. The failure to execute an inquiry of this kind is characteristic of both sides of the dispute, and indeed it is the hallmark of all pre-critical philosophy. It is for this reason that Kant feels himself justified in stating that all philosophies, prior to the *Critique*, are not essentially different from one another (LB XX: 335). And it is, at least in part, because of this failure that the question 'what can I know?' is both the first of Kant's four questions, and a question at all.

The restoration of metaphysics clearly demands an answer to that question, if only as a kind of corrective or discipline. But the implications of the problem are Copernican in their range and depth. The radical quality of Kant's move from the possibility of metaphysics to the limits of experience, which is present in virtually every Kantian argument, explains one part of the analogy between the critical inquiry and Copernicus's revolution. In placing himself alongside Thales, Galileo, and Copernicus, Kant means for us to see the fundamental or radical nature of the transcendental philosophy. But when Kant described his own revolution as Copernican, he intended far more than merely to draw to our attention its radical character. What else Kant and the great astronomer shared can be seen only by turning to the substance of Kant's Copernican revolution.

From the history of human reason, Kant writes, we learn that in all its endeavours, in mathematics, geometry, physics, and philosophy, reason could initially do no more than 'to grope' (herumtappen). In their infancy, these sciences consisted of series of accidental observations, subject to no necessary law (C1 Bxiii). However, by a 'single and sudden' revolution they were able to enter upon a more secure path. This revolution, in geometry as in the other sciences, was accomplished not by the discovery of some new fact or object, but rather by changing the relation between spectator and object. Thales, for example, saw that the most profitable method in geometry was 'to bring out what was necessarily implied in the concepts that he had himself formed a priori, and had put into the figure in the construction by which he presented it to himself' (C1 Bxii). Bacon, Galileo, and Torricelli brought about similar revolutions in the other sciences, and what these revolutions had in common was that each constrained nature to answer to reason's tribunal. The 'groping' of simple empirical observation, which can never yield any greater certainty than that of 'constant conjunction,' was replaced, in the course of these revolutions, by a plan of reason. This is the 'changed way of thinking' (Umänderung der Denkart) that, according to Kant, has been the source of all major scientific advance. An finally, Copernicus himself, finding the existing explanations of planetary motion inadequate, proposed that astronomy might meet with more success were the position of the spectator to be changed. Now, instead of the planets circling the observer, the origin of their movement was to be sought in the spectator himself (C1 Bxvi).

This daring, and counter-intuitive proposition was to change forever the fundamental laws of astronomy.

The two stages of all such revolutions can be enumerated thus: the failure of the existing sciences to 'save the phenomena,' to give coherent accounts of their objects, followed by a revolution that ends this groping about by postulating a new relation between spectator and object, which substitutes the demands of reason for mere accidental observation. Thus, these revolutions all begin with the inadequacy of their received tenets, specifically, a reliance on observation alone, on nature's 'leading-strings.' The relation between subject and object implied in that kind of science can never, for reasons that we shall see shortly, result in the systematic, explicitly law-governed experience that is called science. Science begins only when reason interrogates nature according to a plan of its own, and this new way of treating the relation between object and observer is at the heart of all profitable revolutions (LB xx: 335).

What unites these revolutions and allows them to be entitled 'Copernican' is less their newness, their radical character as it were, than the fact that they make the spectator central to the explanation of the world. The idea of a Copernican revolution suggests that to give an account of any sort of phenomenon, natural or human, a theory of the self is required. This self may be the *res cogitans* of Descartes's *Meditations*, man as he appears in the first part of Hobbes's *Leviathan*, Kant's '*das Ich*' ('the I'), or the player of Wittgenstein's language games. What is crucial is that the new account places the theory of the possessing self at the very root of philosophy.[1] 'What brings the self into philosophy is the fact that "the world is my world." '[2] It is 'my world' in the sense that its boundaries – the limits on what can be known or what can be said – are coextensive or, more precisely, identical with (and are set by) those of the self.

The centre of Kant's concept of a Copernican revolution, then, is the self. Both the failures of earlier theories, scientific and philosophical, and the success of the 'post-revolutionary' endeavours are to be explained by this relation of subject and object. Kant now proposes a similar experiment for the *Critique*: must knowledge conform to the constitution of objects, or must the object conform to the conditions of cognition? Starting from the failure of traditional metaphysics to give an adequate and firmly grounded account of its arguments concerning God, freedom, and the immortality of the soul, Kant proposes a revolutionary 'hypothesis': that the understanding contains within itself rules, the sum of which, when combined with intuition, produces what we call nature. The necessity and priority of the question 'what can I know?' thus become clear: *'The advance from the knowledge of oneself ... to the knowledge of the world*, and by means of this to the original being, is so natural that it seems to resemble the logical advance of reason *from premises to conclusion'* (c1 A337 / B394–5; emphasis added).

The philosophical self, Wittgenstein writes, is not man as he is, the subject of psychology or anthropology, but rather a metaphysical self: the limit of the world – not a part of it.[3] This tells us something of the nature of the self in this first stage of Kant's Copernican revolution. It is not a real subject, not the object of intuition, and it is not a moral agent; this self is rather the formal condition of all knowledge, a logical subject. The *'Ich'* of the *Critique* is the bare form of a possible consciousness, and no further attributes can be ascribed to it, on the basis of this function, than those rules that make experience possible. It is essential, if we are to understand the limits of the *Critique*, to keep in mind that Kant thought it one of the most common errors of past philosophy to try to attach real predicates to the formal unity of the thinking 'I' (c1 A350, 354; LB xx: 338).Nevertheless, as formal and empty as this metaphysical self may be, the role it plays in the edifice of Kantian thought, practical as well as theoretical, is so important that it must at least be sketched here.

The three principal elements of the argument that I shall outline can be expressed in this manner. The introduction to the first edition of the *Critique* states, in the opening sentence, that experience is 'the first product to which our understanding gives rise.' The second edition opens with the words 'There can be no doubt that all our knowledge begins with experience' (c1 A1 and B1 respectively). Taken together, these two propositions do not contradict each other but rather establish the essential ingredients of experience – intuition and judgment, sensibility and understanding. Starting from the relation that exists between sensibility and understanding, as they combine to form experience, Kant states that his Copernican 'hypothesis' will show that there can, and indeed must, be a priori synthetic knowledge. But, for reasons that will be given shortly, this conclusion will lead to the most startling consequence, namely that we can never transcend the limits of possible experience (c1 B xviii–xix). The discussion of how the three elements of the first half of the *Critique*, sensibility, understanding, and the limits of human cognition, are bound together will give us a more complete picture of this phase of Kant's Copernican revolution.

As was just noted, experience consists of sensibility and understanding. Now it is only through sensibility that objects can be given to us in intuition. The subjective condition of sensibility, in regard to outer intuition, is space – the 'necessary a priori representation' that makes intuition possible. Space, in other words, is not an empirical concept, a fact derived from observation, but is itself the basis of all observation. It is the formal character of the intuiting subject; that is, space is the peculiar form of human intuition (c1 A26 / B42). Whether there is another form of intuition, a non-spatial intuition of outer objects, is a possibility that can be neither denied nor affirmed. But in any event, such a form of intuition would be a matter of complete indifference, its capacities being unintelligible to us.

Similarly, time is the a priori condition of all inner intuition. It is the relation among representations ordered, in our inner state, according to the principles of succession and coexistence. And, like space, it has validity only in relation to appearances, to what is given in intuition. What this means is that space and time are not said to inhere in the objects themselves, or to be self-subsistent entities; rather they are the necessary (and hence a priori) forms of human sensibility. They have, to use Kant's words, empirical reality (for the intuiting subject) and transcendental ideality (in relation to things themselves) (c1 A28 / B44, A35 / B52).

These intuitions, based in the spatio-temporal order within which they are made available to receptivity, are the whole field of possible experience (c1 A95). Yet they are not for that reason objective in the full sense of the term and neither is the aggregate of such intuitions experience. For the subjective sequence of perceptions to become an objective ordering, namely rule-governed and independent of any particular subject, requires further steps.

Now the manifold of intuitions can never be combined into a coherent whole through the senses, which have only a power of receptivity. Experience, understood as an ordered whole of intuitions, is possible only where the mass of random intuitions has been combined. The act by which this manifold is combined is the 'figurative' synthesis of the imagination and combination by the understanding. The first of the two forms of combination applies directly to intuition, and it is the process by which intuitions are 'run through and held together.' Appearances must be reproducible if there is to be cohesive experience. Reproducibility in itself is, however, not a guarantee of a rule-determined objective order (c1 A201 / B246). Only when the manifold of intuitions, transformed into cohesive intuition or sense-perception by the imagination, is made subject to the synthetic activity of the understanding can we speak of an objective order.

Without combination, the raw data provided by sense-perception could never be thought and hence could never become knowledge. They would not constitute a coherent experience, where experience could be distinguished from a purely arbitrary, contingent ordering of intuitions (C1 B137). But for reasons already cited, the combination of intuitions cannot be given to us in intuition itself. Rather, combination is the result of an act of synthesis. More than this is implied, however, in the idea of combination, because the combination of the manifold must have, as its foundation, (synthetic) unity. This manifold of intuitions must belong, or must be capable of belonging, to one consciousness. In the words of the famous dictum of the *Critique*, all intuitions, if they are to become part of experience, must allow of being prefaced by the phrase 'I think.'

If this kind of unity is to be possible, then I have to be conscious (or be capable of becoming conscious) of myself as identical with respect to a manifold of intuitions (C1 A401). Without the possibility of this kind of self-consciousness, of the identity of oneself, the unity of experience contained in the words 'I think,' coupled with whatever thoughts it may have as its predicates, would be itself impossible. Thus, Kant concludes, all the conditions of knowledge converge in the identity of self, in that (transcendental) consciousness of self that he entitles the 'transcendental unity of apperception' (C1 A116).

All questions in the theory of knowledge, indeed even the highest question of the critical philosophy, that of the possibility of nature, are at bottom but one problem: that of self-consciousness. That experience has to be, at least *in potentia*, my experience, and that nature, as the whole object of possible experience, must be available for combination in a unitary consciousness, are the preconditions of experience itself and, ultimately, of nature as well. Having radicalized his inquiry to the point that the central issue is now what makes the 'I think' possible, Kant has prepared the basis for his answer to Hume: he will now proceed to demonstrate that neither a unitary self-consciousness or (therefore) coherent experience is possible without synthetic a priori ideas.

What constitutes the unity of self-consciousness essential to all experience is not the empirical, or real, identity of the subject. The logical identity of the transcendental '*Ich*,' the formal unity of self-consciousness, exists even when changes have occurred that do not allow the empirical subject to retain its identity. Consciousness of self-identity, then, not being empirical, is not the result of intuition but is a thought. This 'I,' unlike that of empirical apperception, namely, 'consciousness of self according to the determinations of our state in inner perception' (c1 B132, 158). Why the real identity of the self should be inadequate for Kant's purposes will be discussed shortly, but for a moment what we must ask is how such a transcendental self-consciousness is possible at all, given that this self is not an object of intuition.

Kant's response is that the identity of the subject is possible 'only through the consciousness of this synthesis [of representations] ... Only in so far, therefore, as I can unite a manifold of given representations in *one consciousness*, is it possible for me to represent to myself the *identity of the consciousness in these representations*' (c1 B133). The synthetic unity of a manifold of intuitions, where synthesis is understood as a function of the (transcendental) self, is the basis of the 'identity of apperception itself' (c1 B134,135). Self-consciousness, then, is always the consciousness of an identity of function, or activity, in relation to a manifold of intuition. The identity of synthetic activity across a range of intuitions is what yields identity of self. Consciousness of a unitary self would not be possible without this identity of function. And Kant concludes 'The original and necessary consciousness of the identity of the self is thus at the same time a consciousness of an equally necessary unity of the synthesis of all appearances according to concepts' (c1 A108).[4]

With this, we now have a fuller appreciation of what Kant means when he says that all the conditions of knowledge converge in the identity of self. Like Descartes, Kant brings his argument to a single, incontestable starting point: self-identity. That all experience must be mine, or be capable of becoming mine, presupposes the possibility of a self to whom these experiences could be ascribed. The consciousness of its own unity, the ability to make sense of the word 'mine,' on the part of such a self cannot be the result of empirical intuition, that is, the recognition of the constancy of one's own inner states. Empirical apperception is itself in flux, and even if it were constant the issue is not one of empirical self-consciousness but of what the foundation of identity is, the foundation to which empirical apperception is but an instance given *in concreto* (c1 A107, 116, and B 140).[5]

As we have seen, it is the self's synthetic activity in uniting the representations given to it that makes possible the transcendental unity of apperception. The statement that all experience must be capable of being mine contains two propositions. First, there has to be a unitary self-consciousness to which these experiences belong or could belong. Second, the possibility of this (transcendental) unity requires that the manifold of intuition be subject to the synthetic activity of the self, that activity by means of which the self recognizes itself as identical and so is able to think experience as 'mine.'

Beginning with the idea of a self to whom experiences belong, an idea that, as Descartes realized, even the most thoroughgoing sceptic would have to acknowledge, Kant argues that the world, the sum of representations, must have a certain order. That order must meet those conditions under which alone representations can become 'mine.' In brief, the constancy of Hume's 'constant conjunction' is the identical self that conjoins one intuition to the next. The identity of that self depends upon the possibility of conjoining representations and, therefore, also upon those conditions that would render this combination in one consciousness possible (c1 B132), namely, that the manifold of representations be subject to the synthetic activity of the understanding. This complex relation among objectivity, the coherent, rule-governed order of appearances (c1 A145 / B240, A196–7 / B241 – 2), and the necessity of a unitary self-consciousness is given what may be its most concise expression by Kant. In a passage from the 'A' version of the Transcendental Deduction, he writes that the Deduction 'rests on the relation in which ... all possible appearances stand to original apperception. In original apperception everything must necessarily conform to the conditions of the thoroughgoing unity of self-consciousness, that is, to the universal functions of synthesis ... that synthesis according to concepts in which alone apperception can demonstrate a priori its complete and necessary identity' (c1 A111–12; see also A122, 129). This statement unites the three key concepts of the Deduction – the objective order of appearances, the unitary self-consciousness, and the activity of synthesis.

The Deducation has shown that the categories are an essential condition of experience by demonstrating that they are the logical functions of a judgment by which a manifold of representations is brought under one apperception (c1 B143 and PFM IV: 304-5 / 52). However, the categories, being logical functions, do not produce the least concept of an object. They are, Kant says, rather like the rules of grammar; they serve only 'to spell out' appearances, that we may be able to read them as experience (PFM IV: 312, 323 / 60, 70). To say that categories are logical functions of the understanding amounts to saying that they are the various modes according to which representations are united in one consciousness.

Representations, apart from the categories (those rules by which the understanding combines them), are in the literal sense incoherent. Equally, the categories, apart from intuition, are empty – mere rules that yield no knowledge whatsoever. To give them sense and meaning, it is necessary to combine them with 'our sensible and empirical intuition.' Just as the rules of grammar remain so many empty formulae when they are not applied to words, so, too, it is only when the categories are applied to intuition that they give rise to experience and knowledge. The categories, in short, are limited in their employment to objects of possible experience, and thus the understanding, of which they are the rules, is, like the categories themselves, both 'realized' and 'restricted' by sensibility (c1 A147 / B187 and PFM IV: 308, 324 / 56, 72).

The manifold of representations, subject to the conditions of space and time, is thus transformed by the synthetic activity of the understanding into experience. And the a priori conditions of all possible experience are, at the same time, the conditions of the possibility of the objects of experience. If there are objects that are not available to us in any possible experience, and we cannot positively deny (any more than we can affirm) their existence, they would remain nothing for us, things about which we could neither know nor say anything. The possibility of experience is, therefore, the universal law of nature (c1 B159–60, 165, and PFM IV: 318–19 / 65–6). It is clear how this radical proposition is the direct consequence of the Transcendental Deduction: nature can only be said to be the whole object of possible experience. Nature, in its formal sense, is the synthetic unity of appearances (c1 A126–7, 383). And this unity is given to appearances by means of the universal laws prescribed by the understanding. The boundaries of possible experience and of the world, or nature, are thus one and the same.

We may now return once more to the idea of a Copernican revolution and set out its principal features. We recall Wittgenstein writing that it is the fact of this world being mine that 'brings the self into philosophy.' Kant's Copernican revolution has the self as its central concern, for very much the same reason that Wittgenstein suggests. By turning from what is accidental and contingent, namely, from mere observation of empirical events, to legislative reason, Thales had set geometry on a solid foundation, and Copernicus had given a more adequate explanation than was previously available of planetary motion. Kant extends this revolution so that its fundamental tenet, the centrality of the spectator, is now employed not in the explanation of this or that particular set of phenomena but rather in the description of the possibility of all experience and nature as such. The radical character of Kant's Copernican revolution sets it apart from all earlier revolutions in thought. Its claims are no longer 'hypotheses,' thought-experiments awaiting empirical confirmation, but apodictically certain propositions (c1 Bxxii note). The radicalness and the certainty of Kant's propositions concerning the legislative self and self-consciousness, connected as they are to each other, are combined in the term 'transcendental.' The self of the first *Critique*, like Wittgenstein's, is not empirical but transcendental, the limit of the world, not a part of it.

'*The limits of my language* mean the limits of my world.'[6] This thought brings into relief the second principal theme of Kant's Copernican revolution. All experience, and hence nature, considered as the whole object of possible experience, must be capable of becoming mine. The conditions under which it can become mine are its limits as well. These limits are the categories and the pure form of sensibility (space and time) by which sense-perception is transformed into a coherent whole, called experience. And, as we have seen, the categories are restricted, in their application, to the field of sensibility, of intuition. To translate the language of Wittgenstein's *Tractatus* into that of the *Critique*, we might say that the limits of what can be brought to the unity of apperception, combined by this identical self, are the boundaries of the world.

'The world is all that is the case.'[7] What cannot be contained within the boundaries set by space and time and by the categories, that is, those 'events' or 'objects' not bound by the rules of this law-governed order, cannot be known – in the broad sense of known, namely, cannot become experience. To understand Kant's Copernican revolution one must first see the relation between the three propositions: the world is my world, my limits are its limits, and the world is all that is the case. The sum of these statements is what Kant was referring to when he spoke of the 'astonishing' (*befremdlich*) consequence of the proof of 'our power of knowing a priori': that we 'can never transcend the limits of possible experience' (c1 Bxix). It is the connection between the first proposition and the two others that is frequently ignored in discussions of Kant's *Critique of Pure Reason*.

The principal theme of Kant's Copernican revolution, which emphasizes the concept of the self as active and as legislating for the whole of nature, has led some to interpret it in almost Apollonian terms. Here, human reason is seen as the great form-giver of nature, the Kantian *Ich* as the 'proprietor of the world.'[8] This interpretation of the role of the self in the first *Critique*, while partially accurate, fails to understand that though the Copernican revolution may make of man the proprietor of the world, it also, and consequently, allows him a very small domain indeed. It should be recalled that Copernicus sought the source of the motion of planets in the spectator, and removed that spectator from the centre of creation. Perhaps Nietzsche was not entirely wrong in claiming that, for Kant, astronomy reduced the importance of man in his own eyes: 'The observations and calculations of astronomers have taught us much that is wonderful; but that most important lesson that they have taught us has been revealing the abyss of our *ignorance* ... Reflection upon the ignorance thus disclosed must produce a great change in our estimate of the ultimate purposes [*Endabsichten*] for which our reason should be employed' (c1 A575 / B603 note and context).

# 2

# The moral implications

We have found, indeed, that although we had contemplated building a tower
which should reach to the heavens, the supply of materials suffices only
for a dwelling-house, just sufficiently commodious for our business on the
level of experience, and just sufficiently high to allow of our overlooking it.

Kant, *Critique of Pure Reason*

We are a part of nature, and want to be the whole of it.

Kant, *Geschichte und Naturbeschreibung der merkwürdigsten Vorfälle des
Erdbebens*

How little we have accomplished, Wittgenstein wrote, when we have
successfully demarcated the limits of what can be said or thought.[1]
Once all the questions of natural science, broadly understood, have
been answered, the great problems of what we ought to do, of what
we may hope for, and of what man is remain unsolved. Wittgenstein
adds that these questions cannot even be intelligibly posed, since their
'objects' are, strictly speaking, transcendent. And so these problems,
if not the impulse to them, vanish into silence.[2] Note that Wittengstein
does not deny the reality of ethics, for example, or of the transcendent
in general, but rather relegates their concerns to a domain in which
no sensible statements can be made about them. Yet the fact of a
limited world, which reduces us to silence on those problems that we
feel to be most important, compels us to seek the transcendent. 'The
drive to mysticism arises from the failure of science to satisfy our
wishes. We *feel* that even if all *possible* scientific questions are answered, our problem has still not been met at all.'[3]

It is this 'peculiar fate' of reason that Kant speaks of at the beginning of the first *Critique*: 'In one species of its knowledge it is burdened by questions which, as prescribed by the very nature of reason itself, it is not able to ignore, but which, as transcending all its powers, it is also not able to answer' (c1 Avii). All men desire by nature to know, and metaphysics has, since its inception, sought to know the suprasensible (LB xx: 335). The source of this desire to know the suprasensible is, as we shall see, practical rather than theoretical. 'True metaphysics,' however, recognizes the limits of human reason (UGP VIII: 180), and it shows us the 'ultimate purposes for which our reason should be employed.'

Kant's Copernican revolution, in its first phase, sets the foundation for a 'true metaphysics' by describing the sources and limits of knowledge. These limts are, as we have seen, the dependence of the mind on what can be given in sensible intuition and the rules according to which intuition is transformed into experience. That intellectual (non-sensible) intuition is not available to human beings means that knowledge rests ultimately on sensible intuition. And what can be given in such intuition is, in turn, restricted by those conditions under which it could be united in one consciousness. The *Critique*, then, has done what the sceptics were unable to do – show our necessary ignorance in regard to all questions with answers that would transcend possible experience (KEC VIII: 226 / 139, and see also c1 A261 / B789).

Kant's *Critique* can thus be read as the most radical sceptical argument: previous metaphysics had not only failed to answer its central questions (those concerning the transcendent), but could not have answered them. In this sense, the value of the *Critique* is purely negative. It is a discipline limiting the claims of reason, and it has the modest task of calling the mind back from its pleasant, but fruitless, dreams. It teaches us that our knowledge is a plane with a horizon or, to use the constructive metaphor more appropriate to a theory that emphasizes the role of spontaneity in experience, it invites us to consider the materials available for building our edifice, and the height to which the building may rise (c1 A759 / B787 and A738 / B766). The structure can be high enough, Kant wrote, for our business here on earth, our practical purposes, but not of sufficient height to allow us certain knowledge of the suprasensible.

Kant's Copernican revolution places man at the centre of its account of nature but at the same time limits and undermines his pretensions. It tells man that the world is his, his property, the edifice that he has constructed, but it also tells him that the world is all that is the case. 'Where determination by laws of nature comes to an end, all *expla-*

*nation* comes to an end as well. Nothing is left but *defence'* (GMM IV: 459 / 127).

Where the possibility of explaination ends, there knowledge ends as well, and so too does experience. By the 'laws of nature' Kant means not any specific law governing the behaviour of objects in nature, but the transcendental laws of nature, the categories which, when combined with intuition, yield experience (FI xx: 203–4 note / 9–10 note). What can be experienced and known must be explicable according to those fundamental laws that are, at the same time, the laws of nature. All knowledge, then, it governed by these laws. Beyond the explainable, there does indeed lie what can be thought.

The rules that determine what can be thought are those of logical possibility, particularly the law of non-contradiction. So long as they are not self-contradictory, thoughts are always possible (C1 A596 / B624 note and BXXVI). Yet there is a sharp difference between logical and real possibility, the former governed principally by the law of non-contradiction, and the latter by the fundamental laws of nature. And there is no deductive path from logical to real possibility. Mere thought, which does not submit itself to the conditions of real possibility and which is combined with no intuition, possesses the charm of not being refutable by experience. However, since it can make no claim to knowledge it also has no response to the citation of other logical possibilities (C1 B416 note and A4 / B8). The person who asserts that a unicorn's horn is white has little with which to defend himself against someone who insists that its horn is blue.

Knowledge, then, as distinct from thought, is limited by the (transcendental) laws of nature. Crucial for our purposes here, and in fact for the whole of Kant's writings (since it touches so centrally upon both his theoretical and practical philosophy), is the notion of casuality – that all events must be part of a casual nexus in which there are no uncaused, or first (free) causes. To be able to explain means to be able to give a causal account of an event. This rules out the idea of a free or first cause, because such a cause, being itself not a member of any further causal chain, would be inexplicable and incoherent. Because only explanations of this kind (empirical and capable of causal formulation) can make supportable knowledge claims (all other varieties of explanation having presumably to invoke principles that cannot possibly be proved), they always have a priority in regard to knowledge (C1 A546 / B574).

What, then, of the great questions, concerning God, freedom, and the immortality of the soul? All earlier metaphysics has wanted to know the suprasensible, but Kant seems to have affirmed and even grounded the central proposition of a very radical scepticism: that the world, governed by its natural laws, is all that is the case. It is difficult to see, in the light of the first phase of the Copernican revolution, just how metaphysics, that old dowager, has been restored to her former position, or even to a more modest, but nevertheless honoured, condition. Having hoped for a renewed metaphysics, a rigorous and scientific philosophy, we are told that we must remain content with our modest dwelling place, with this 'land of truth' beyond which there is no further shore but only an unending 'sea of illusion' (c1 A235–6 / B294–5). Into the innermost secrets of nature we are permitted to enter, but beyond nature's limits there is nothing for us. Eager as we may be to know the answers to the questions that burden philosopher and non-philosopher alike, we shall never be able to do so (c1 A702 / B730, A278 / B334).

What is at issue here is, again, more than simply the possibility of one kind of philosophy. In the first sentence of his *Metaphysics*, Aristotle wrote that all men by nature desire to know. Kant tells us that metaphysics is placed in us by our nature (DV VI: 376 / 33 and c1 A797 / B825). Nature is to be understood not simply or even primarily as curiosity, but rather as the practically or morally rooted desire to know of God, freedom, and the soul. It is to this fact that Kant is referring when, at the beginning of the *Critique of Pure Reason*, he speaks of reason's 'peculiar fate' and this is also the sense of his statement that man is a 'needy being' – *'ein bedürftiges Wesen'* (c2 v: 61 / 63). He is needy because burdened with desires that cannot be satisfied as such. The desire to know, which implies the incompleteness of our knowledge and thus our neediness, is, according to Aristotle, the source of all philosophy.[4] Perplexity or wonderment (for Aristotle) and our practical needs (in Kant's account) – in both cases, the inadequacy of what we have when compared with what we want – constitute the impulse that gives birth to metaphysics. For Kant, that impulse is also the origin of dialectic.

Kant referes to dialectic as the 'logic of illusion' (c1 A293 / B349). But the ideas of reason are no mere illusion, in the ordinary sense of that term, no simple conjurer's trick, but an illusion implanted in us by nature itself (c1 A298 / B354). Kant draws an analogy between dialectical illusion and the observation that the moon appears larger to us during its ascent than at its zenith in the night sky. We know, of course, that the moon's circumference does not change, yet we never-theless cannot help but view it as larger at the beginning of its climb. There is, however, an essential difference between this kind of optical illusion and the dialectical illusion of reason. The former is the result of the failure of our passive faculties, of our receptivity, and it is in no way bound up with our interests or desires. The latter begins with the limits of experience and is driven by the needs of reason to seek sat-isfaction elsewhere. Like Platonic *eros*, the needs of reason are the dynamic force that compel ascent.[5]

Experience never fully satisfies reason. Indeed, the very fact that reason is incessantly urged on by its questions shows that what is answered in experience is very little. 'Who can satisfy himself,' Kant writes, 'with mere empirical knowledge in all the cosmological ques-tion of the duration and of the magnitude of the world, of freedom?' (PFM IV: 352 / 100). Experience denies us knowledge of what is tran-scendental, namely, of what cannot be given in sensible intuition and subjected to the laws of experience, that is, to the categories. Reasons's desire for the unconditioned, for absolute totality, and for the ideas of God and the soul is never answered by experience. The limits of ex-perience and explanation command us, so to speak, to remain on that little isle of truth and certainty that is ours, and not to be lured by empty hopes for the discovery of a new land (c1 A236 / B295). What we are left with is a world governed by mechanical causality with no freedom and no first beginning of the world (no God), and in which the idea of the soul is unintelligible. Here man is a mere speck in nature, a 'trifle' (*kleinigkeit*), whose presence on earth is as inexplicable as his fate is certain. We are beings who find ourselves endowed, for a time, with life – how and for what reason we do not know – at the end of which we are returned to the soil. 'We know not how ...', nor, we may add, why (c2 V: 162 / 166 and OQ VII: 89 / 148). The sense of the world and what, if anything, distinguishes man from the other creatures who join him here on earth must be outside the world, outside its laws and the sort of explanations they present.[6]

Reason finds itself dissatisfied with the knowledge provided, and limited, by experience, and it follows its urgent and lofty inquiries, tearing down the 'boundary fences' of explanation, until it reaches a domain without limits, the 'empty space' of thought without intuition (c1 A296 / B352). Not content with the exposition of what is true, we demand that what we desire to know shold also be taken into account. The aim of this 'natural disposition' (*Naturanlage*) is to free our concepts from the 'fetters of experience' and from the contemplation of mere nature (PFM IV: 362 / 111). This demand for an extension of knowledge beyond what can be known is, Kant says, like a dove which, feeling too much resistance to its flight, seeks an empty space where no air or gravity will impede its rise. On the 'wings of mere ideas' is how Kant describes the natural desire to ascend that he attributes to reason (c1 A5 / B8–9, A638 / B666).

Kant's writing on this impulse to illusion abounds in uncharacteristically embroidered prose, which, as seductive as it may be, does not advance our understanding of that disposition. Is Kant offering us a grand descriptive psychology, or claiming that a full account of what is the case requires explanatory devices for which there can be no direct proof? I wish to postpone consideration of this question to a subsequent chapter. For my purposes here – a brief sketch of the dialectic, its source, and its solution – it is sufficient to remark that reason finds the limits of explanation, as set by the (transcendental) laws of nature, too narrow, particularly in regard to those concepts that Kant calls 'unconditioned.'

Reason fails to see that need alone is not a sufficient deduction for its ideas (that is, a proof of their legitimacy – that they are not mere illusions – and of their necessity) (PFM IV: 259 / 7). It then attempts to extend its knowledge claims, into the non-empirical, transcendental realm. But this transcendental domain is an 'empty space' in relation to precisely those knowledge claims that reason wants to make. Much ink has been spent examining Kant's concept of the noumenal and transcendental. These efforts are due, in no small part, to the obscurity and even contradictory character of his pronouncements on this topic. The weakest line of argument in the first *Critique* (on this particular question) need only be mentioned here: the understanding, by assuming appearances, grants the 'existence' (*Dasein*) of things in themselves that constitute the 'basis' of those appearances (PFM IV: 315 / 62 and c1 A252). It is almost as if Kant thinks himself compelled to adopt this conclusion by his use of the term 'appearance' – in English, as in German, a noun formed from a verb. If there are 'appearances' (*Erscheinungen*), then there must be something that 'appears' (*erscheinen*). Though we can know that 'something' only through its appearances, the latter compel us to grant the former (c1 BXXVI and A540 / B568). Kant is thus led to speak of the two worlds (c1 A249), the phenomenal and the noumenal, and even to the suggestion that the one world may be the (causal?) ground of the other.

It will be clear from our earlier discussion of the Deduction that words such as 'world' and 'causality' are misused, and dangerously misused, when applied to this 'empty space.' For they allow and encourage a slide from an explanatory hypothesis of dubious necessity (that of things in themselves, or transcendental objects) into the language of ontology, of transcendental objects, worlds, and causes. The move from the need for a heuristic device to the description of that device in object language was just the sort of illegitimate move that Kant condemned throughout the first *Critique*. The ontological flavour of some of Kant's reflections on the noumenal is distinctly at odds with what he correctly took to be one of the key methodological advances of the *Critique*: the idea that ontology must give way to the theory of knowledge (c1 A247 / B303).[7]

A more sound approach, and one for which there is a substantial textual basis, is to treat the noumenal as being a strictly negative concept – the 'transcendental object = x' (c1 A250). This negative concept uses the idea of the noumenal or transcendental not as a pseudo-object, but as a marker for the limits of explanation and for a 'problem' or 'task' (*Aufgabe*) bound up with the limitations inherent in our sensibility (c1 A287 / B343–4 and PFM IV: 316–17 / 63–4). Here we are once again on the solid ground of the critical philosophy – the noumenal is an empty sphere, a problem (for reasons that we shall examine in the next chapter) perhaps, but not the bizarre 'world' of transcendental objects. Experience cannot provide, or even allow, answers to those questions that burden reason, and this failure leads the mind to that empty space. But there it finds no satisfaction, or only illusory satisfaction, the mirage of an answer. Yet, while denying reason its satisfaction, this privative concept of the noumenal also limits the use of empirical principles. By pointing to this empty sphere, and by restricting the range of use of the transcendental laws of nature to what can be given in sensible intuition, Kant's *Critique of Pure Reason* curbs the pretensions of mechanical causality and sensibility (c1 A255 / B310 –11).

The ideas of reason – freedom, God, immortality of the soul – show the boundaries of materialistic explanation while in the same moment they are themselves denied by Kant the title of knowledge. The mind, in acknowledging this empty space, restricts sensibility without thereby extending its own domain (PFM IV: 352 / 101). The notion of a boundary, however, offers the possibility of a space without as well as within its domain; materialism is limited to what can be given in intuition, and so at least the possibility of, for example, another type of causality is kept open (c1 Bxxx). This is the sense of Kant's now famous statement: 'I have therefore found it necessary to deny *knowledge* in order to make room for *faith*.' Many problems and nuances in this last thought will have to remain, for the moment, unexplored. What I wish to do here is to turn to Kant's third Antinomy in order to show how this distinction between phenomena and noumena permits Kant to settle the competing claims of reason, which are at the very heart of the Dialectic.

My intention is not to review the whole of Kant's argument in the first *Critique* concerning the Antinomies, but only to sketch the third Antinomy. The solution to the third Antinomy is representative of Kant's answer to the 'dynamical' Antinomies in general, and, more important, Kant attached great significance to this particular problem and its resolution in the light of its consequences for his moral theory. Kant's question, then, is: how can one render compatible two types of explanation, one based on the possibility of a causality through freedom, and the other making mechanical causality universal? Freedom, in this context, should not be understood as specifically moral freedom, the free agency of the will or submission to self-given law. It has here the rather more general sense of the power of beginning a state spontaneously. In the cosmological language of the Antinomies, the questions is one of the first origin of the world.

Kant sets out his argument in the following manner. The 'thesis' of the third Antinomy states: 'Causality in accordance with laws of nature is not the only causality from which the appearances of the world can one and all be derived. To explain these appearances it is necessary to assume that there is also another causality, that of freedom' (c1 A444 / B472). The 'antithesis' adopts the position that there is no uncaused or free cause, but that everything that happens must necessarily obey the laws of nature (c1 A445 / B473). The proof of the 'thesis' proceeds thus: take the argument of the 'antithesis' that everything is subject to natural laws, and search for the consequences of such a position. If that view is granted, everything must have a preceding state. But that state, being itself an 'event,' must be preceded by another state. There will always be a relative and never a first beginning. However, the law of nature is just this, Kant writes, that nothing occurs 'without a cause *sufficiently* determined a priori' (c1 A446 / B474).

The key to Kant's argument in the 'thesis' is to be found in the phrase '*sufficiently* determined a priori.' Although the significance of that phrase is somewhat obscure, the context provides us with the required information. The point that Kant wants to make is fairly clear: this first cause must not require any further (causal) explanation.[8] This amounts to the claim that a first cause is not to be found in the chain of natural causes that are always, and in principle, capable of further causal explanation. That tells us what a first cause is, but why must there be such a cause? Though the genealogy of the answer to this question is much disputed in the Kant literature, it seems that Kant is presenting a version (cast in epistemological terms) of Aristotle's idea that an infinite regress in the series of causes is impossible.[9] Were an infinite regress possible, there would be no (sufficient) explanation and hence no science. The thesis has also been interpreted as an expression of Samuel Clark and Isaac Newton's postulate of two kinds of causality as against Leibniz's theory of universal determinism.[10] Apart from its less interesting problem of the pedigree of the thesis, the debate between Kant's commentators centres around the issue of whether the Antinomies are cosmological in the sense that Kant claims they are. Beck favours the moral interpretation of the Antinomies, and particularly the third Antinomy, whereas Al-Azm tends to read them as Kant's entry into the Leibniz / Clarke-Newton fray over cosmology.

The weight of evidence, particularly that offered in Kant's commentary on the third Antinomy and, later, in the *Critique of Practical Reason*, clearly rests with the view that the Antinomy is intended to establish the possibility of freedom with the ultimate purpose of showing the posibility of morality. Indeed, it is reasonable to speculate that the moral question stands at the centre of the entire *Critique*, and becomes plainly visible in the Dialectic. Kant himself suggests as much in his *Lose Blätter* (LB xx: 335). To be sure, Kant thought that, within the limits of the first *Critique*, the moral question could be touched only obliquely, and thus the definition of freedom that he employs in the third Antinomy is not that of specifically moral freedom. Yet, as will become clear further on, Kant's overriding interest was in the practical implications of these questions, and their cosmological language should not conceal from us the primacy of this moral concern. When Kant wrote that reason 'is impelled by a tendency of its nature to go out beyond the field of its empirical employment' and that the source of that impulse is not theoretical but practical (c1 A797 / B825), he meant that metaphysics and its dialectic are rooted in our need to act, our moral needs in this world.

The antithesis of the third Antinomy claims that there is no freedom:

everything that occurs does so in accordance with the laws of nature, which preclude uncaused or freely caused events. The proof of the antithesis takes much the same form as that of the thesis. It asks us to adopt the argument that there is freedom, the power of spontaneously beginning a series, and then it seeks to show that were this the case, the unity of experience would be violated. The conflict here, then, is between a kind of explanation that permits freely caused events and what Kant terms 'transcendental physiocracy.' Stated in the language of Kant's theory of the dialectic, we find reason, in its search for the unconditioned, contradicting the requirements of experience as set out in the Aesthetic and Deduction of the first *Critique*.

Kant puts his solution to the third Antinomy into the unsatisfactory and misleading language of appearances and things in themselves. For the sake of exegetical fidelity, I shall briefly recapitulate that solution and then reconstruct from Kant's ideas, if not his words, a more comprehensible answer. Kant resolves the conflict between the thesis and antithesis by the proof that a heterogeneous condition 'not itself a part of the series [of sensible conditions], but *purely intelligible*, and as such outside the series, can be allowed' (c1 A530 / B558). In the 'dynamical' Antinomies, the completely conditioned is bound up with an empirically unconditioned and non-sensible condition. Consequently, the possibility of a resolution satisfying both reason and the demands of experience is permitted. The two types of causality coexist and can even be found in the same event.

The reason that the antithesis was incapable of grasping this possibility was that it asserted the absolute reality of appearances; it treated appearances as if they were things in themselves. 'If appearances were things in themselves, and space and time forms of the existence of things in themselves, the conditions would always be members of the same series as the conditioned (c1 A535 / B563)'. However, if appearances are understood as representations, then they must have a ground that is not itself an appearance: 'The effects of such an intelligible cause appear, and accordingly can be determined through other appearances, but its causality is not so determined' (c1 A537 / B565). In other words, the effect is in space and time, a phenomenal event, and it is for that reason subject to the laws of natural causality. The cause of the effect, however, stands outside the empirical series and so is not bound by the latter's rules. The same event may be viewed as free with respect to its intelligible cause, while, regarded as phenomenal, it is governed by the law of mechanical causality.

We can, I think, profitably ignore such quasi-ontological distinctions as that between apperances and things in themselves, and we can certainly avoid, again with no loss, discussions of noumenal causality. Better that we employ the term 'thing in itself' in the exclusively privative sense that Kant suggests in the *Critique*, or at least in parts of the *Critique*. Only this approach can be reconciled with Kant's theory of knowledge. How, then, can we recast the third Antinomy and its solution? Let us imagine an event or rather an explanation of an event being given before a court. A murder has been committed, and a defendant is being tried for it. Viewing this as an event in nature, a phenomenon, we can give a complete and self-contained explanation (requiring for its coherence no further and extraneous explanatory principles) in terms of natural, mechanical causality: electronic signals in the brain, a movement of a finger, a mechanical reaction in a weapon, an explosion, the trajectory of a projectile through space, a wound, and the cessation of a life.

Insofar as this particular form of explanation has as its horizon the events viewed as natural phenomena, differing in no fundamental way from other natural events, its principles (especially that of efficient causality) are wholly adequate, necessary, and exclusive. Within the given horizon of that kind of explanation, the events are exhaustively described using the principle of natural causation as the thread uniting the disparate events in one coherent account. Everything in the empirical series is to be explained according to the basic laws of all natural phenomena; no spontaneous, uncaused, or miraculous incidents can be introduced into the explanation. This murder, viewed as an empirical event – one given, to use Kant's expression, in sensible intuition – is wholly explained by a chain of cause-and-effect relations.

But the fact that as an empirical event this murder can be thoroughly analysed into cause-and-effect relations does not preclude the possibility of examining this same event from a different perspective – for example, with regard to the intention of the actors. What is precluded, on Kant's account, is the right of this new sort of 'explanation' to make the same kind of knowledge claim as that put forward by empirical explanation. Thus, while the knowledge claims of statements relating to the quality of a person's will are, at best, weak in Kant's argument (cf RWL VI: 63 / 56–7), by limiting the explanatory power of the laws of nature to the 'empirical series' (what is or can be presented in intuition) of events, Kant has left open the possibility of other ways of viewing that series.

In short, the crime (to conclude our illustration), as an empirical event, can and must be subject to that type of explanation of which the principal premises are the transcendental laws of nature. Within this horizon, marked out for us by sensibility and the categories that order them, these principles reign supreme; they are sufficient and exclusive. And all that can properly be called knowledge must conform to them. Yet beyond this horizon, these principles do not hold; another point of view is possible. But it is more than merely possible. Having bowed before the claim of scientific explanation to give an exhaustive account of the murder, we still feel that something is lacking, not from the standpoing of knowledge, but from a moral or practical perspective. We therefore take this same event and describe it in the light of accountability, or moral agency, rights, and duties. Beyond the horizon of empirical explanation, another (moral) point of view is allowed and needed. The reverse side of this proposition, however, is that because knowledge ceases where that horizon ends, there remains only an 'empty space,' empty with regard to what can be known of it. Experience is thereby preserved in its coherence against those who would disrupt its order by allowing uncaused, miraculous events in it, and at least the possibility of freedom is granted by the *Critique* (c1 A558 / B586).

In review, then, we have noted that the requirements of experience and knowledge on the one side and the needs of reason on the other are central elements of Kant's Copernican revolution. That revolution also claims to provide us with a key to the solution of the conflict between them. The limits of experience – of what can be given in intuition and combined in one consciousness – are also the limits of the laws that govern experience. Since these laws, or boundaries, define a space without (not bound by the transcendental laws of nature) as well as one within, the former, at a minimum, allows for the possibility of some viewpoint other than that of natural explanation. The error of 'transcendental physiocracy' is that it oversteps the boundaries of explanation by presuming that everything, not simply what can be given in sensible intuition, is governed by the transcendental laws of nature. Just as metaphysics overreaches itself when it vainly attempts to make knowledge claims about ideas that could never be given in possible experience, so too empircal explanation tears down its barriers when it applies its principles beyond the realm of phenomena.

The narrow limits of experience are thus the impulse that causes reason to 'ascend' in search of answers; but those same limits deny it, in its suprasensible ventures, the knowledge for which it is so eager. We wanted, Kant said, to build a tower that would reach to the heavens, but we found that our materials were sufficient only for a commodious home, suited for overseeing our business here on earth (c1 A707 / B735). Yet the boundaries that make impossible any solution to the urgent and pressing questions that burden our minds also restrict the field that empirical explanation can claim for its own. An empty space is thereby granted, and freedom is at least possible. These three characteristics of thought – the limits of experience and explanation, the need to transcend those limits, and the empty space beyond them – are, as we can now see, simply different, but related, facets of what Kant called his Copernican revolution.

At the end of the Antinomies, Kant tells us that freedom has been shown to be possible, nothing more. The noumenal, the 'empty space,' remains just that, empty. It is, however, a task, Kant says, to which we are unavoidably drawn by reasons's peculiar fate. We must now leave the dry language of Kant's theory of knowledge, which (to use Kant's metaphor from the *Groundwork of the Metaphysic of Morals*) defended the possibility of freedom, but did not establish its reality. We shall, in the next chapter, turn to the needs of reason. It is there that Kant's Copernican revolution first reveals its crucial moral side. We have thus made the natural and consequential transition from the question 'what can I know?' to the moral problem of what I ought to do.

# 3

# The needs of reason

Kant acted with a playful irony in that, on the one hand, he seemed to strive to set the most narrow limits on the faculty of knowledge while, on the other hand, and with a wink from the corner of his eye, he pointed beyond the limits which he himself had set.

Goethe

## KANT'S CONCEPT OF ORIENTATION

The *Critique of Pure Reason* concludes that the limits of explanation make any answer to the great questions of metaphysics impossible, at least from the point of view of the theory of knowledge. The corollary of this conclusion is that beyond those limits an 'empty space' is left, and so freedom is shown to be thinkable. This odd phrase, 'empty space,' is to be found throughout Kant's mature writings. In one sense its meaning is quite clear: what cannot be explained, that is, described in the language of the universal laws of nature, is empty – it cannot become knowledge and hence is nothing for us from a theoretical point of view (as knowledge of objects or events), merely a chimera or thought-entity. This use of the word 'empty' turns our attention to the range of supportable claims to knowledge. The 'empty space' is what one is left with after all that is knowable has been catalogued.

There is another, more elusive sense that Kant attaches to the phrase 'empty space.' 'Empty' here refers not so much to the necessary inadequacy of statements about the suprasensible as to the unsatisfactory character of what can be known when compared with our needs. The adjective 'empty', then, describes both a domain whose objects could never be given in any possible experience and the set of pseudopropositions about that domain. 'Empty' also characterizes the world and the legitimate propositions that can be made about it when the question is one of satisfying our moral or practical needs. Experience, one might say, is empty in relation to those questions which, by nature, burden our reason. This play on the meaning of 'empty' is at the very heart of Kant's theory of the dialectic, and it is what he means when he calls the noumenal an *Aufgabe*, a 'problem' or 'task.'

The ascent from what can be known to what we desire to know is thus reflected in this double meaning of the term 'empty'. If that word meant nothing more, in Kant's account of experience, than baseless claims to knowledge, then its significance would be confined to the theory of knowledge. Yet Kant calls that empty space a task and states that we are not only permitted to enter it (allowed to assert the possibility of freedom) but are compelled to do so: 'We are at *liberty*, indeed we are *summoned* [*aufgefordert*] to take occupation of it, if we can, by practical data of reason' (c1 Bxxi–xxii; emphasis added). Once all the questions that can be answered within the horizon of the world and the laws of its explanation have been answered, there remains an emptiness. The prospect of a world without purpose in which man is a mere trifle and the idea of men without freedom and of no hope for a life after death compel us, Kant seems to suggest, to take hold of this empty space. Put in another manner, the *Critique of Pure Reason*'s answer to the question 'what can I know?' is satisfactory only so long as the practical or moral is not taken into consideration (c1 A805 / B833). What we must now do is examine Kant's theory of the needs of reason, since it is precisely those needs that express the emptiness of experience (for moral purposes), on the one side, and the need to ascend from experience to the suprasensible, on the other.

The tribunal that Kant spoke of at the beginning of the first *Critique* was that of the theory of knowledge. It was the court before which the claims of reason and experience were to be judged. In its 'dry formulas' the *Critique* had set out 'merely the ground [*bloss den Grund*] of their legal claims' (c1 A462–3 / B490–1). Having determined the rightfulness (judged from the standpoint of the theory of knowledge) of these claims, when they are given a suitably modest form, we have to turn to those claims themselves, for which the rigours of the *Critique* were but a necessary prelude. These claims of reason are to be made about a domain that Kant likens to a room blanketed in a darkness into which no light can penetrate. Many things may be imagined in such darkness, but nothing can be seen; likewise, many suprasensible objects may be thought, but which of them are the 'phantoms of a magic lantern' (*Zauberlaterne von Hirngespenstern*), and which are necessry and just? It will be left to another court, not the tribunal of the theory of knowledge, to answer this question.

The very needs, the 'felt needs of reason,' that compel our ascent also serve as our guides in this 'realm of impenetrable darkness.' In an empty space within which no objects are given to us, the needs of reason allow us to distinguish what is capricious from what is necessary (c1 A259 / B315 and WOT VIII: 137 / 297). We have already noted Kant's remark that the need of reason is one of seeking the unconditioned. If this idea is to be of use to us we have to examine it further, as to what Kant intends both by a need and by the unconditioned. To orient oneself, Kant writes, 'means to find, from one given direction in the world ... the others' (WOT VIII: 134 / 294). The sun in the noon-time sky (an objective datum) combined with my subjective sense of left and right (the 'feeling of distinction in my own person') allows me to determine the other directions.

In Kant's next illustration the objective data are somewhat dimmer, the stars at night. His final example, that of a dark room, presents a situation in which nothing can be seen, where no objective data are available, but only objects remembered. Now in the problem of orienting oneself at night, Kant says that even if a miracle occurred and the direction of all the stars were reversed from east to west, yet keeping the same pattern, vision alone would notice no change. But the feeling of left and right would come to the person's aid, and he would not only 'notice the change but would orient himself regardless of it' (WOT VIII: 135 / 295). However, if in the darkened room this same evil genie were to rearrange the room's contents, an observer would be unable to orient himself relying on the now inaccurate data provided by recollection of the room's furnishings. Only the feeling of left and right would permit him to navigate in a room with four identical walls.

Kant's imagery, while itself somewhat opaque, nevertheless reveals the direction of his argument. The suprasensible is equivalent to the impenetrable darkness of the room described above. Nothing in it can be 'seen' (known), and no experience can provide us, directly at least, with information about it. Vision, in this metaphor, stands for knowledge, and Kant is simply maintaining the position he put forward in the *Critique* that what cannot be given in any possible experience cannot be known. This room, the suprasensible domain, has neither a sun nor stars that might provide an objective reference point, a bench-mark against which we might determine direction. In the first two of Kant's three illustrations, it is just this objective point of reference that aids us in finding the four directions. Here the subjective sense is not forced to rely solely on its own capacities but rather finds a guide in what is external to it. The darkened room has no such point of reference, no North Star or sun, and it thus forces us to depend exclusively on our subjective sense. The first of Kant's images, the sun at midday, establishes a clear and reciprocal relation between an objective signpost and the subjective sense of left and right. Orientation here means taking one's bearings by correlating two sets of data, that of the senses and that of a 'feeling.'

This process is analogous to the use of hypotheses in the natural sciences: objective data are mixed with speculation (for example, the notion that nature always seeks the most economical path in her actions), and new insight is gained into nature's operations from the exchange between the facts as they are known and the postulated condition. The third of Kant's examples portrays a situation in which this exchange – speculation pulling empirical research toward its postulated ideal state while at the same time being restrained in its flights of fancy by the hard empirical facts – is not possible. This is plainly meant to parallel reason's adventures in the suprasensible, where there is no intuition or experience (in general, no nature) to aid us in finding our direction.

It is necessary to note, in order that we may avoid a misrepresentation of Kant's argument, that while reason's ascent is altogether lacking in objective signposts, narrowly understood (objects given in intuition), the practical or moral needs of reason have, in Kant's account, a higher status than that of mere hypotheses. This higher status rests on the claim that they are the corollaries of what Kant terms a 'fact of reason,' namely the moral law and freedom. What is meant by 'necessary corollaries' and by a 'fact of reason' we shall see at a later point, but the words 'necessity,' 'fact,' and 'objective' (as applied to this 'fact') are usually prefaced by the phrase 'for practical purposes.' Thus, when we say that there are no objective data that reason can employ, we mean objective in the theoretical sense (from the point of view of knowledge), not in the practical sense (in relation to action). Yet even this statement requires one further qualification. There are no positive data, no intuitions or experiences, that mark out a path for reason, but, in a privative sense, experience does point the way. Reason 'sees its lack and, through the impulse to cognize, it effects the feeling of a need' (WOT VIII: 139 note / 299 note). This need is, therefore, not called into being *ex nihilo* but rather has its origins in the inadequacies of what is given us in experience, and in the necessity of making judgments despite these inadequacies.

To orient oneself in thought, then, means 'to determine one's assent according to a subjective principle of reason because of the inadequacy of its objective principles' (WOT VIII: 136 note / 296 note). Certain propositions, hypotheses, or postulates are allowed even though, judged according to the standards of what knowledge is, they lack a sufficient objective foundation. The postulates or hypotheses claim no insight into their objects and can compel our assent only on a subjective basis. We must not permit such 'exacted presuppositions' to masquerade as knowledge, but we may not deny reason the satisfaction of its legitimate needs. These two requirements, seemingly in conflict with one another, are recognized as compatible once it is seen that the ideas of reason are not, in themselves, dialectical but become so only in their employment. When we assent to a principle on the basis of a subjective need, and when that assent is coupled with a consciousness of its objective insufficiency, no violence is done to the distinction made in the *Critique* between what can be known and what merely thought. And within the realm of what can be thought, Kant separates those ideas that are 'corollaries' of a need of reason and therefore both subjective and universal from those ideas that rest solely on our 'inclinations' (*Neigungen*) and thus possess no necessity or universality (C2 V: 144 note / 149 note and WOT VIII: 136 / 296).

We have just remarked that the needs of reason give rise to principles which, while unable to carry the proud title of knowledge, nevertheless have a certain universality and necessity. What precisely Kant means by 'needs' is, however, not yet clear. Here we are helped by the idea of orientation. We orient ourselves by the sun, stars, or our subjective senses alone; in so doing, we find a direction – the four divisions of the horizon, the road home, or our way about a room. We wish to go somewhere, to do something. We do not orient ourselves in order to know about the sun, for example, or the stars, but we need to know their location so that, with their help, we may move from one point to another. Orientation is a navigator's word, not that of an astronomer. Navigators, unlike astronomers, are not in search of knowledge of the stars for its own sake but only of such knowledge as will be of use to them in determining the direction in which they are to go. Similarly, we need these principles of reason in order to extend our knowledge of nature or to act in a moral manner. Their employment is, therefore immanent, not transcendent.

Our need to act well, not the ultimately futile desire to have knowledge of suprasensible, of God, freedom, or the soul, is what compels us to adopt those principles of reason. The necessity of judging and of acting leads us to adopt as subjectively sufficient ideas that are not (and cannot be) supported by experience. The needs of reason ultimately amount to the need to act, and that need in turn points to man's practical or moral side. This suggests that the formal 'Ich,' the self that determines the boundaries of the world, considered as an object of possible experience, is not the whole self. The acting self, the 'Ich' as a moral agent, sets a second boundary to the world, now viewed as a world constituted by rational and moral beings. The knowing self, the self of pure, formal consciousness, and the world whose limits it prescribes are now seen to be complemented by an acting self and its world, the world bounded not by the laws of what is but the laws of what ought to be.

## THE NEEDS OF THEORETICAL REASON: TELEOLOGY AND THE EXPLANATION OF NATURE

The needs of reason are two-fold, Kant writes, speculative and practical. Since the practical needs of reason have a clear priority in Kant's eyes [WOT VIII: 139 / 298], it is to them that we shall devote special attention. First, however, reason in its speculative interests should be discussed; with that done, we shall have a more complete picture of the theoretical side of Kant's Copernican revolution. Now experience, according to Kant, can be viewed in two ways: as a system according to transcendental laws, and as a system according to empirical laws (FI XX: 208 / 14). Kant defines a system as a 'body of knowledge ordered according to principles' (MAN IV: 467 / 3). The former system consists of those rules (categories) by which intuitions can be united in one consciousness: its rules are at the same moment the conditions of all possible experience. But experience must also be viewed as a system of potential empirical knowledge, as an object fit for scientific inquiry. The order of nature created by the transcendental laws of experience makes our intuitions a possible object of coherent experience, of experience in the most rudimentary sense. Before these rudimentary experiences can be said to make systematic knowledge, or science, possible, further 'ingredients' are required. This distinction between experience as a system according to transcendental laws and as something that can be worked up into scientific knowledge clearly shows that the first *Critique* was intended to demonstrate the possibility not of science as such but only of simple experience – the combination of intuitions in a single consciousness.[1]

The understanding is 'in possession a priori of universal laws of nature ... but it needs in addition a certain order of nature in its particular rules, which can only be empirically known' (C3 v: 184 / 21). The transcendental laws are the necessary conditions of experience, but the aggregate of those experiences need not form a system. While every event must, for example, follow a causal pattern according to the formula 'every event B is preceded by an event A according to a rule,' there might be such a bewildering diversity of rules, not combinable with each other, that events would be so heterogenous as to render systematic knowledge impossible.

Science depends on the possibility of subsuming groups of events under laws and, in turn, combining those laws in a larger system of law. Thus the classificiation of empirical phenomena is a pre-condition of science. Science, then, might be said to require a 'connected empirical cognition' (C3 v: 386 / 233). It must assume not only that all objects are knowable in the weak sense of being objects of possible experience but also that they can be connectd to other like phenomena in a rule-governed system. If events and objects were so diverse as to defy classification, we would indeed still have experience but not science. We assert, therefore, that nature, in its organization, must conform to our capacity for judging it (FI xx: 202, 209 / 9, 15, and C3 v: 360–1 / 207). Nature's objects and events have to be classifiable into genera and species, nature must exhibit a parsimony in its laws and forms, and those laws cannot be so discrete and unique as to make a system of related laws impossible. In short, if we are to study nature, and if we are to have systematic knowledge of it, then nature has to be viewed as a lawful system arranged as if to suit our judgment.

To see this more clearly, consider Wittgenstein's account of how we describe the world. Imagine, he writes, a white sheet of paper dotted with irregular black marks. I place a square mesh over it and then identify every square in that mesh as either black or white or mixed. 'In this way I shall have imposed a unified form on the description of the surface.'[2] Without the mesh there would remain black marks and white marks but no unified form or systematic description. We could choose other meshes, hexagonal or triangular, for instance, and these different meshes are analogous to the various ways we have of describing the world. But if the dots on that paper were so constituted (though it is difficult to imagine quite how this could be done) that no mesh could be placed over them, then description and ultimately science would be impossible. The world must be ordered in such a way that at least some 'mesh' can be used to present its elements in a cohesive and systematic manner.

Here we have to do with a need of judgment, a need for systematic unity in nature, indeed the greatest possible systematic unity (c1 A686–7 / B714–15). This sort of judgment Kant calls reflective: it is one in which the law or major premise is not given to us. In determinant judgment, the act of judging consists in the application of a known principle to a set of particular circumstances or facts. Judgment is here required to supply no concepts of its own; it is rather a relation, or function, by which one kind of data is brought to bear on another. But in those cases where no principle is supplied, the faculty of judgment must supply its own, and, according to Kant, the only standard it can employ in selecting this principle is the requirements of judging itself. The person who is judging says something like this to himself. I am faced with a collection of facts, phenomena, say, and I have no principle under which they can be subsumed and hence judged. I am therefore entitled to produce such a principle or premise as would permit my judgment its exercise. All the while I must remain aware of the fact that this postulated major premise rests its legitimacy on the needs of judgment and not on any supposed insight into the objective reality of the hypothesis itself. The deduction of the hypothesis is thus based on a subjective need, the need of judgment.

This hypothesis, in its most general form, is the interrelation posited between one cluster of phenomena and the next, which makes them available for inclusion in a system of empirical laws (FI xx: 216 / 21). Kant designates this unity a 'logical finality'; it is a purposive system, consisting not of individual forms explicable on teleological principles, but of phenomena tied to one another as if they had been arranged that way in order to make science possible. Now a 'purposive phenomenon' Kant defines as something the existence of which seems to presuppose the antecedent representation of it (FI xx: 215 / 20). The greatest possible unity is purposive unity: nothing is contingent here, but everything has its place and function in a system that we are capable of comprehending only on an analogy with designed objects (c1 A698 / B726).

Kant's argument can best be undestood by using the watch metaphor so popular in the teleological writings of his day. A watch consists of an aggregate of parts, and taking them as an aggregate, a mere heap, we can do no more than to catalogue them. Were nature, like this watch, simply an aggregate of parts, only the most elementary sort of description would be possible, and the enormity of even that task would be daunting. But the watch can also be described as one part meshes with another, according to its function, wheels turning wheels and pins moving hands, so that all the parts constitute a system, an aggregate raised above the level of a heap of discrete units by a set of connected laws of behaviour.

Science requires more than an aggregate, a collection of facts; it demands a system, a set of laws under which the particulars can be subsumed. The first *Critique*, it might be said, showed us how experience and nature are possible but left unexamined how nature could be made subject to a systematic description. The need of judgment to suppose the accessibility of nature to a process by which particulars are subsumed under more specific laws than those provided by the categories suggests to us a principle by which nature as a whole is to be judged: as purposive in that it satisfies the need of reason for systematic unity.

What we have been discussing is the formal or logical teleology of nature. Material purposiveness is distinguished from its formal counterpart in that here purposiveness is not so much introduced by the subject as it is rather we who are 'instructed' by the object to think it as purposive (c3 v: 365 / 211). To be more precise, the kind of logical purposiveness analysed above introduces the idea of purpose into the investigation of nature not as the result of any direct perception of purpose there, not because we see something whose form clearly tells us that it is purposive, but because the possibility of science requires of us that we assume nature, as a whole, to be designed in a way that meets the need that we have to inquire into it.

What Kant terms 'organized beings,' however, are objects with a form that compels us to think of it as purposive. And it is called internally purposive because the form of the object is seen as being both cause and effect of itself. In other words, it is not purposive in the sense of being of use to some other natural being (utility), but rather it is teleological in its inner constitution. In an organized being, the final or mature form is taken as the cause and the effect of the various parts. This distinguishes it from a mere art product, where the purposiveness resides not in an internally generated final form but in the idea of a designer or artificer.

The somewhat convoluted statement that the effect in an organized being is reciprocally cause and effect amounts to this: we take this being, the human body, for example, to be the effect of the working of its parts, the supply of oxygen, blood, the generation of tissue, and so on. Yet when we examine the function of those parts we find ourselves compelled to adopt the language of teleology and to leave aside the principle of efficient, non-purposive causality. The heart exists in order to circulate the blood, and blood exists in order to carry oxygen, until the 'sum' of these 'in order to' propositions yields the whole that we call the concept of a body. The living body is, then, at once the effect of the workings of its constituent parts and the 'goal' or end that allows us to account for their existence and function. Plainly, such natural products are purposive only by analogy; we attribute no purpose, in the strict sense (acting according to an idea of an end), to them but use that sort of language in order to account for phenomena that seem to defy explanation in the terms of mechanical causality.

It is Kant's contention that certain natural objects require purposive explanation (UGP VIII: 179); mechanism alone does not allow us to think the possibility of such objects (c3 v: 421–2 / 271). This is not to say that we can, with certainty, deny the possibility of a mechanical explanation being given for them; rather we can claim no more than that these organized beings must be considered by us as purposive (c3 v: 405–6, 408 / 253–4, 257). This is what Kant means when he says that there will never be another Newton 'who shall make comprehensible ... the production of a blade of grass according to natural laws which no design has ordered' (c3 v: 400, 409 / 248, 258). The same Newton who had set the planets on their geometrical course cannot explain something so insignificant as a blade of grass. To be able to cognize, to account for organized beings, we must regard nature or certain of its objects as purposive. Formal teleology was needed in order that science might be possible. Material teleology, insofar as it is concerned with inner purposiveness, is made necessary by objects with a form that is inexplicable on any other grounds. The possibility of science in the one case and of organized beings in the other (more exactly:

the possibility of our comprehending them) is the deduction or justification of the use of teleological principles in these cases.

The third, and last, kind of natural teleology that we want to consider is relative purposiveness: objects that, exhibiting no internal purposiveness, are nevertheless, in virtue of their usefulness for some other object or being, designated as purposive. This type of teleological judgment was thought by Kant to be the weakest of the three that we have considered. It is weak because the explanation of no phenomenon depends on it. And further, in order to claim validity for itself it must be able to determine some ultimate purpose of nature because without that ultimate purpose the whole range of subordinate utilities are denied their purposive status and revert once more to the level of contingent phenomena.

Let us think about the example that appears throughout Kant's writings: Laplanders and the peoples of the earth's frigid zones find themselves provided with firewood and building materials in the form of driftwood. In these inhospitable lands, the animals of the sea supply oil and furs. It would seem almost as if nature had placed driftwood and sea animals there so as to support human life in an otherwise barren region. But why do people find themselves there at all? If they are there by accident or by free choice, we can hardly maintain that the driftwood they discover or the animals they hunt are there in order to support their settlements, since those settlements are contingent in the first place.

To make a claim of a relative teleological character we would have to know that the populating of the northernmost areas was also a purpose of nature. We are thus led, Kant writes, along a chain of relative purposes, of utilities the purposive nature of which cannot be established until a final purpose is discovered to which all others are subordinate. But as a final purpose it must be something unconditioned, and, as was mentioned in our discussion of the third Antinomy, nothing unconditioned is to be found in nature.

Kant says that if there is such a purpose it must be man viewed as personality, that is, as a being possessing moral agency. Yet Kant clearly understood the weakness inherent in the move from this final purpose back into a series of subordinate utilities. Even if we allow that man is the final purpose of nature, the particular phenomena that we might wish to describe as teleological could not be so described simply on the basis of the kind of being man is.

To assert, for instance, that oil-bearing sea creatures exist to serve man, it is not sufficient to show that man is a final purpose. One would have to prove also, as we said above, that he is placed by nature in those areas where animals that yield fur and oil would be essential to his survival. If his being there is contingent, or if his need for these creatures is, then the purposive argument would be weak at best. Without this further specificaton of the more general claim about man as a final purpose, the purposive connection remains tenuous indeed.

The end result of this analysis is that while evidence of purposiveness in organized beings may lead us to make the leap to the idea of nature as a purposive whole, that type of teleological judgment lacks the necessity that attaches to the idea of internal purposiveness. Nothing about nature requires that kind of explanation, and the evidence for it, given its reliance on a general notion of what a final purpose would have to be, is somewhat thin (c3 v: 378–9, 398–9 / 225, 246). The doubts that Kant had about such a line of reasoning are strikingly revealed in this remark from his essay on the various races of men: 'To say with Voltaire that God, who has created the reindeer in Lapland in order to consume the moss of these cold regions, has also created Laplanders in order to eat these reindeer is not a bad notion for a poet. But it is a poor expedient for the philosopher who is not permitted to abandon the chain of natural causes' (vvr ii: 440).

Theoretical reason, then, has an interest and a need; an interest in advancing its exercise, in extending its knowledge of objects 'up to the highest a priori principles' (c2 v: 120 / 124), and a need to assume those conditions under which alone this advance would be possible at all and, indeed, under which science itself could be considered as a feasible enterprise. What science or theoretical reason seeks to do is to explain, to exhibit phenomena in a law-governed order, and to give to that order the greatest attainable systematic unity. For the purposes of explanation, theoretical reason adopts hypotheses, not in order to give objective reality to the objects of those hypotheses (for example, organized beings) but so as to satisfy inquiring reason in its desire for a coherent account of the world, and to give occasion for further investigation into the postulated ideal order of nature. By attempting to approximate this ideal, empirical science orients itself, according to Kant, and is continually drawn forward in its researches. The basic vocabulary of experience, namely the categories, is insufficient when we want to give a systematic description of natural phenomena, be that description science in general or the more specific interest in purposive biological systems. A need is thereby established to adopt those hypotheses that are necessary for the satisfaction of reason's desire to explain.

## THE NEEDS OF PRACTICAL REASON: FREEDOM, FAITH, AND THE STOIC IDEAL

There is another need of reason, however, now taken not as theoretical or scientific but as practical reason. This is the need to assume the existence of a moral Designer of the world and to postulate the immortality of the soul so that the idea of the highest good may then be possible. My intention here is not to attempt a summary of Kant's moral theory but rather to show how the idea of the *summum bonum*, together with the necessary postulates, emerges from it.

Freedom, Kant tells us in the first *Critique* and at the end of the *Groundwork*, is possible but inexplicable – the idea of a freely caused event does not and cannot mesh with the fundamental laws of nature. But of one thing we are certain: the moral law. We construct for our wills maxims to which we ascribe necessity and universality and which we call law only when they have been separated from all empirical considerations. In short, we pronounce to ourselves the word 'ought'. It is the exercise of this faculty of moral judgment, not the external practice of virtue, that stands at the centre of morality. The conduct of the virtuous man, that he acts well, is of less importance for Kant than the fact that we are beings capable of making judgments with the status of law, necessary and universal judgments. That we can think something like an 'ought,' a counter-factual, a law that speaks unequivocally and that we employ in our judgments is what marks man off as unique.

In the Aristotelian practical syllogism, the major premise of which is a rule or maxim and the conclusion of which is an action, Kant's concern is principally with the former. This sort of argument allows one to concede, at the extreme, that all behaviour has its origins in a stimulus-response mechanism, in the pleasure principle, or whatever source of action we might care to name, and nevertheless to allow man a special place in the realm of sentient creatures. His right to claim this position rests not on his behaviour, which, as we have just conceded, is learnt in much the same way as the laboratory animal learns to press a lever in order to get food, but rather on the fact that he judges, that he speaks the word 'ought.' The moral law, the imperative contained in the 'ought,' is inexplicable on any natural grounds (C2 V: 43 /

44). We may learn our behaviour in a manner similar to that of other living things, but we differ from them in that we judge our behaviour. The behaviour itself is, like all phenomena, explainable on natural grounds: 'if we could exhaustively investigate all the appearances of men's wills [i.e. their empirical character], there would not be found a single human action which we could not predict with certainty, and recognise as proceeding necessarily from its antecedent conditions' (c1 a549–50 / b577–8). But nothing in nature can give rise to the idea of an 'ought.' The moral law, the possibility of which depends on our independence from nature and on our ability to prescribe laws to ourselves, is thus the *ratio cognoscendi* of freedom. That law makes of freedom a 'fact of reason,' since freedom is the only possible basis, the *ratio essendi*, of the categorical imperative (c2 v: 4 note / 4 note).

The moral law establishes the practical reality of freedom as a 'fact of reason' (c2 v: 94, 133 / 97, 138). Now a postulate is, as we saw earlier, a proposition about the nature of things to which we give subjectively sufficient and objectively insufficient (as regards knowledge) assent. We shall have to expand this definition, but for the present it should be remarked that a practical postulate differs from a hypothesis not only in the need that gives birth to it but also in the fact that whereas a hypothesis may be rendered false by an advance in our knowledge, a postulate, which rests only on the 'data of pure reason' and our finite nature, will never be confirmed or denied by experience (c2 v: 94, 133 / 97, 138). Hypotheses, then, stand to be corrected, while a postulate or, as Kant frequently refers to it, a rational belief is unchanging. One is a theory about objects given in experience, the other postulates facts that, by their nature, will never be met with in experience. However, more important than the epistemological claims made by the postulates is their source. We have seen above that they arise not from a need to explain, but rather a need to act. To see why the need to act should require postulates we must turn to Kant's distinction between law and will, between the form and the object of moral action.

The word 'ought' expresses the relation of a law to the will of a limited, finite being. The categorical imperative, which that 'ought' gives voice to, is what is required for a being whose will is not, of itself and necessarily, good, but requires a command in order to adhere to the law. If, in other words, the will were necessarily determined by the 'law of the good,' the phrase 'I ought' would be completely interchangeable with an 'I will' (gmm iv: 414 / 81). The *'principle'* of morality is a law (c2 v: 132 / 137 and tp viii: 280 / 47). It is the formal, necessary, and universal character of an imperative that binds our will, if it is to be moral, to an action irrespective of the purposes that that will may have. The crucial point here is that if the 'I ought to' is accompanied by an 'in order to' clause, the imperative becomes at once hypothetical, no longer a necessary law but a command contingent upon the end to be achieved and my desire to achieve it. The heart of the moral law, then, is its non-teleological quality or, in the more modern jargon, its deontological character. It is the purity of this concept of duty and law, the complete abstraction from any end whatsoever, that gives morality its dignity and uniqueness (TP VIII: 284 / 51).

The emphasis that Kant places on the quality of the will, its disposition in relation to the law rather than on virtuous deeds, separates him sharply from the classical tradition of ethics, with Aristotle as its principal figure. Moral judgments, in Kant's account, are about the disposition of a will, and here the formal character of the will's law-abidingness is central (RWL VI: 66–7, 72–3 / 60–1, 67). 'The fulfilling of duty consists in the *form of the earnest will*' (C3 V: 451 / 302). The moral law, and I wish to emphasize the word 'law' here, stands alone, and it is the essential ingredient in all morality. Its imperative nature, that it commands, is in no way bound up with some further end or purpose that we may have; on the contrary, it depends, for its law-like status, precisely on abstraction from such ends.

This has led some students of Kant, among them Christian Garve, one of Kant's contemporaries and the subject of the important first chapter of *On the Old Saw ...* to attribute to him a somewhat implausible, if exhilarating, theory of moral behaviour. According to this account, Kant's doctrine portrays the moral life as one free of desire or longing, a life without purposes, in short one governed exclusively by the moral law. This is the deontological argument taken to an extreme, and to see why it is an inaccurate description of Kant's theory one can do no better than to look at the latter's rejection of Stoicism.

The Stoics, Kant writes, 'left out of the highest good the second element (personal happiness), since they placed the highest good only in acting and in contentment with one's own personal worth, including in it the consciousness of moral character' (C2 V: 127 / 132). The Stoic sage was like a god, independent of nature and finding within himself a wholly self-sufficient source of contentment. Such a being would, of course, not know of desire, since desire implies a want, a lack of something, and hence the absence of self-sufficiency. But the 'voice of their own nature' should have shown them the faults in that argument. Here we find Kant making the seemingly curious case that Stoic moral theory was impoverished by its failure to consider the role of desire in human actions. Yet this should come as no surprise to us, since Kant had defined life as the 'faculty of a being by which it acts according to the laws of the *faculty of desire'* (c2 V: 9 note / 9 note; emphasis added).

Kant distinguishes desire from pleasure, referring to the former as the purposive or teleogical faculty by which one causes through 'ideas, the reality of the objects of these ideas.' Kantian desire, de-eroticized as it is, amounts to purposiveness, the capacity to act according to the idea of an end. That desire, for Kant, means nothing other than the will can be seen in a passage from the *Critique of Judgment* where he distinguishes between the sort of desire that ties men to nature and a free desire, or good will (c3 v: 443 / 293). Thus, when Kant says of the Stoics that they ignored desire, what he means is that they did not have an adequate theory of the will. What was lacking was exactly what is implied in the equation of desire and will: that the activity of the will is always a willing for something. That we must will for something shows that we are not as self-sufficient as a god might be, that we, as worldly beings, must look beyond ourselves and our moral worth to nature if it is happiness that we want (gmm iv: 438–9 / 105–6 and rwl vi: 7 note / 6 note).

The deontological side of Kant's argument must be brought into balance with his theory of the will. To be able to achieve this balance, we have to realize that his full account of moral behaviour ( a practical anthropology) includes both a conception of a formal, namely non-teleological, law and a theory of an essentially purposive will. What is deontological is Kant's idea of the moral law – but he was careful not to mistake a theory of law for an exhaustive description of moral life;[3] not to mistake, that is, a theory of judgment for a theory of behaviour. The theory of law has to be complemented by an account of the limited human will, the 'how' of our actions (rwl vi: 4 / 4). Against the Stoic denial of desire, Kant insists on a recognition of the teleological character of the human will, that it requires an object.

But we would do well not to draw too sharp a line between Kant and the Stoics; indeed Kant's own position will ultimately emerge as a sort of Stoicism itself, with this one alteration – that it recognizes the imperfection of the will. To see this, we should look more closely at the idea of desire, of an object of the will, and at the role of law in moral action. Kantian desire is, as we have seen, separated from pleasure. We are then left with a desire that amounts simply to willing for an object. Even this theory, however, is reduced, for Kant wants to play on the ambiguity of the notion that a will must have an object: an object of the will could be understood, on a strong purposive account of the will, as an end that is the cause of the actions that produce it – in other words, the 'final causality' of the third *Critique*. Here the idea of the end, the purpose or object, determines the will. In a weaker sense, an objet of the will could mean the expected or anticipated effect. This object does not determine the will but is merely what we expect, or hope, to follow from our actions (cf GMM IV: 413–14 note / 81 note). Kant transforms desire, strips it of pleasure, and then denies to its object the authority to guide the will. Desire, one might say, is reduced to a hope, a wish as to what will follow from our deeds.

Against those who collapse the distinction between law and will or desire, Kant insists on the primacy of the law in everything moral. The moral law is self-sufficient and needs no object; it is the principle, the *conditio sine qua non*, of a moral deed. Were our wills stronger, we might not need an end, and in such a case the moral law would remain untouched. Without that law, however, no will could be moral. How I ought to act can never be in doubt; to what end is often obscure. The former is objective, which means necessary and universal; the latter is subjective, bound up with our particular constitution (c2 v: 125 / 130).

The primacy of the moral law over any object of the will can best be seen in the making of moral judgments: here we have to do only with the conformity of the will to the moral law, the quality of the will as it follows the categorical imperative. The object of the will, from this point of view, can only enter into consideration as a factor destroying the moral character of a will by offering some particular, contingent end in the place of disinterested obedience to the law. Moral judgment concerns itself neither with the individual's external circumstances, his history, for example, nor with his desires or purposes, but only with the unqualified subjection of his will to the categorical imperative (TP VIII: 283 / 50 and c2 v: 117 / 121).

Nevertheless (and this is where Kant disagrees with the Stoic account), we are beings dependent upon sensuous objects for our welfare, and when nature is seen to comply with our wishes we call this happiness. And happiness, Kant writes, is a universal subjective end, which we have in virtue of being 'rational worldly' creatures – only as rational do we have ends, and as 'worldly' we desire happiness (RWL VI: 7 note and 46 note / 6 note and 41 note). We want happiness, and Kant seems to suggest that willing, considered as a purposive activity, is, in one form or another, willing for happiness. But not all of us will in the same way, and it is at this point that Kant once more picks up the thread of the Stoic account of virtue, albeit in a somewhat modified form.

Some make this necessary object of our sensuous wills, happiness, into the principal impulse behind their actions. Others subordinate this desire to the moral law, and allow their desire for happiness the status of a wish or hope. Still others seek to live like the Stoic sage mentioned earlier, to be courageous and to act without even the hope for happiness. Kant takes the thought of that sage and transforms it into a Platonic Ideal, an 'archetype' for how we are to live (c1 A569 / B597 and DV VI: 383 / 41). Kant preserves here what he considered Christianity's most important teaching, namely modesty, by presenting the sage as an ideal, to whose perfection we may only try to approximate our own lives. But in offering the sage rather than Christ as an archetype, Kant shows his preference for the Stoic conception of virtue over the hopeful point of view of the Christian's *summum bonum*. His argument against the Stoics has nothing to do with their emphasis on duty – rather, it is directed against the claim that virtue produces its own happiness. If the best life is the one led according to the moral law, it does not follow that happiness will necessarily be its reward.

Kant's modified Stoicism retains the ideal of the courageous sage but rejects the notion that happiness is a part of his condition. A god, a perfect being without a body or desires, might find happiness in the exercise of virtue alone – but not man. Men are free to ignore duty and to pursue only happiness, or to transform desire into a mere wish that is not permitted to act as an incentive for the will (and thus to bring happiness into harmony with virtue), or to attempt to approximate this (modified) Stoic Ideal – to ignore hope and happiness, looking instead only to the commands of duty.

As free beings, subject to the self-given moral law, we give happiness a very secondary role, but as creatures of flesh and blood, who depend on the 'circumstances of sensibility,' we want happiness. Kant recognizes, as Aristotle had before him, that a life well lived and yet full of misfortune is not complete.[4] Even the virtuous may desire happiness, but they desire it in a different way from those who are unvirtuous. Kant emphasizes what Aristotle did not: that the good life (or what is supremely good, without qualification) is the life of virtue, irrespective of the happiness or misery that may befall the virtuous man.

There is a distinction to be made, though, between the supreme good, which is the good will, and the complete good, which is happiness in proportion to virtue or, more exactly, the greatest happiness as a reward for perfect virtue. The Stoics and the Epicureans made a similar error: both equated virtue and happiness, the former by collapsing happiness into virtue and claiming that happiness is to be found in the exercise of virtue alone, and the latter by collapsing virtue into happiness or pleasure, implying that what is good is identical with the pleasurable. Kant separates morality from happiness in order to preserve the former from a heteronomous incentive and to use the latter to provide an account of our nature more in line with the facts of the matter than the Stoic theory. Yet he also says that they can be combined in the will of the virtuous person, and it is to that combination that we shall now turn.

It will be clear from the preceding analysis that morality and happiness are not combined as means and ends are. The truly moral will pays strict and exclusive attention to the categorical imperative, not to the results of its actions, when it is making a moral judgment. And since happiness is a condition bound up with our dependence on nature in general, the well-intentioned will, which has to do above all with our freedom, has no necessary relation to the harmony of nature with our desires. In sum, for Kant, morality does not provide its own pleasure or happiness (the latter being, as Kant maintained against the Stoics, a condition that involves the satisfaction of our worldly, sensuous wants), and morality cannot be treated as a prescription for how we may attain that condition. Nor, finally, does the moral will produce in nature that correspondence to our wishes that we call happiness. This is what Kant means when he says that the highest good is a 'synthetic proposition' – the proposition's two terms, morality and happiness, are not analytically derived from one another.

How then are morality and happiness to be united? How is this wish of mankind for a proportion between reward and virtue to be realized? In order for this object of the will to be possible – and only as possible could it be an object of the will – we have to postulate the existence of a moral governor of the world who will secure, in this life or in the one to come, the proportion we desire between our worth and our happiness. We have also to postulate the immorality of the soul because we are capable only of an infinite progress, or approximation, to that state of moral perfection that would warrant the complete happiness we seek. A new nature is neded, and so, too, is a soul that endures beyond the short span of time given to us here. We can never know that these conditions of the *summum bonum*, the highest object of our wills, are actual, but we can have faith. This faith, unlike the historical faith that relies on the testimony of people about past events (c3 v: 469 / 321), has the charm of never being refutable by experience or by an extension of our knowledge. To be sure, rational faith shares this charm with the pseudo-propositions of pre-critical metaphysics, but it differs from the latter by casting its claims not on the level of knowledge of God and the soul but rather as belief, and by the fact that it emerges from a practical need of reason. Faith is the 'moral attitude' (*Denkungsart*) of reason, a trust in the attainment of what we believe ought to be ours. The *summum bonum*, which demands worthiness of us and for the sake of which we postulate the conditions whereby that virtue will be rewarded, is the object of our faith. Its kind of happiness is the happiness that the virtuous desire. We trust in the 'promise of the moral law,' a promise not contained as such in the moral law but one that we 'put into it' (c3 v: 471 note / 324 note). Belief is an expression of our trust and our modesty (c1 A827 / B855) about the extent of our wisdom – we believe because we are unable to know. But the *summum bonum* and its postulates reveal our limitations in other ways: we assume the immortality of the soul because we are incapable of achieving moral perfection or holiness. And we postulate the existence of a moral God because we are not masters of nature. The limits of our knowledge, of our moral wills, and of our power over nature create in us the need to trust, to be faithful.

The step into religion (and that is, after a fashion, what Kant is discussing in his remarks on the highest good) is taken on behalf of a 'wish' (c2 v: 130 / 135) not within our power to grant. This faith is not a trust in revelation but a result of our moral reason (c3 v: 451 note / 301 note). We have no insight into an afterlife: no revelation has told us – as it promised St Augustine's pilgrims – of a City of God, of a salvation that we can confidently await. Rather, our needs, our weaknesses urge us on to a trust in the promise of the moral law, to hope. Faith is a source of hope, the moral law a source of worthiness (c2 v: 130 / 134). What Christianity calls divine commandments are holy not because they are commanded by God, but because they are the 'essential laws of any free will as such' (c2 v: 129 / 134). Kantian faith will take an even more radical step away from its Christian counterpart.

Faith has its origin in our moral needs, not in revelation. The promise that our wish will be fulfilled is, however, different from our worthiness to have it satisfied. Hope is different from a pattern for our conduct – the former contains what only nature or Providence can provide for us, worthiness is that which nobody but the person can give to or take from himself (TP VIII: 283 note / 50 note). The law-governed quality of our moral actions is within our power and, indeed, must abstract from all purposes. While the *summum bonum* is a good conditional upon our worthiness (C3 V: 451 note / 301 note) and upon the soul and world that it requires, the moral principle is absolutely self-sufficient. The principle of morality is not a postulate, but a law, and it can do without the highest good (C2 V: 132 / 137; TP VIII: 280 / 47; GMM IV: 450 / 117). In short, the practical principle is independent of our faculty of desire and of the object to which that faculty gives rise. The basis of obligation is the moral law, and no end is needed in order to know what duty is or to command its performance (RWL VI: 3 – 4 / 3–4). We know what we ought to do, and the law-abiding character of our actions in accordance with this 'ought' is within our power.

Kant's 'rational beliefs' (*Vernunftglauben*) are meant to serve the purposes of action. Faith is not commanded, as the moral law is, but chosen (C2 V: 144–5 / 149–50). And we choose it because of a subjective need related to the limits of a finite being -- the need to believe that our deeds will have the outcome that we wish. Were faith to be denied, the moral law would remain, though we would have to give up our hope in the moral law's promise. We believe in order that we may think possible that promise (which we attribute to the moral law) of a reward for our worthiness. Moral theology is thus of immanent use only: it serves the needs of that peculiar being who both desires and wills freely.

But moral theology is immanent in two ways that must be distinguished: one (the Christian version), which we have already seen, offers belief (the *summum bonum* and the postulates) as a source of hope in the realization of an end for which we have a subjective need. The idea of a moral Architect of the world and of the immortality of the soul allows a hope for a nature other than the one we know, a world where the coincidence of virtue and happiness would be secured. So as to think of a world of this kind, we have to postulate the existence of two 'objects,' God and the immortal soul. There is a second (Kantian Stoic) sense in which moral 'theology' is immanent; here the postulates speak not of imagined worlds and objects, but of duty: 'A postulate is a practical imperative, given a priori, for whose possibility no explanations (and therefore no proof) can be given. Thus one postulates not states of affairs [*Sachen*] or, in general, the existence of objects but rather only a maxim (rule) for the action of a subject' (VAT VIII: 418 note).

This formulation of the idea of a postulate shifts the emphasis away from a future world to the acting subject. It suggests that Kant has so transformed rational faith that it is now less concerned with the reward that we may hope for than with how we are to conduct ourselves. 'Rational belief is ... the signpost or compass ... It can show the way in ... a practical sense' (WOT VIII: 142 / 301). Rational belief, understood in this manner, amounts to another formula of the categorical imperative: it says, '*Act* so as to be worthy of the highest good.' Duty, not hope, our wills, not a world to come are to be our principal concern. Moral 'theology' (though it is difficult to see just how this doctrine can still be called a theology) in this second sense enables us to fulfil our vocation here on earth, to govern our wills according to the moral law. Indeed, Kant is reported to have said (in reference to his moral interpretation of the Bible) that if the Bible did not already exist, there would be no need for it to be written at all.[5] All the postulates, Kant writes, are, at bottom, answers to a single problem: what ought we to do (c1 A799–800 / B827–8)?

When we have properly understood moral theology (its proper use and limits), even the uncertainty we have, which is expressed in the idea of belief, appears as a blessing. That we are permitted only belief in, and not knowledge of, God and a life to come does not, as one might think, show the niggardliness of nature. For what if we did know with certainty of God, in his awful majesty, or of eternal punishment and reward? Our actions would then conform, in their external features, to the requirements of morality, but most would be done from fear or hope, the two great religious incentives, not duty (c2 v: 147–8 / 152–3 and c3 v: 481 / 335). This suggests again that Kant's argument is a sort of modified Stoicism: Kant shares with the Stoics an emphasis on duty. For Kant, our principal concern must be with the moral law, the 'moral standpoint' as he calls it, not salvation. But the Stoics made their virtuous man into a near-God and seemed to think moral perfection possible. They failed to take into account the limits of human nature. Kant, as we remarked above, sought to combine the Stoic conception of virtue with the recognition of those limits in his idea of the archetype of the sage, whose perfection we cannot realize but can approximate.

Christianity taught man humility by holding before him a 'pure and uncompromising' moral ideal: it 'destroyed man's confidence of being wholly adequate' to that ideal. Christianity did more, however, than teach man his limits. It threatened to turn the moral law into the commandments of an all-powerful God, and to offer, in place of respect for the law, hope and fear as the incentives for our actions. By adding hope to duty, Christianity turned man's eyes from the quality of the will and deeds in this world to the promise of salvation. Kant transforms the Christian highest good so that it serves Stoic, or Kantian ends: he takes the hope for salvation, deprives it of its character as an incentive, and remakes it into an imperative. Kant's Stoicism tells us that we must pay attention to duty above all else, but that we must also realize that, according to our nature, as finite worldly beings endowed with desire, we cannot obtain moral perfection. To say that the world is all that is the case is to say, against Christianity, that our concern must be with what we do here and now, not with what we may hope for, and it is also to say, against the Stoics, that we are not gods but men, imperfect men.

PART TWO

# Interpreting the world

# 4

# The origins of Kant's philosophy of history and politics

## THE PRIMACY OF THE PRACTICAL

Copernicus taught us that the source of the planets' motion was to be sought in the observer. We also learned from him that man does not stand at the centre of creation. In discovering the true origins of the movements of the heavens, we come to understand that we are simply one planet among many, that we are not the jewel crowning the starry firmament.

The lessons of astronomy are many, Kant wrote, but its most important lesson is the revelation of the 'abyss of our ignorance' (c1 A575 / B603 note), of how little we do or can know. Astronomy has shown us the insignificance of our knowledge, and it has pointed to our unimportance in the natural order of things: the sight 'of a countless multitude of worlds annihilates ... my importance as an animal creature, which must give back to the planet (a mere speck in the universe) the matter from which it came' (c2 v: 162 / 166). The depth of our ignorance and our insignificance as natural beings is what we have learned from Copernicus. But in turning back our pretensions, the Copernican revolution directed reason to its true vocation, to its 'ultimate purpose,' that is, to our affairs here on earth. So, too, has Kant's rational theology taught us not to abandon 'the guidance of a morally legislative reason' (c1 A819 / B847) in our actions for the sake of an ultimately fruitless search for knowledge of God and of his commands.

Once we have discovered the limits of what can be known, we also learn how vain our earlier efforts were. This is the 'startling consequence' that Kant mentions at the beginning of the *Critique of Pure Reason*: that a priori knowledge is possible, that the understanding is the law-giver to nature (c1 B159–60), but that beyond what can be given to us in possible experience, in the spatio-temporal framework of appearances governed by the categories, nothing can be known, and what cannot be known, in the broad sense, cannot be experienced. This in itself would pose no problem were it not for the fact that our reason is burdened by nature with questions, at once unavoidable and unanswerable, about God, freedom, and the immortality of the soul. These Kant describes as the 'needs' of reason, and the distance between those needs and our limited materials, our inability to meet them, is what gives rise to dialectical illusion.

The world viewed as an object of possible experience is radically empty and meaningless, in relation not to knowledge (on the contrary, only propositions that remain within the boundaries of that world can make a supportable claim to knowedge) but rather to our moral or practical needs. The world as described in the *Critique of Pure Reason* denies purpose and intelligent causation and does not permit us to distinguish what is most divine in us, our freedom, from what is merely natural. The natural world, seen in this way, is a sort of 'abyss' (compare c1 B21 to c2 v: 162 / 166), and the people in it are nothing but natural beings. In the 'starry heavens' passage just cited, Kant is saying that, viewed as part of nature, we can see ourselves only as matter endowed with life – how and why we do not know – but having no higher purpose than to return to the earth whence we came. We simply find ourselves here, mere specks in the universe, about whom it would be as silly to ask after a higher purpose as it would be to inquire about a stone's destiny. Man, taken as a more natural being, is bounded by the unintelligibility of his presence here, of the reason for his being endowed with life, and by the open grave that awaits him at the end. The deeply disorienting and unacceptable implications of such a view (the loss of our long-held sense of place in the order of things and consequently of our sense of direction as well) are revealed in Kant's claim that man has, by nature, a disposition to metaphysics. Kant repeats here the first sentence of Aristotle's *Metaphysics*: 'All men desire by nature to know.' Yet it is not Aristotle but Plato whom Kant has in mind. Plato, he writes, realized that our 'faculty of knowledge feels a much higher need than merely to spell out appearances according to a synthetic unity' (c1 A314 / B370–1).

Plato's Ideas, Kant adds, 'rose higher' (*übersteigen*) than Aristotle's concepts of the understanding. Plato, like that 'light dove' to which Kant compares reason, leaves the empirical world, the boundaries of which he finds too narrow, and joins the flight of ideas in the 'empty space of pure understanding' (c1 A5 / B8–9). For Kant, then, Plato stands for the needs of reason and, no doubt, for the errors into which those needs can lead us. The limits that we are given by nature, limits of our knowledge, of our wills, and of our mastery over nature, create in us needs, and the power that our reason has to rise above experience gives those needs an illusory satisfaction.

But philosophy's true purpose is to expose precisely those illusions by demonstrating that what cannot be given in experience is, for us, nothing. Kant, like Socrates, brings philosophy down from the heavens to human beings. The Copernican Kant tells us that we must give up all sterile and presumptuous speculation about God and the soul. Our reason is thus called back to a more modest self-knowledge (c1 A735 / B763), to its practical employment. Our 'materials,' though not sufficient to allow us to build that tower that we hoped would reach to the heavens, are nevertheless adequate for our purposes here on earth. When the question is 'what can I know?,' Kant's answer is that the world is all that is the case; no passageway leads out of this cave. But Platonic Ideas can be taken and turned into archetypes, patterns as Plato called them, for our conduct in this world (c1 A315–18 / B371–4). The needs of reason, when they lead us to claim certain knowledge of the suprasensible, are the source of all that is vain and empty. Yet the ideas to which they give birth can, if understood correctly, serve our purposes here, our practical or moral purposes (c1 B421).

Ultimately reason is guided by its practical, not by its speculative interests, by its need for a compass, for orientation rather than for theoretical wisdom. Whether we choose to find our direction using faith in the *summum bonum* as a guide (together with its postulates about God and the world) or turning instead to the moral law alone is an issue that will be taken up later. The point here is that once the needs of reason have shed the unrealizable desire to know (in the strong, speculative sense of know: to grasp fully their objects) and are governed instead by the practical end of acting well, questions about the existence of God, the immortality of the soul, or a purposively ordered world are freed of their dialectical qualities and become various ways in which we answer the problem of what we ought to do. The needs of reason, made harmonious with the 'ultimate purpose' (our business here on earth) of reason, lead to hope, to consolation, and to maxims for our conduct.

As was suggested in the previous chapter, it is these maxims, the formulations of the categorical imperative, that have a certain priority, even over hope and consolation. This priority rests on the independence of the moral law from all considerations of subjective human limitations. Our practical needs (whether for an imperative or for a reward to match our good deeds) have a priority over the interests of knowledge or speculation. Our pretensions to knowledge of the suprasensible having vanished, our reason is then turned to its true purpose, how we act in this world. And recognizing how limited our capacity for knowledge is, we can no longer hold contemplation to be what gives man his worth. What does make man unique is his possession of the only unconditional good that there is: the moral law. He is thus distinguished from other creatures by 'how and according to what principles he acts' (c3 v: 443 / 293, and see also GMM IV: 393 / 61). Contemplation has worth, Kant says, only in relation to this capacity for free actions. This is one of the senses in which the practical has an undisputed primacy over the theoretical for Kant.

A second sense is suggested to us by the following thought: the immediate task of the critical philosophy was to clip the wings of reason's free flight into the suprasensible. But in so doing, it made room for faith and freedom. By reducing theoretical knowledge to the range of things and events given in possible experience, it permitted faith. This is what Kant intended when he said that he had to limit knowledge in order to make room for faith. Faith is, as we shall see, one of the ways in which knowledge is extended practically. This idea in turn leads us to suspect that Kant's notion of the primacy of the practical over the speculative or theoretical has little to do with the sort of argument commonly associated with Marx. Kant's version has, one might say, a marked Copernican flavour, and to see how that differs from other accounts of the priority of the practical I want to consider briefly the Marxist version of this argument.

MARX AND THE PRIMACY OF PRAXIS

The primacy of the practical meant, for Marx, the dismissal of philosophical questions and ultimately of philosophy itself in favour of revolutionary praxis. This rejection itself, however, rested on a prior theory of what man is: essentially a producing being, who works up nature, who, in other words, creates, through his activity, the world around him.[1] Now animals produce as well; they, too, transform the nature that surrounds them. We differ from them, Marx writes, in that we labour consciously.

In the *Economic and Philosophic Manuscripts*, Marx formulates this idea in the language of Feuerbach – labour, which is man's 'life-activity,' his 'species-being' is itself an object of the will, whereas animals are immediately (and hence not via the will) related to their production. This same thought, now freed from Feuerbach's terminology, reappears throughout Marx's mature writings: 'a bee shames, through the construction of its wax cells, many a human architect. But what distinguishes in advance the worst architect from the best of bees is that he builds the cell in his mind before he constructs it in wax. At the end of the process of work a result emerges that from the beginning of that process was already present, ideally present, in his imagination.'[2] Note that man is still, first and foremost, a producer, who transforms nature. He is also a conscious being, and consciousness is always consciousness of existence. But existence means production, hence man is a producing being.

Man makes the world according to his ideas or purposes – nature is made subordinate to him. Indeed man is, Marx says, the centre of the universe. And here philosophy, in the form of the criticism of religion, has a useful role to play: to be radical means, Marx writes, to go to the root. 'But for man the root is man himself.' Just as man makes the world by humanizing nature, so, too, he makes religion.[3] The 'criticism of religion disillusions man to make him think and act and shape his reality like a man who has been disillusioned and has come to reason, *so that he will revolve round himself and therefore round his true sun'*.[4] True philosophy, which is radical in the sense mentioned above, places man at the centre of nature – more, at the centre of all that is. It shows man the source of real happiness and reveals the illusory consolation of religion. In this way, philosophy serves history or, what amounts to much the same thing, it serves man.

But the Young Hegelians' criticism of religion is not sufficient, Marx writes. The Young and Old Hegelians agree on the importance of religion, the one to condemn, the other to praise it.[5] The fundamentally conservative character of even the most radical of philosophies is shown in the fact that the materialist philosophers, the atheists, demand only a change of consciousness, another way of interpreting the world.[6] To be radical means, in Marx's view, to grasp the matter at its roots, that is, to recognize the primacy of the practical in human affairs. Thus the truly critical philosophy does not remain within its own horizon of interpretation, but leads to practical tasks.[7] True philosophy reveals its truth to us by transforming itself into practice (abolishing itself).

This is the central point of Marx's *Theses on Feuerbach*. Thesis I states that materialism has thought only of objects and of the contemplation of objects and has consequently ignored the acting subject. The idea of an active subject has been left to idealism, which does not know the meaning of real action and practice. The materialist criticism of religion 'overlooks the fact that after completing this work, the chief thing still remains to be done.'[8] The critique of religion has made man the centre of the universe, but it has done this only in the realm of thought. It has failed to show that man must become the actual 'sovereign of nature,' to take that final step to the realization that man is a producing, active being. Only when philosophy has made this leap, its last hurdle, will it have grasped the heart of the matter – and then it will cease to exist. 'The philosophers have only interpreted the world in various ways; the point, however, is to change it.'[9]

The sum of Marx's argument can be seen in this passage from the introduction to the *Contribution to the Critique of Hegel's Philosophy of Right*: 'The criticism of religion ends with the teaching that *man is the highest being for man*, hence with the *categorical imperative to overthrow all relations* in which man is a debased, enslaved, forsaken despicable being.'[10] This is Marx's version of Wittgenstein's idea that having climbed the 'ladder' of philosophy, properly understood, we realize that we must throw that ladder away.[11] At the end of Wittgenstein's 'ladder' we find silence[12], and so, too, at the end of Marx's critique of philosophy. Philosophy is there reduced to speechlessness, and we are left with action alone. Real philosophy, which can mean only the knowledge of man, leads inexorably to a single, clear conclusion: that philosophy must be transformed into practice, the contemplation of the world into the task of changing it. There are no more speculative questions to be answered, only things to be done.

The relation between some of these points and Kant's theories cannot be denied. Marx's idea that the root for man, and hence for philosophy, is man himself – in other words, that the subject, acting or knowing, is central to philosophy – is certainly something with which Kant would have concurred. Moreover, Marx's genealogy of religion and his call for a return from the heavens to man are perhaps not that far distant from Kant's own ideas. But man, for Marx, is a tool-using, a producing being – above all a historical being, where history is to be understood as the production and reproduction in various forms of his life and the means for its continuation.

This anthropology gives Marx's theory of the primacy of the practical its distinctive character: here practice means change, changing nature, both human and physical.[13] Man, to use Marx's words, has to become the centre of the world, his own sun: Marx (not Kant, as Bertrand Russell and others have suggested) thus overturns the conclusion of the Copernican revolution. Copernicus, Marx said, freed astronomy from theology as Machiavelli had freed politics from religion.[14] Philosophy, for Marx, is the beginning of man's conquest of the world and of himself. Radical philosophy liberates him from his illusions and makes him master of the world of consciousness – it is not an expression of the modesty of man's intellectual powers, but rather the first stage of a Promethean revolution. And this liberation is, as we have seen, only the prelude to practice – man is made free of religion so that he may truly liberate himself by his actions and become the master of his history. Seeing the world with human eyes, the freeing of human things from the mystical shroud of religion, is followed by Marx's inversion of Copernicus's heliocentrism: man once more becomes his own sun. This inversion leads Marx to his 'categorical imperative': the command to change the world.

Recent attempts to draw a parallel between Kant's Copernican revolution and Marxist theories of praxis[15] and humanism fail to understand what Kant meant by this revolution. Marx himself did acknowledge the profound difference between Kant's theories and his own, though in the typically perverse language that he regularly adopted when discussing philosophical issues.[16] There can be little doubt, though, that his attack on the 'idealists' in the *Theses on Feuerbach* is aimed, at least in part, at Kant. The crucial difference between Marx and Kant, on the particular problem, can tentatively be expressed thus: whereas Marx argued for the primacy of the practical, Kant asserted the primacy of the practical point of view. What Marx called his own 'categorical imperative' was the command to change the world, to educate the educator – in short, to master nature, human and physical. Kant's concept of the practical raises the issue of orientation, of how we are to guide ourselves within that realm of affairs, moral and political, over which we are indeed sovereign. It is this problem that stands at the heart of Kant's Copernican revolution, in politics and history, which we must now examine.

KANT AND THE PRIMACY OF MORAL JUDGMENT

In the *Critique of Judgment*, Kant distinguished between two kinds of arguments – one that he called *kat' aletheian* (according to the truth), and the other *kat' anthropon* (according to man). The first considers its object as it is in itself, the second what that object 'is for us' (c3 v: 462–3 / 314). This second sort of argument may, in turn, be subdivided into theoretical propositions (hypotheses about nature, for instance) and practical principles (for example, the *summum bonum* and its postulates). Theoretical propositions, *kat' anthropon*, can never yield firm conviction, since they remain always contingent hypotheses that must be prepared to give way to scientific explanation. Practical principles result in a moral conviction – that is, in a certainty adequate *in praktischer Absicht*, for practical purposes (c3 v: 463 / 314). To look at something 'according to man,' then, is to consider what it can be for us: and this means to ask what use can be made of it for our theoretical or practical purposes (c3 v: 467 / 318–19).

From the theoretical point of view, the admission that a proof can be offered only *kat' anthropon* implies the realization of the limits of human reason. It is a confession that, 'according to the truth,' this proof might carry no weight whatsoever. When Kant says that there will never be a Newton who can explain the growth of a blade of grass on mechanical principles, what he means is that for us, *kat' anthropon*, mechanical explanation is, in this case, inadequate, though for some superior being with greater powers of insight (*kat' aletheian*), the non-teleological basis of such growth would be intelligible. This same inadequacy is also characteristic of practical reason – that we cannot know of God, of the immortality of the soul, or even of the foundation of our own freedom. But here we need never fear refutation. More importantly, the use of the postulates is for practical purposes, which means that their adequacy is determined, *kat' anthropon*, in relation to those purposes. Theoretical hypotheses, which are adopted for the purpose of obtaining knowledge of nature, are, from the outset, a kind of argument that announces its own inadequacy – that, by the use of the term 'hypothesis,' defines itself in contrast to a perfect condition (*kat' aletheian*). There is no such 'perfect condition' for a practical postulate, since it shows its validity in moral judgments and action, not in an (as yet unachieved) state of complete knowledge.

Thus Kant can ask: what is lost for us if, for example, the idea of God is sufficient for every human purpose (*Absicht*) yet unprovable on higher, objective grounds (c3 v: 400 / 248)? Nothing is lost for the practical use of our reason. We cannot know certain things, but we do not need to know them – this is precisely what we were speaking of when we discussed orientation. Orientation, it will be remembered, is subjective assent that is demanded of us by our needs and for which no objectively sufficient assent is either possible or required. And orientation is a word that indicates that we wish or need to go in some direction or other; it is, in short, a word that suggests use or purpose.

This is one sense, then, in which we may take the idea of the primacy of the practical point of view: unlike theoretical hypotheses, which are always judged inferior, *kat' aletheian*, practical postulates (which do not measure themselves against the standard of knowledge but by the interests of our moral conduct) are self-sufficient. In some of their forms, they make and need to make no claims to theoretical knowledge, to the knowledge of the objects of nature. But this is a secondary sense for Kant.

Primacy, Kant says, is the prerogative of something by which it determines the combination in which it stands with others (c2 v: 119 / 124). What is at issue here is the contrast between the speculative and practical interests of reason: which is to have the prerogative? Now the third Antinomy showed that freedom was at least thinkable, though problematic. Speculative reason, if it could free itself from all interest, theoretical or practical, would waver between denial and affirmation of the reality of freedom, between nature and morality. Unable to decide clearly one way or the other, it would try to preserve a fine balance between the two interests. But we are not free of such interest, and these needs or interests impose upon us a 'duty to decide.' These 'ugent motives,' pleas that carry the greatest possible weight with us, compel us to give our assent to objectively insufficient principles (c1 A589 / B617).

The indifference of this imaginary pure speculative standpoint, its precious balance and aloofness – an indifference that might, perhaps, be available to a being without needs or interests – is shattered by our need to make judgments, particularly moral ones. Nowhere is this clearer than in Kant's own critical endeavours. The first *Critique* is constructed around this artificially created indifference of reason: reason's impartiality is the basis of its role as a tribunal before which competing interests are to be judged. But this indifference, required of a tribunal that is to legislate over various factions, is as artificial as Hobbes's Leviathan, to which Kant compares his *Critique*. We know from Kant's statement about why he felt it necessary to limit knowledge that even the impartial justice of the Kantian tribunal had to yield to more pressing concerns.

Thus, while as contemplative beings we must not give in, straight away, to those interests (c1 A475–6 / B503–4) but rather must attempt to demonstrate the compatibility of reason's interests, we are nevertheless, in the last analysis, won over by our practical, moral needs. We are active as well as contemplative beings, and 'active' means, for Kant, in its principal signification, that freedom whereby a supreme maxim is adopted by our will. Only derivatively does 'action' refer to the deeds themselves performed in accordance with the free will. The exercise of moral judgment, then, is what Kant understands by 'action,' and it is the needs associated with that judgment that undermine reason's studied posture of indifference.

This indifference now having vanished, the question for Kant becomes one of whether reason's theoretical interests, including the desire to restrict reason in its flights of fancy, should weigh more heavily in the balance than the wish of moral reason to make assumptions (postulates) about God, freedom, immortality, and purposive nature. Kant answers that these practical interests do indeed have a priority. This is to put the matter too simply, though. The speculative interests of reason are not forced to yield to the practical, nor could they be without thereby destroying the integrity of knowledge and science. One simple solution, already hinted at, is that speculative reason has nothing to say against the postulates so long as they remain just that, postulates, and not claims to theoretical knowledge. The postulates, according to this solution, are merely allowed. But it would not be adequate, Kant says, for the two spheres simply to be co-ordinates, to stand beside one another, as it were, each making propositions within its own realm. For were this the case, were the range of legitimate knowledge claims to be confined to possible experience, then we would have to agree with Epicurus that everything else is an empty, though allowable sophism (c2 v: 120 / 125).

Reason's two employments cannot merely be co-ordinated and kept separate from one another. The question of hope, of the *summum bonum*, is after all both practical and theoretical – about what ought to be done and about what may be expected as a result of those actions. Kant's point is difficult to see if it is kept within the confines of a vocabulary that speaks of two reasons, two distinct minds. Such a language is at once exotic and implausible. It is one and the same reason which is employed in the study of nature and for practical purposes. When we postulate the existence of God and of the soul we do, in fact, extend the claims of reason, and either this extension amounts to nothing more than an empty sophism or it is legitimate. The practical interests of reason lead it beyond what can be given in experience to God and the soul. And it leads to the latter, not as to the illusions of a magic lantern, but rather as an extension of knowledge of a specific sort. Not only has speculative reason nothing to object to this extension, but its own limitations find in this advance the transcendence that was denied them on purely theoretical grounds.

Practical reason thus shows its primcy over theoretical reason not simply by proving that it cannot be refuted by experience but by showing the justice of its claims to constitute an extension of reason. Now this extension is of a unique kind: all the very familiar language of the theory of knowledge reappears here, for example, objects, certainty, knowledge, but now accompanied by the phrase *in praktischer Absicht*, for practical purposes or from a practical point of view. It is this latter phrase that is the core of Kant's argument for the primacy of practical reason.

The extension of our knowledge that is necessarily implied in the idea of a postulate (if it is to be more than a convenient fiction) is permitted for practical purposes (c2 v: 133 / 138). This knowledge is not sufficient for a speculative extension of reason – which is to say that no use can be made of these ideas in the study of nature (since they provide no knowledge of objects per se). Nevertheless, they are definable in a practical sense, namely in a manner adequate to the maxims of our rational conduct, and they can claim for themselves objective reality, again, for practicl purposes (c3 v: 175, 453 / 11–12, 304). They are, in brief, speculatively subjective and practically objective.

At first glance, this argument has the distinct appearance of a philosophic slight-of-hand. It seems as though Kant has merely taken the vocabulary of knowledge, so carefully defined and limited in the first *Critique*, and added to it a qualifying clause, *in praktischer Absicht* (from a practical point of view, or with a practical intent). Certainly the use of identical terms in two quite separate types of argument, is, at the very least, confusing. This confusion is, however, not accidental; as we shall see, it emerges from the nature of arguments such as that given in the *summum bonum*, namely a morally inspired interpretation of things, of the world. The attempt to combine the practical and theoretical in this way is what gives the ideas we are considering their rather unsettled appearance. Yet these ideas are so crucial that we must try to sort out what exactly Kant wants us to understand by them.

Let us turn once again to the idea of orientation, in the hope of seeing what Kant means by a practical extension of reason. In the act of orienting ourselves we combine our subjective sense of direction with the data provided us by the noonday sun or the North Star in order to determine the direction in which we are to travel. We extend our knowledge by determining this direction, though we learn nothing further about the stars, the planets, or the world around us. This new piece of knowledge is knowledge of direction. And even in that dark room, where there are no visible objective data, our ability to navigate according to our subjective sense of left and right provides us with knowledge, not of the room, the contents of which are completely shrouded in darkness, but of the direction in which we must travel. We mark a path for ourselves through the world – whether with the aid of landmarks (immortality, a morally governed world) supplied us by revelation and the Christian view of the world or by means of our own capacity for self-legislation (freedom, autonomy). The extension of our knowledge consists in the setting out of this path. Nothing is learned, thereby, of the stars or of the sun which may have aided us in determining our course or about the world through which it passes.

The world can be viewed as a whole organized according to the principles of possible experience (the categories), of a moral teleological order (postulates), or of an intelligible world (the categorical impera-tive), a world of freely acting agents governed by the moral law, not the laws of nature. The practical knowledge of this intelligible world is identical to the knowledge of what ought to be, and its practical reality amounts to another formulation of the categorical imperative: to act as if there were another (intelligible) world (VAT VIII: 416, 418, and LB XX: 341). And the sufficiency of practical arguments is to be measured by their practical use, namely how they serve to mark out that path that we are commanded to follow but which itself is often only dimly visible (GMM IV: 461 / 129). Practical ideas are for immanent use alone, and that use gives them a reality no less firmly established for being practical rather than theoretical. They are practically objec-tive in that they offer us a way in which the world can be viewed, sufficient to allow us, with the help of that standpoint, to make our way through it. They give us direction, and direction, even though exclusively bound up with the purposes of the traveller and therefore saying nothing about the world, is real, practically real.[17]

Practical ideas have a reality for us *kat' anthropon*, as moral beings. This thought can best be grasped by reflecting on Kant's comments on Plato:[18] Platonic Ideas, if they claim to be theoretical knowledge, imply an intellectual intuition of which we are not capable, and one impossible on the only sort of intuition we do possess, namely empirical intuition. As pretensions to theoretical knowledge, from which further synthetic propositions about nature can be worked up, they are chimerical. But these same ideas, now freed from their theoretical claims, can be given a more moderate form, which also establishes their practical reality: as moral archetypes they serve to guide our actions. Boundaries are set on our understanding of the world and on the propositions that we can make about it. These boundaries indirectly influence the language in which we express other standpoints: they exercise this influence by forcing us to adopt the distinction discussed above between what is simply true and what is true for us, between stating 'it is certain' and 'I am certain' (c1 A829 / B857). It is as a result of these boundaries that the set of practical ideas is bracketed by the qualifier *in praktischer Absicht*.

It is these practical ideas, however, in the various formulations of the categorical imperative or cloaked in the modest garb of rational faith, that have a primacy over speculative reason. The indifference, or even the hostility, that theoretical reason shows toward the needs of practical reason is overcome both by its inability to refute practical ideas and by the legitimate claims made by those ideas to offer an extension of a certain kind of knowledge. We are, as Kant writes in the Transcendental Deduction, the law-givers to nature; but as moral beings we also give the law to ourselves. By the first, we view nature as an object of possible experience; by the second, we create an intelligible world of moral beings, or we see a moral God standing above the world, holding out to us the possibility of a reward for our virtue, in this life or the next. We are not merely permitted to adopt a moral point of view, we are commanded by practical reason, by our needs, to take possession of this 'empty space' in order to fill it with practical data. The moral standpoint may not extend our knowledge of nature, but it is adequate for its purpose, the finding of the path we are to travel.

In the 'starry heavens' passage from the second *Critique*, we are shown man from two points of view. We see him as a natural being, as matter trivial in relation to the countless multitudes of other bodies and the great emptiness that surrounds him. But we can see him also as personality, as a moral being, and now his worth is raised infinitely above that of the world around him. The change from a mere speck in the universe to a being near-divine is brought about by viewing man from a different standpoint. Our moral needs, to act well, to recognize our superiority over nature, and to believe in a moral governor of the world and an immortal soul, force us to quit the inadequate standpoint of nature and to adopt instead the moral point of view, be that submission to the law or rational faith. This is the sum of Kant's Copernican revolution: that revolution made the spectator, the self, into the centre of its account of nature. The world is always something that appears to me. The way in which the world appears depends on the standpoint of the spectator – it can be seen as a whole acting according to the fundamental laws of nature, or as governed in a purposeful manner by a moral God, or as an intelligible world of moral agents.

The standpoints of nature, faith, and morality are, at bottom, just so many ways of expressing the fact that the observing self is at once the source of the formal conditions of nature and experience *and* a practical (moral) self. The description of the world that takes those formal conditions as the core of its account is not exhaustive precisely because the self that describes the world is not exclusively contemplative. We are free, with a capacity for moral judgments, and as such we have another standpoint from which to view the world. As faithful beings, we can see, in its order and design, evidence of a moral purposiveness at work, which lends further support to our belief in the *summum bonum*, in God and the soul. From the moral point of view, we turn our attention from nature, mechanical or purposive, to moral judgment alone, to the quality of our wills. And finally, from the theoretical perspective, nature is regarded as a manifold worked up according to the categories into coherent experience, and fit for inclusion into a systematic description that we call science.

Kant's Copernican revolution showed us the limits of what we are, of the place that we occupy in the universe, and of what we can know. But within this modest dwelling-place, we are the authors of the formal conditons of the world and of our own judgments and conduct. Marx's anti-Copernican revolution does just the reverse: it teaches us that we can master nature, that there are no incorrigible givens, either in external nature (there is thus no nature that cannot be 'humanized') or in our own. This revolution is Promethean, it wants to make gods out of men. We are the producers, according to Marx, both of nature and of our own infinitely malleable selves: the point, then, is to change the world, not to interpret it. Kant taught us that we are finite in our capacity to know and to do – we do not have the power that a god might have to know without having to depend on empirical intuitions, to master nature, or to will what is right without the need for an imperative. Nor would we need hope – then everything would happen according to our wishes. These limitations cannot be changed: not the insignificant place that we occupy in the natural order of things, not the circumscribed range of things that can be known, and not the 'crooked wood' of which we are made. But our will is ours, and so too is the ability to judge and interpret the world, according to our theoretical or practical interests – to see it from the perspective of a being who desires knowledge of nature or from the point of view of the free beings we are.

Kant, it might be said, did not seek to show how the world could be changed. Rather, he set himself the more modest task of showing how we can make our way through a world of which the familiar 'landmarks' (those of tranditional metaphysics, revelation, and natural law) have disappeared. He made this argument not because of the historical 'limits of his vision,' not as a result of the backward social and political conditions of eighteenth-century East Prussia,[19] but because he saw more clearly than Marx did both man's limits and the heights he could reach. Kant thought that a mere glance at the boundless vault of the night sky would be sufficient to instruct us that we are not, as Marx was later to write, the 'sovereigns of nature.' He was by no means unaware of the progress of civilization and science in extending our control over the small corner of nature that we occupy, but of that, too, he was sceptical: and not only sceptical of its success, but wary of the *glänzende Elend*, the glittering misery, that it produced (c3 v: 432 / 282). Knowing that this 'sovereign of nature' in the end himself returns to the dust of that puny kingdom over which he sought to rule, Kant also saw what infinitely raises man's worth. To the 'glittering misery' of civilization he contrasted the true brilliance of the moral will which 'would ... shine (*glänzen*) like a jewel for its own sake as something which has its full value in itself' (GMM IV: 394 / 62).

FOUNDATIONS OF KANT'S CONCEPT OF HISTORY

Men make their own history, Marx wrote. Kant, too, thought that we are the authors of our own history. But he meant this in a more literal way than Marx had. We are the authors of history because it is we who are at liberty to choose the standpoint from which we are to view the world. And history is one of those standpoints. We write and we think stories about the world. Now story-telling is a unique human ability.

It presupposes not only the capacity for language, for knowledge and memory, but also the power to run through, as it were, a series of discrete events so as to transform them from a simple aggregate into a cohesive whole. Were we able only to know and to recollect, we could indeed produce a catalogue of events, a methodical classification and description of events, but not a story or history of them.

Kant suggests that the meaning of the word 'history' that has come down to us from the ancients is not adequate. It understands history as description but does not allow us to distinguish between a description that is a systematic classification of a set of givens and one that accounts for their genealogy (UGP VIII: 160–1, 162–3). Kant wants to separate *Beschreibung* (description) from *Geschichte* (history). *Beschreibung* aims only at a classification of phenomena by means of their common traits – it seeks to categorize phenomena under nominal categories, divisions introduced solely for the purposes of classification (BBM VIII: 100 note and VVR II: 429). *Geschichte*, in contrast, attempts to show the genealogy of events by connecting them with their causes in a temporal sequence according to a principle, to a law of their development. Description has as its foundation a system of classification, whereas history is organized around the study of the laws of development of a particular set of phenomena (VVR II: 429).

For a history of events – both natural and human history – we need a 'guiding-thread' (*Leitfaden*) along which the various discrete events can be arranged and that will give them a unity and a certain kind of connection with one another. And this unity will not be of the sort employed in systematic description: an artificial group of classes, similarities, or differences among species for example (Kant calls these academic or nominal species *species artificialis*). Rather, the unity of events will be causal and developmental, organized around a principle of explanation, a guiding-thread into a cohesive story or history. The guiding-thread, because it deals with a relation between events across a given span of time, is necessarily a causal principle for explaining their relation. Indeed, the definition of an event is a sequential and irreversible chain of 'happenings' (*Geschehen*) according to a determinate (causal) order (CI A192 / B237). Typically, that is, history is a causal account of a process of generation or degeneration. The temporal-causal relation of these events is at the centre of the idea of history.

But this is to say too little. How we choose to unite these facts, what guiding-thread we make use of and for what purpose, is something in which we have a say – though in a historical account we must choose within the limits of what is required for a story, that is, a causal and chronological relating of events. We provide the guiding-thread but since it is to be used in an interpretation of events in the world, it has to conform to the nature of all phenomenal events – it must be sequential and consequential.

What we see here is a theory of historical explanation, a characteristically Kantian theory of the origins and legitimacy of that sort of explanation. To be a historian means to be a narrator of events; but events, in their raw state, present themselves to us in a contingent cluster of discrete units subject to no law or connection save that minimal, formal law that makes experience possible. The historian (and we are all, to some extent, historians, according to Kant) is a viewer of the world, a navigator in thought through that world, and as such has a right and even a need 'to think into' (*hinzudenken*) the world the order that is found lacking there. The capacity, the right, and the need together form the heart of Kant's general theory of explanation and of his Copernican revolution. We have the capacity, in virtue of the spontaneity of our reason, to think a connection into events. And we have a right to introduce principles that make events conform to our need to explain them, because, well understood, such principles are restricted to the level of reflective propositions and do not claim for themselves the proud title of knowledge. Finally, we have a need to think about the world using these guiding-threads – both for theoretical purposes and for our practical interests.

The limits of the world, as defined by the formal conditions of the possibility of experience and of knowledge, are too narrow when we come to view that world as moral beings. The self, the Copernican '*Ich*' – that formal self whose laws are at the same time the laws of nature – would, if it were the only self, be able to make its way through the world without difficulty. Or, to be more precise, it, too, would need teleological principles, but more for the extension of its knowledge than to give reality to its objects, which are, with absolute certainty, presented to us by experience. But reason is, at one and the same time, practical and theoretical, and so it needs to think the world as an intelligible order of rational, moral beings and also, perhaps, to see the hope for a reward in proportion to virtue, a hope supported by evidence of purposiveness at work in nature. The need to think of the world, not as a mechanically ordered whole with no freedom or morality, but as a kingdom of ends, or to think of it as having a morally purposive arrangement, emerges from the 'empty space' offered us by the world as it is given us immediately in experience. We are called upon by the practical need to find our direction (to determine what we ought to do) – a need not answered by the study of nature, shrouded as it is (for our moral purposes) in the blackest night – to think a moral order into the world, or to reconize ourselves as autonomous legislators, indifferent to the rewards or trials that nature may bestow on us.

The basis of historical explanation, broadly conceived, is thus practical. It has its source not so much in the desire to know but in a need to give a moral account of the world or to interpret that world as a store-house of prudential maxims, or justifications, for our present course. The practical foundation of history is best grasped in the idea of a guiding-thread. In the history of nature as well as of human affairs, the given facts are both unchangeable and unsuitable for our purposes; we therefore take up these facts but order them according to a guiding principle. We think this principle into the data so that our reflection upon them may be more adequate to the purposes we have (c3 v: 399 / 247 and c2 v: 121 / 126).

We choose the principle because we are capable of such spontaneity and because we find the world as it is inadequate. This suggests that its employment in reflective judgment is related to some purpose or interest that we may have. History, then, taken as a way of viewing the world, is reflective, arising from a need and especially a practical need, and it is chosen. Urged on by our practical needs, we choose how to see the world. We do not choose how we may change it, though – for that, Kant thought, a new creation would be required. How the world may be seen or interpreted has already been hinted at: one standpoint, beginning from the language of need and desire, reads back into nature the purposiveness that it seeks. It derives hope and consolation from the idea of the possibility of the *summum bonum*, and so it postulates the existence of God in order to secure in thought nature's compliance with its wishes, here or in another world. It looks for evidence of purposiveness in nature, it tells a story about nature and ascends from there to a kind of theology. Its hopes are given support by the order and beauty it sees in nature. This is the modest language of rational faith.

A second standpoint begins from the same failure of nature to supply direct evidence of moral purposiveness in its workings, but instead of thinking that purposiveness into nature, it replaces the modest language of need and faith with that of courage and sublimity. It turns its attention not to a romance, a fiction written about nature, but to that inner quality – moral freedom – that infinitely raises us above nature. The Christian and the Kantian Stoic viewpoints, the beautiful and the sublime are the great aesthetic views of the world, two of the ways by which we find our way through the world. It is to them that we shall now turn.

# PART THREE

# Kant's positive revolution:
# Reason interpreting the world

# 5

# Nature: The sublime and the beautiful

Nature never set forth the earth in so rich tapestry as divers poets have done; neither with so pleasant rivers, fruitful trees, sweet-smelling flowers, nor whatsoever else may make the too much loved earth more lovely. Her world is brazen, the poets only deliver a golden.

Sir Philip Sidney, An Apology for Poetry

## INTRODUCTION

Part i of this book (chapters 1–3) sets out what might be called the negative, or Wittgensteinian, side of Kant's Copernican revolution. There we learned of the limits of what can be known and of the inadequacy of the knowable world when our practical needs are at stake. Our limits and needs were the central concern in those pages. This rejection of the pretensions of past philosophy led Wittgenstein, at the end of the *Tractatus*, to silence, and Marx in the *Theses on Feuerbach*, to the imperative to change the world.

Kant, in the positive or artistic side of his Copernican revolution, shows how the world can be interpreted, that it can be re-presented for practical purposes. Having lost nature and revelation as guides by which to orient ourselves, it is we who must establish our own path and markers for our sojourn here. The recognition of the bounded character of human understanding and of our practical needs – in sum, the 'peculiar fate' that Kant spoke of in the first *Critique* – compels us to take our bearings unaided by fixed, external reference points. The spontaneity of reason, its artistic quality or legislative capacity, makes this orientation possible.

Part III (chapters 5–7) forms a whole centred around this positive element of Kant's Copernican revolution. This chapter (5) shows that nature can be viewed as beautiful, but also that we can stand in a sublime relation to it. As beautiful, nature is portrayed in such a way that our attention is turned outward, toward the world. We take an interest in the beauty displayed in nature's forms, which suggest design, as if nature's purpose (or that of its Maker) was to please man. Nature is represented as supporting and as being in harmony with man. That thought leads us to the idea of a wise designer of nature, and to gratitude – a type of theodicy. This is the Christian, sanguine view of the world, and it teaches contentment both with God and with our fellow humans. But we can also stand in a sublime relation to nature. Here our attention is turned to our moral selves, to the capacity that we have for resisting nature. The world is formless, and nature is violent and seems to oppose man. No designer is evident here, and thus there is neither gratitude nor a theodicy. We are left with the recognition of man's moral worth, though with no source of hope or optimism. The beautiful portrayal of nature offers us the world and its creator as the means by which we may determine our course. The sublime leaves us with a moral, self-legislating capacity as our only guide.

Chapters 6 and 7 take this analysis and apply it now not to inanimate nature but to human phenomena, our external affairs. Chapter 6 contains an examination of the beautiful representation of those affairs in philosophical history. Once more our attention is turned toward nature, humans considered as a class of animal, but a class that exhibits, in its history, a purposeful design. Progress and teleology are at the heart of this account, and nature (or Providence) is seen as a well-meaning tutor. Man emerges as lovable, and God is justified in history. We are thus permitted hope and consolation. Yet in order to console, philosophical history must present design in the world as visible, that is, as knowable. But the negative critique has shown that it is not knowable in the beautiful (purposeful and just) sense intended here. This viewpoint is weak theoretically, and, more important it is misleading from a moral perspective, since it makes hope and benevolence into standards for our judgment rather than right and duty. The consequences of this account of the human world are displayed in the philosophical historian's depiction of the French Revolution.

Chapter 7 represents human affairs according to the principle of (political) right. The focus here is not upon teleology or progress (evolution) but upon a priori right or justice. And nature is no longer our tutor, but rather we are shown as subject to self-given law. The result is not a hopeful interpretation of human phenomena, nor is it a theodicy. Rather, it is a theory of the *Rechtsstaat*, an ideal of respect for man's moral and civil personality which commands sovereigns and subjects alike to approximate it in their actions. With this as a standard, we do not need to have nature's order made visible for us – all can be concealed in darkness – and despite that we can still find a path, and this without the danger of being led astray, either by a theoretically implausible account of nature or by false moral incentives.

The conclusion (chapter 8) draws together these themes of Kant's Copernican revolution, the sublime and the beautiful, justice and history, and orientation in the form of a commentary on Kant's essay on theory and praxis. That we can view the world in various ways and why we feel the need to do so is the idea that stands at the centre of Kant's Copernican revolution. From this idea, we learn something about the world, about its inadequacy for our moral purposes, and about ourselves, our interests, and our desires. The givens, the incorrigible data of experience, and the 'guiding-thread' that we use to unite and interpret them are the warp and woof of history. But what this tells us is that history rests on a more primitive foundation, that of the relation in which we stand to the world around us. This foundation I have called, in the previous chapter, the aesthetic standpoint – and indeed, the heart of Kant's Copernican revolution is just that: showing how the world can be worked up or represented in a manner that conforms to the needs of knowledge (experience) or morality. The pictorial representation of nature, if it is to be a representation at all, must, to be sure, agree at least to some extent with the laws of perspective, of space, and of the form of its subject (corresponding to the transcendental laws of experience, the categories). Beyond this, however, nature can be portrayed as in El Greco's *Laocoön* or his *View of Toledo* as the terrifying and ominous storm approaching the city, or it can be shown as serene and grand, as in Constable's work. The sublime and the beautiful: these were, Kant thought, the two great standpoints from which nature can be viewed, and not merely by the artist, the painter or the composer.

Kant's Copernican revolution has taught us that man is an artist, in the literal meaning of the word. With his synthetic powers he weaves together information from the senses into coherent experience, and since he is a moral as well as a knowing being he reworks nature using a different cement than that required for experience as such. He re-fashions nature *in praktischer Absicht*, according to his moral inter-ests. The world can be seen, as the faithful see it, in the light of a moral governor who secures its harmony with our presence here, or, as Kant's version of Stoicism interprets it, as a test of our courage and virtue.

Kant divided his critique of taste (aesthetics) into two principal sec-tions: the beautiful and the sublime. And by this division he intended to speak not only of the arts but also of the ways in which we judge nature. How we judge nature, this Copernican theme, containing as it does both the givens of the sensory experience of nature and our in-terests (desires), is the foundation on which Kant's theory of history and of politics rests. In its division into the beautiful and sublime we find a key to the understanding of those theories. In the section that follows, I want first to discuss the formal properties of aesthetic judg-ment (free, interestless, and universal) and natural and artificial beauty in their relation to morality, and then proceed from there to Kant's analysis of the sublime.

AESTHETIC JUDGMENT: THE BEAUTIFUL

Reflective judgment, both aesthetic and teleological, considers nature as purposive in respect to its products: in the former, subjectively, in the later, objectively (that is, having to do with the possibility of the object). In the representation of the beautiful in nature, nature is judged to be subjectively purposive: as if it were designed for our judgment. This judgment also differs from its teleological counterpart in that it occurs prior to any concept of the object. The subjective formal pur-posiveness of the aesthetic object is expressed, Kant writes, in the pleasure of the free play of our cognitive faculties, our imagnination and understanding (c3 v: 189–90 / 26). Thus, in aesthetic statements, a given representation is indeed related to an object, but it is a judgment that conveys a determination of the subject, not any essential property of the object as such (FI xx: 248 / 52). It announces the subject's feelings of pleasure or pain in the presence of that object. The subjective ele-ment in this representation is precisely the feeling of pleasure, and through pleasure nothing is cognized and no concept is needed for the feeling of pleasure obtained in reflection upon beauty in nature.

When we come to ask if something is beautiful, we do not refer the representation to a concept, to the notion of an end or purpose that the thing may have, either in itself or for us; rather, we relate that

representation to our feelings (c3 v: 204 / 38). To use Kant's own example: when it is said that 'the wine is pleasant,' the predicate 'pleasant' expresses the relation of our sense of pleasure to the representation
of the wine and thus involves no concept (FI xx: 224 / 28). In sum, we
can say that the division of the third *Critique* into an Aesthetics and
a Logic, respectively concerned with beauty and sublimity in the first
and teleology in the second, reflects the distinction between two ways
of relating the notion of purposiveness in reflective judgment to an
object (FI xx: 250–1 / 54–5).

The beautiful pleases apart from any concept of the object. Beauty
is thereby distinguished from perfection in nature as well as from
utility. The latter two qualities depend on the concept of a purpose, a
final end toward which a thing strives, or an external end, in which
case it is called simply useful. The beautiful, since it pleases immediately and in the mere act of reflection requires no idea, is thus 'purposiveness without a purpose.' It seems designed (speaking now of
natural beauty) as if to cause pleasure in us, yet when we pronounce
it beautiful we do not put the idea of a design or end at the basis of
our judgment (c3 v: 226 / 62). This same principle tells us that the
good cannot be called beautiful, since it too depends on a concept of
what ought to be. Neither the perfect in nature nor the good correspond,
then, to the beautiful. They may well evoke pleasure, but not that sort
of pleasure that could properly be called aesthetic.

And the beautiful is not identical with gratification, with what is
merely pleasant. The pleasant depends entirely on sensation, whereas
the beautiful needs reflection. What is still more crucial, the pleasant
arises from or creates in us a need, a desire or interest in its source (c3
v: 205 / 39). Here our satisfaction is combined with an interest in the
existence of the object – it is pleasure that desires to continue, and
that consequently wishes for the means for further gratification. The
good and the crudest sort of gratification share this one trait: both
unite their pleasure (or esteem) with an interest in the existence of its
object – in the one instance, an interest in the reality or coming into
being of the good, and, in the second sense, a desire for the source of
satisfaction. In the good and the merely pleasant, the judgment is not
free because it is not disinterested. It is bound down in the good by
the moral law, which commands that a certain state of affairs be brought
into existence, and, in so doing, it produces a desire or want in us
(though this desire cannot, as we have previously remarked, precede
the moral determination of the will) (c3 v: 210 / 45 and c3 v: 353–4 /

199). And the pleasant renders us unfree, interested, by creating a desire in us for the existence of that which gratifies us.

Aesthetic pleasure, in contrast, is a contemplative or passive satisfaction not coupled with desire. Not being bound by desire, it is disinterested – a pleasure taken in the mere representation of the object and the free judgment made about it. Beauty, in short, is independent both of concepts (perfection, utility, the good) and of desire (the pleasant and the good). Aesthetic judgments are free in a very special sense, which cannot be obtained in the realm of the pleasant or of the morally good (as an 'object of the will'). In both of the latter, interest is central (c3 v: 209, 270–4 / 43–4, 111).

The disinterestedness of aesthetic judgments about the beautiful sets the foundation for their claim to universality. Kant wants to distinguish purely subjective statements such as 'I find this food pleasant' from aesthetic judgments proper: 'such and such is beautiful.' The former makes only an empirical claim about the pleasure caused in me by an object; the latter claims universal agreement for itself. Now the distinterestedness of genuine aesthetic propositions means that they rest on no arbitrary inclination of the subject, no particular interest or desire (c3 v: 211 / 45–6). Yet their universality is not based on a concept of an object demanding assent from everyone.

It is just this that is the curious feature of the beautiful: these judgments extend to the whole sphere of rational subjects, though they do not rest on a concept of an object. Their universality is thus not objective but subjective: it is the attribution of a similar pleasure to all persons in the presence of a given representation. The crucial difference that separates aesthetic judgments from statements of personal preference is precisely this universality and the idea implied by that universality of the communicability of the mental state that accompanies the representation of a beautiful object – that 'mental state' being, according to Kant, the pleasure derived from the interplay of our imagination and understanding. Thus, in addition to disinterestedness, which might be called the negative condition of universality, aesthetic judgments require a kind of *sensus communis* (in the literal meaning, a free play of our cognitive faculties), which, being both disinterested and non-conceptual, is nevertheless universal (c3 v: 217, 238–9 / 51–2, 75–6). This common sense is not determined through empirical psychology but is rather an ideal form, an 'ought,' which says not that all people will in fact find something beautiful but that they should do so. The existence of something like this *sensus communis* is postulated in order to make possible the distinction referred to above between the universal claims of aesthetic taste and the private claim of preference.

What we have described here are the formal properties of aesthetic judgment: that it pleases immediately, that it is disinterested (not determined by desire), free, and universal. These formal qualities of the beautiful make of it a symbol (applying the same rule of reflection in two otherwise distinct cases) of morality. Both free, or pure, beauty and morality are elevated above mere sensibility (gratification): both are free in that their determing ground is not to be found in desire, though freedom in beauty consists in play, a sort of liberality, not in the self-given law of morality. The beautiful and the moral please immediately, the one in sense, the other in a concept, and they both ascribe universality to their judgments (c3 v: 353 / 198–9). These formal or symbolic properties shared by moral and aesthetic judgments – the rules of reflection that they have in common – are, however, only one side of their relationship.

As we saw in chapter 3, desire or interest is an unchangeable quality of the finite beings that we are, endowed with bodies and needs. And just as morality, given expression in human volition, can be united with an object for the will (the *summum bonum*), so too can the purity of aesthetic judgment yield to the interest we have in the beauty of nature. In both instances, the formal conditions of the judgment remain – no act can be called moral nor judgment aesthetic unless it meets those requirements enumerated above. Those conditions are the logical determinants, the rules for judging (subsuming a particular under a universal), which permit us to distinguish between a truly moral judgment and those with subjective and particular origins, and between aesthetic propositions proper and mere statements of preference based on empirical pleasure. But no more than in the case of morality does Kant mean to exclude interest and desire from his account of the beautiful.[1] His method in the two types of argument that we are considering here is two-fold. He wants, first, to isolate those rudimentary conditions the presence of which is a necessary feature of any judgment that is to be called aesthetic or moral. And he wants, second, to show how these central properties may be taken up by man, a needy and therefore desiring being, and by a 'synthetic' step be transformed into a kind of experience of the beautiful and into one possible guide for our moral conduct.

The beautiful can have no interest as its determining ground, nor can it be forced on us by nature itself: in pure aesthetic judgment, it is rather we who view nature with favour. When we speak of the liberality of taste, it is, in part, that favouring that we have in mind. Free beauty (to be distinguished from dependent beauty, which we shall discuss later) would not be free were it to arise from an interest or to be forced upon us by nature in the way that some natural objects require teleological principles in order to be comprehensible to us at all. The freedom, the playfulness, and the liberality of aesthetic judgments depend on an absence of any restriction whatsoever, be it interest, the moral law, or the requirements of explanation. But this is not to say that the beautiful cannot be combined with an interest that is, however, not its determining ground (c3 v: 296 / 138–9). (This argument parallels exactly Kant's analysis of the *summum bonum* in the second *Critique*.) This interest would give us pleasure in the existence of the beautiful rather than simply a pleasure in its representation.

Now Kant writes that the pleasure and satisfaction can be of two kinds: empirical and intellectual. Beauty interests us empirically only in society, and it involves the communication of our feelings to other people: this interest is thus part of our natural sociability. More important, we have an 'intellectual interest' in the beautiful things of nature. This intellectual interest is, in fact, a moral interest in natural beauty. Nature can be represented, Kant writes, as being subject to 'an irregularity which must be far more revolting to the human mind than the blind chance that we sometimes wish to use as a principle for judging of nature' (c3 v: 458 / 310). This irregularity is one between worth and reward, where the just, whose actions are worthy of reward, nevertheless suffer equally with the evil. But the revulsion, the disorientation that we feel at the sight of such a world, our interest in a harmony between nature, and our moral wills (given voice most clearly in the idea of the highest good) would, Kant suggests, direct our attention to the beauty and purposiveness of nature.

The particular value that we attach to natural as opposed to man-made beauty rests on precisely this moral interest: we seek the agreement of nature with our presence here (c3 v: 299–301 / 142–3). Beauty reveals nature to us as art, and nature is beautiful because it looks like art. And all art implies an artificer; art in nature shows us, perhaps, a moral Governor of the world whose intentions in regard to us are evidenced in the abundant beauty he has scattered throughout nature. Beauty, when combined with a moral interest, leads beyond mechanism to teleology in nature and it leads us also (c3 v: 246, 301 / 84, 143–4), beyond the playful freedom of pure aesthetic judgment, which is satisfied immediately in the mere representation of the object, to an interest in its existence and thus to the conditions of its existence – purposiveness and God.

Beauty in nature and our moral interest in seeing our ideas given objective reality are, as we now recognize, bound to one another. The wonders of nature, Kant says, arouse reason from its melancholy by supplying empirical evidence of a God who favours us. The order and beauty displayed in nature turn our attention to design and from there to a designer. Natural beauty and purposiveness both point to faith and to God (c1 в xxxii–xxxiii, a622–4 / в650–2): beauty because it is art (even in nature it is art) and purposiveness because we are led from particular purposive organisms to the idea of a purposive world-whole, and from there to an intelligent Being. The appearance of such order and regularity in nature (though those purposive beings themselves are 'self-contained': cause and effect are to be found within the same organism, and thus there is no absolute need to seek an outside cause) suggests to us that if nature is purposive in its parts it must be purposive as a whole.

Physical teleology and beauty thus point the way to theology. This is what Kant called the *Abenteuer der Vernunft* – the adventure of reason (c3 v: 419 note / 268 note). It is an adventure because physical teleology, while impelling us to seek a theology, can itself provide neither evidence of God's existence, nor any idea of the purposes he might have, nor, finally, any insight into the nature of his being. It can offer only an artistic understanding of scattered purposes, but no concept of a wise final purpose. In this sense, a 'physico-theology,' a theological argument derived from or based on evidence of purposiveness in nature, is little more than a physical teleology that has overstepped its limits (c3 v: 442 / 292). Only a moral teleology (and by this Kant means something akin to the argument for the *summum bonum* presented in the second *Critique*) can give us a final purpose to which all others, indeed all of nature, would be subordinate. The *summum bonum*, at least to the extent that it can be approximated in this world, depends on a certain constitution of nature. Physical teleology and natural beauty suggest such a purposive constitution, but it is left to the practical, moral side of the argument to display man as that final purpose and

God, a moral world architect, as nature's sovereign. Nevertheless, natural teleology, and the empirical evidence of purposiveness in the world, precede moral teleology and the theory of final purposes by pointing to the latter and, though falling short of it, presenting physical 'evidence' of its reality (c3 v: 444–5, 456, 478–9 / 295, 307, 331–2).

Moral teleology, then, concerns us as worldly beings, *Weltwesen*, bound up unavoidably with the things of that world. The name itself implies a reciprocal reference between our own causality as moral agents and the relation of the world to that causality. It gives voice to our interest in nature: not merely the contemplative, passive satisfaction of the pure aesthetic judgment or the other contemplative pleasure we feel at seeing nature accord with the theoretical laws we employ to study it, but an interest in the existence of a certain kind of order in nature. Our mind is turned from an immediate pleasure in the work of art to the Artist and his intention; we feel gratitude to nature or, more exactly, to God.

Beauty shows a kind of favour that nature or Providence has felt for us; we are thus led to the love of nature, Kant writes. It will be remembered that in pure aesthetic judgment it is we who view nature with favour; it is we who are 'liberal', we receive it generously (c3 v: 350, 268 / 196, 109). But when the aesthetic judgment is mixed with moral interest, we look beyond the immediate representation of nature to the purpose of natural beauty and so to its author as well. And then it is we who are filled with gratitude for the favour shown us by Providence. Kant is here contrasting the pure aesthetic judgment, in which man stands at the centre and is himself the one who is generous, or liberal, in his view of nature, and the Christian attitude toward natural beauty, in which beauty is a signpost, a visible manifestation of God's benevolence. Purposiveness and beauty both lead us to gratitude to God (c3 v: 380 note / 227 note). It is worth repeating here that the original aesthetic judgment, the recognition of beauty in nature, is a mark of our liberality, the favour that we show nature.

This contrast is similar to one made in Kant's moral theory: there, pure moral judgment, self-given law, leads to no gratitude to God or nature but to a stern disregard of everything save the quality of one's own will. Morality, however, when mixed with interest and desire (the 'matter' of the will) turns our attention to nature and to a postulated God who secures the harmony of that nature with our morality. Christian gratitude is the end result. In both instances, Christianity enters so as to allow an interpretation of the world that meets our moral need for hope in the 'promise' of the moral law (the *summmum bonum*). Christianity concerns us, as was said above, as worldly beings who have an interest in a particular consitution of nature: it concerns us, that is, when we move from what we ourselves are capable of, namely living well, to the hope for a world that will not show a repulsive 'irregularity' between what we do and what our fate is.

We have finally to consider beautiful art. We have seen that there is an immediate interest attached to natural beauty, an interest in the purposive harmony that it exhibits between ourselves and nature. Now if, Kant writes, we were to discover that some beautiful object in nature was not a natural product but a human artefact, our interest in it would disappear. Our interest (though not necessarily the aesthetic judgment as to its beauty) would be lost precisely because it could no longer be taken as evidence of the work of Providence (c3 v: 299–300 / 141–2). Art does, however, have one crucial advantage over natural beauty. The appreciation of natural beauty is passive and contemplative, and it is immediate, not governed by concepts. Natural beauty is, in brief, a beautiful thing. But art is a beautiful re-presentation, and in its representative quality, art shows its superiority: it does not depend on the thing being given to it, but rather renders even the ugly in nature beautiful (c3 v: 312 / 154–5). War, suffering, and natural cataclysms can all be made beautiful as they are worked up, transformed, and represented in art. The beautiful in nature is occasioned by mere reflection on a given intuition; art, by a concept of an object (c3 v: 320 / 164).

Thus in the artistic representation of the human figure an ideal represenation is possible. This possibility tells us two things, one about us, the other about art. There is no ideal flower, for example, since an ideal is a kind of perfection and so rests on a concept of the inner purposiveness of a thing. And only man, Kant argued, has the purpose of his existence in himself; thus man alone is capable of being a final purpose of nature. Only the human form, therefore, is susceptible of an ideal representation. This ideal form is not simply an empirical composite of human features, a 'normal idea' of man, as Kant calls it, but a phenomenal form which gives expression to our innter purposiveness (c3 v: 233–6 / 70–2). It is the visible embodiment of moral ideas.

We have a great interest (a moral interest), Kant writes, in the ideal of beauty (c3 v: 235–6 / 72). Indeed, it would seem that since all art has its origins in a concept or purpose, representational art – the reworking of nature – is bound up with an interest, or more properly, a guiding-thread and consequently lacks the immediacy and intuitive character of natural beauty. Art, then, both in its represention of nature and in its ideal portrayal of man is able to take what is ugly or merely ordinary, war for example, or the physical human form, and render it beautiful. In speech, sculpture, and the pictorial arts is shown our productive power; and in presenting an ideal, they offer us things that exist in thought, or art, alone, that have no empirical existence.

The beautiful in nature reveals design to us and the work of a divine artificer; beauty in art, be it the representation of nature or of the human form, shows us that even in what is ugly and without purpose we can, if we view it from the right perspective, see the physical manifestation of design. Where nature does not give us such evidence directly, we can transform it in thought so that it meets our needs, though the fact that it is not given to us but created suggests a certain romance-like, or fictional quality about it. Beauty in nature and beautiful art, whatever the formal properties of the aesthetic judgment about them, are nevertheless intimately related to our interests. And interests, or what amounts to the same thing, desires or needs, are as we have seen above all practical. Natural beauty and man-made beauty allow us ways of seeing the world that satisfy our moral need to find something other than a shocking irregularity in nature's workings. They also lend support to one another, natural beauty (and teleology) by presenting empirical traces of purposiveness in nature and art by transforming what is not given immediately as beautiful, that which in its ugliness shows no sign of art, into a beautiful thing.

MORAL LIFE, THE SUBLIME, AND THE BEAUTIFUL

Now Kant, as is well known, rejected Burke's psychological approach to aesthetics in the third *Critique* (c3 v: 277–8 / 118–20). In so doing, he rejected also much of hiw own early work on aesthetics (the *Observations on the Feeling of the Beautiful and Sublime*). There is, however, a clear parallel between that earlier piece and Kant's later transcendental grounding of aesthetics and that parallel will provide us with some key ideas with which to study the essays on history. The pure aesthetic judgment is free: it is not bound down by desire for the existence of the source of pleasure or by a moral desire for the reality of the *summum bonum*. But the freedom associated with the beautiful is not that of self-given law; rather, it is a kind of lawless play, a mere liberality of spirit (c3 v: 292 / 134). Lacking the cold voice of principle or law, it is, Kant writes, like female or 'beautiful virtue' – the world of the gentle, charitable, and graceful: the stern compulsion of duty is not to be found there (OBS II: 231 / 81).

Pure aesthetic judgment is also universal or, to be more exact, makes universal claims for itself: thus the precondition of aesthetics is a 'common sense,' a literal sympathy among people and perhaps even a certain sociability. The capacity to recognize the beautiful, being strictly aesthetic (based on the senses and a shared feeling of pleasure), is a universal faculty. In the *Observations*, the beautiful, because it is a shared pleasure common among people, is said to be related to sympathy in a broader sense, to love of one's fellows rather than respect or esteem for them (OBS II: 215–18 / 58–61). What is beautiful in nature and the common capacity we have to perceive it is the source of love; the law – obedience to the principles of morality – may inspire respect but not affection. The beautiful is thus tied to a sanguine temperment (OBS II: 219 / 63), hopeful because of its philanthropy and because of what beauty in nature points to.

Beauty and the philanthropy that is part of it put love and charity at the source of our actions – making, Kant says, for beautiful, not virtuous deeds: 'It is a very beautiful thing to do good to men because of love and a sympathetic good will ... But this is not the genuine moral maxim of our conduct' (c2 v: 82 / 85). And when beauty leads us to think of the cause of the wonders of nature, we are grateful to their Author. Gratitude toward God and philanthropy toward our fellows – in other words, hope for the betterment of the world, arising from faith and from love of man – are the attitudes that form the heart of the beautiful view of the world.

'*Der Tag ist schön*' (OBS II: 208–9 / 47) – the day is beautiful. In daylight all is illuminated, the manifold beauty of nature is laid out before us. The beautiful is found in nature, in beautiful things given to us directly by the senses. In daylight we are worldly beings, immersed in the world about us. We orient ourselves in daytime by visible nature – the distant shoreline or other landmarks. Beauty too, visible or phenomenal beauty, serves to orient us – by suggesting an Artificer to us, by showing us the ugly now made beautiful: by giving reality to the promise of the *summum bonum*. Beauty needs daylight – it depends on nature made visible, given to us, presented or represented in art.

'*Die Nacht ist erhaben*' (OBS II: 208 / 47) – the night is sublime. At night, nature disappears from sight, familiar places lose their familiarity. In the deepest night that Kant speaks of in his essay on orientation, not even the stars guide us; even in our own room, we fear to lose our way – darkness concealing its order from us. The most important distinction between the beautiful and the sublime is that in natural beauty the object brings with it a purposiveness in its form, by which it seems preadapted to our judgment. The sublime, in contrast, violates purposiveness in the form of the object – the nature that awakens this sense in us is, in its essence, formless, though it reveals a different kind of purposiveness, a moral nature in the subject (c3 v: 192, 245 / 28–9, 83). The beautiful, then, attributes a purpose to nature itself, whereas the sublime begins with the formlessness of nature and arouses a feeling of purposiveness in the spectator. We thus seek a ground external to ourselves for beauty, but the sublime we discover within us (c3 v: 246 / 84).

The sublime is found in the formlessness of nature, in storm-tossed oceans, for example. The sublime emerges from violence and the destruction of order in nature. The purposiveness seen in natural beauty extends our concept of nature beyond mechanism to art or design; the sublime extends not our idea of nature, but rather the concept we have of ourselves. Nature may properly be called beautiful but not sublime. The latter involves no teleological assertions about nature, the former depends upon just such propositions. The beautiful calls forth an interest in nature, its design and Designer and forms a part of the guiding-thread out of which a faithful interpretation of the world is woven. The sublime leads to no interest in nature; in the formlessness that inspires it no guiding-thread is to be seen. Now Kant distinguishes two kinds of sublimity, the dynamic and the mathematical, and it is in the dynamically sublime that the feeling of moral courage is most apparent.

Here, in the dynamically sublime, we realize our superiority over even the greatest horrors that nature confronts us with. We discover in ourselves a 'faculty of resistance' to nature. The resemblance to courage is obvious, and Kant explicitly draws the analogy between sublimity and military virtue or courage. War can, when represented in art, be made beautiful – as, for instance, in a statue of Mars: the terrible is thereby rendered beautiful, the repugnant attractive (c3 v: 312 / 155). War may also be seen in all its fearfulness and ugliness, and viewed in this manner it can arouse a sense of courage in us (c3 v:262–3 / 102).

Kant gives two parallel examples from nature: the heavens and the oceans. The heavens and oceans can be seen in two quite different ways. The heavens can be viewed as a system of bodies moving 'in circles purposefully fixed' (c3 v: 270 / 110), as Copernicus and Newton described them, and the oceans as a kingdom of aquatic creatures or as designed to facilitate commerce between the continents. However, the heavens can be seen also as 'a wide vault' (*Gewölbe*), and the oceans as a 'restless, threatening abyss' (*Abgrund*) (c3 v: 270 / 111). Only as a limitless vault or as an abyss do they awaken in us a sense of sublimity. Considered as designed, as being systematic, unified, and purposive, they may strike us as beautiful perhaps, but not sublime.

Both beauty and sublimity are related to our moral feelings, the first by the disinterest that is a part of pure aesthetic judgment and by calling our attention to design in nature; the second, by pointing to our superiority over nature, our capacity for resisting and overcoming nature. When Kant, in the *Critique of Practical Reason*, describes the 'unbounded magnitude of worlds beyond worlds and systems of systems ... a countless multitude of worlds' (c2 v: 162 / 166) and then states that a person's moral worth infinitely raises him above nature, what he is portraying is the sublime – looking into the boundless vault of the heavens and knowing oneself to be above it. And the seat of this superiority is to be found in oneself, in the moral law. The beautiful only dimly reflects this victory in the disinterest that its judgments display.

Kant is here drawing a clear parallel between the beautiful and the sublime on the one side and faith (the *summum bonum* and its postulates), and moral courage (Kant's modified Stoicism, cf chapter 3) on the other. Both the beautiful and the beliefs of reason see design in the world and therefore the work of a Designer – a thought which, as Kant points out at the end of the third *Critique*, acts as a support for the hope that we have in the 'promise' of the moral law. They differ, of course, in that one emerges from sense, while the other arises from the moral law itself. Yet they converge in the idea of a wise Architect of nature; and the purposiveness that the former claims to see represented in beauty lends weight and points to the idea of God postulated by the *summum bonum*.

The sublime and the pure moral standpoint, the courage not to turn to faith but to cling to morality alone, share the same kind of relation as that between the beautiful and the beliefs of reason. The sublime begins with the world – with the violent formlessness of nature – and ends by revealing our superiority over it; the pure moral standpoint shows us the strength of a person who governs himself according to the consciousness of duty alone, and it displays the triumph of that consciousness over a world that may indeed offer little hope of reward for a life well led.

In the beautiful and the beliefs of reason, the concern is with the constitution of nature, seen or postulated; in the sublime and the moral standpoint, only the moral will, the inner worth of man, is the object of attention. The beautiful becomes visible only in daylight because only in that light can we see what is external to us, nature. The *summum bonum* and its postulates make nature visible too, though in a different manner, through concepts. The world made visible (be it in the immediate perception of natural beauty, in represented beauty, or in faith) is the means by which, from this standpoint, we orient ourselves here on earth. Night, the formlessness of nature, and a rejection of faith render nature (creation) useless as a guide: we are then left with our moral will, and that may be sufficient.

A void is created by experience, which Kant calls the repulsive irregularity of nature: the denial of the possibility of a direct (empirical) inference of purposiveness from the facts of nature. When the spectator changes viewpoint so as to be no longer bound by the narrow limits of possible experience the world can be seen in the light of faith (the subjective assent to moral purposiveness in nature) or, as in the 'starry heavens' passage quoted above, as a challenge to duty and to courage. From this second standpoint, we are invited to reflect upon what raises us above mere animality – and that is not the coincidence of virtue and happiness, but virtue alone. Faith and a sense of inner worth or moral nobility are two great ways of viewing the world.

In sections 86 and 87 of the *Critique of Judgment*, three men and their standpoints can be seen. 'Suppose the case of a man ...' Kant writes (c3 v: 445 / 296), a man surrounded by beautiful nature, who sees beauty in the things around him. His mind is at rest in the 'serene enjoyment of his being' and he feels a need to be grateful for that beauty and serenity. The world seems to favour him, and he is thankful to its Creator. This same person, when pressed by duty, interprets those duties as the commands of a supreme Lord, and should he violate them it is the voice of a Judge that calls him to account. This is the religious view of the world. It consists in gratitude for the evidence supplied us by nature of God's generosity, obedience to moral laws expressed as his commands, and humiliation when we fall short of those imperatives (c3 v: 446 / 296). It is 'at least possible,' Kant concludes, to represent to ourselves such a Being and to see in the world his works. This person's morality is thus given strength (c3 v: 446 / 296–7).

Then 'suppose the case of a righteous man,' Kant begins again, a Spinoza, let us say (c3 v: 452 / 303). Spinoza, Kant writes, does not believe in a wise Artificer. Or, more accurately, he does allow an original Being as the ground of the things of nature and thereby hopes to secure the unity of nature inhering in this one Substance. But the unity of appearance in a Being of this kind is different from purposive unity. Spinoza's original Being, or Substance, is not an intelligent, moral (having a will) Designer of the world, but only the basis of its formal (non-purposive) unity. Thus, Kant says, Spinoza has chosen to see only mechanical necessity where he could well have seen design, at least from a practical point of view or 'with a practical intent' (in praktischer Absicht) (c3 v: 453 / 304).

What does the world look like to one who sees it as Spinoza does, who does not adopt faith or the practical point of view? Kant's description is graphic: this man can see no harmony of nature with his moral worth – nature does not reward the sort of life he feels himself bound to lead. Deceit and violence surround him, and the just suffer equally with the evil. 'So it will be until one wide grave engulfs them together (honest or not, it makes no difference) and throws them back ... into the abyss of the purposeless chaos of matter from which they were drawn' (c3 v: 452 / 303). The denial of purposiveness in nature results in a view both deeply pessimistic and fearful, and one that would seem to threaten morality by calling into question the reality of its 'promise' (the summum bonum). But it is revealing that Kant does not suggest that a man like Spinoza would cease being moral; on the contrary, the emphasis is upon a person who, despite such a bleak view of the world, nevertheless perseveres. The 'indelible idea of morality' remains even if the 'senses see nothing before them' (c3 v: 274 / 115). Moral sentiment (Gesinnung) (c3 v: 452 / 303) may be threatened by the denial of purposiveness in nature, but not the moral law. This picture of Spinoza should be contrasted with that of the third and last of Kant's three portraits. Like Spinoza, this man is not faithful and does not believe in design in nature. But having no faith, he, unlike Spinoza, considers himself relieved of all moral duty (c3 v: 451 / 302).

Kant's own work of art: in these few pages portraits of three kinds of men emerge – of those who have faith, who for practical purposes choose to give their assent to the idea of a moral Governor of nature (the beautiful); of those who do not share this faith but whose courage, based on a recognition of moral duty and worth allows them to lead a good life without consolation (the sublime); and, finally, those who, finding in themselves no capacity for belief and thus seeing no hope for the reality of the moral law's promise, choose to deny duty (the worldly-wise). All three begin from the same fact, the emptiness of nature in relation to morality, its repulsive 'irregularity' as it is given to us directly in experience. But they choose to view it in different ways – as a call to faith, an inducement to courage, or as an apology for immorality. Looking at his art work, at his portraits of the beautiful, the sublime and the prudent, did the artist, Kant himself, have a preference? It is perhaps too early to say; he did remark, however, that the moral law 'awakens a *sense of the sublimity* of our own destiny which enraptures us more than all beauty' (RWL VI: 23 note / 19 note) (*was uns mehr hinreisst als alles Schöne*).

# 6

# Philosophical history and the beautiful

The love of history seems inseparable from human nature, because it seems inseparable from self-love.

Lord Bolingbroke

## INTRODUCTION

Kant tells us of a certain innkeeper in Holland who announced his establishment to passers-by with a sign. But no ordinary sign, this; for on it was painted not the usual cluster of grapes or kegs of beer but the dismal scene of a graveyard. Inscribed above this odd vista were the words *Zum ewigen Frieden*, 'Perpetual Peace.' The inscription, we are informed, is satirical, but satirical of what we do not know. Is the object of this satire the whole of mankind, the worldly-wise statesmen, or the dreamers of sweet dreams, the philosophical millenarians? Could the sign painter have been a misanthrope who viewed the victims in the graveyard and the authors of the optimistic thought 'perpetual peace' with equal disdain? Or then again, might this painting have been intended as a judgment upon statesmen, who never weary of the long strife; a moral judgment, perhaps, taking as its standard the ideal of perpetual peace? And finally, it could be suggested that the artist was satirizing visionary dreamers, the philosophical optimists who arouse great hopes by building beautiful cities to come, in speech alone, oblivious of history's bloody reproach to their comforting tales.

The problem of the Dutch innkeeper's sign provides us with a point from which we may begin to study Kant's historical essays. For it captures the questions central to those essays: how can we view history, what makes us adopt a viewpoint at all, and, lastly, how is a history a priori possible? The contrast between the words – the short speech, *Zum ewigen Frieden* – and the fact of the graveyard mirrors the principal theme of Kant's essays on history. Kant's doubts about the artist's intentions, the many possible ways of interpreting his work, point to the variety of standpoints from which history can be seen. The artist has not told us of his purpose, and there is no way in which we can discover it. History, as Kant frequently remarks, is like a theatrical spectacle – a tragedy, a comedy, or both. But what a curious sort of play! In it we are actors, authors, and spectators. On the one side, then, we are like that weary traveller standing, perplexed, before the inn's sign, bemused as to the painter's purpose. But his difficulty is purely aesthetic and passive: a question simply of interpretation. We, on the other side, are both observers and actors, and what we are to make of this play of human affairs is very much a practical as well as an aesthetic problem.

Kant's intention, I will argue, is to make sense of this play; or, more exactly, to show that we are to some extent at liberty to rewrite its scenes and to turn away from it at the end, elevated or degraded by what we have chosen to make of it. The bare facts displayed outside of that Dutch inn are less important than whether the way we choose to interpret them produces in us fear and moral cowardice, a comforting hope and a certain philanthropic sense, or a recognition of our moral superiority to its many horrors. This liberty that we have, the freedom to choose a viewpoint, is a mark both of the spontaneity of our reason and of the failure of nature or God to provide any clear answer as to the purpose of the world and of the people who inhabit it. The Artist himself has not instructed us in the sense of his play, in which we are and must be actors, and so we are left free to interpret it for our practical purposes here and now. This freedom reveals our unique capacities, our limits, and our needs. Our liberty is at once a power and a consequence of our limits, a problem.

The *Idea for a Universal History with a Cosmopolitan Intent* begins with a dismissal of the metaphysical, or moral, problem of the freedom of the will. Whatever one may think to be the forces determining the will, the will nevertheless gives rise to appearances, to human actions. And history is concerned with the narration of those actions. Not the form of the will, its submission to or rejection of the moral law, but only its manifestations are of interest here. Man is now considered as a natural being, and his deeds are subject to the same universal laws as those that govern all natural phenomena. The transition from the problem of the will and its maxims to the narration of human events prepares the ground for the ignoring of the person, moral or civil, who is the ultimate locus of moral accountability, and for the emphasis upon the species, the vehicle of historical evolution. The moral notions of responsibility and worth give way to species-related ideas of evolution and progress. This is not, therefore, a history written with a moral and didactic purpose, but rather a universal history of mankind. Animals can have a history of this kind. We are reduced to what we possess in common, to our species-being (to use Marx's phrase), and not to virtue, which is rare, and which is in any event not amenable to historical explanation.

But man is unique among the species of living beings in that his actions are subject, to some extent, to caprice, to a negative sort of freedom. The human world, in other words, is not governed by instinct in the way that a bee's would be. A history of bees would, Kant suggests, be a relatively simple matter, since their actions occur according to instinct and with as much order and regularity as the cycle of day and night. Nor yet would a history of a species of entirely rational beings offer any difficulty (UH VIII: 17 / 12). In the former case, instinct and, in the latter, a consciously adopted plan would provide the historian with a guiding-thread with which to compose a cohesive narrative. However, humans live neither wholly according to reason nor according to instinct. Where, then, is the historian to look for an organizing principle? Kant had elsewhere maintained that there are various ways in which human actions can be interpreted, but all these varieties of explanation are passed over in his philosophy of history. Why he rejects them, and what leading principle he ultimately proposes, are crucial questions for us here, since an insight into Kant's intention in these essays depends on an answer to the problem of the different types of available explanation.

A person's actions can be judged not from the point of view of nature but from a moral standpoint, as reflections of the quality of will that is at their source. Take the example of a liar, Kant writes – his misdeeds can be explained in a temporal-causal, historical (evolutionary) manner. That is, we can look at his bad education, his poor upbringing, or his evil friends. We are, however, able to (and indeed to make a moral judgment we must) abstract from that history: 'We can leave out of consideration what this way of life may have been, ... we can regard the past series of conditions as not having occurred and the act as being completely unconditioned by any preceding state ... Our blame is based on a law of reason ... This causality of reason we ... regard ... as complete in itself' (c1 A555 / B583).

Kant concludes: 'Although *difference of time* makes a fundamental difference to appearances in their relation to one another ... it can make no difference to the relation in which the action stands to reason' (c1 A556 / B584; emphasis added). Here the temporal order, the series of events, is ignored, and so a guiding-thread, a history, of the person is not needed. From the point of view of the (moral) law of reason, not the temporal origin but solely the rational origin of a person's actions is what is at issue (RWL VI: 41 / 36).

Now clearly such a way of judging the will's appearances or manifestations cannot yield (as it does not require) a history that, as we have seen, is a temporal-causal account of a sequence of events bound together by a leading principle. Nor, by the same token, is any 'universal' point of view possible, any consideration of the species: the 'species' has no will, only individuals do, and consequently moral attribution can be made only to individuals. What Kant argues is the only unqualified good thing in the world, and what separates man from the other creatures of the earth – the moral will – is an inadequate guide for the historian. Further on, we shall discuss other reasons why the moral account fails to satisfy the historian's needs.

Now, Kant says, people have an empirical character, the actions of which, 'as appearances, stand in thoroughgoing connection with other appearances in accordance with unvarying laws of nature' (c1 A539 / B567). Considered as phenomenal, as events in time, subject, as the *Idea for a Universal History* argues, to those same laws that bind all nature, human actions could be predicted with absolute certainty (c1 A550 / B578). Kant, in his later essays, moderates this statement somewhat: the new hope is that some ordering principle may be found which, while not allowing prediction in the strong sense, will nevertheless display the coherence of human actions, and point to the course that those actions will take. If we look, he writes, at the unstable weather, we find that we cannot determine in advance what weather we shall have, but we do see that, looked at over the years, weather helps maintain the cycle of nature, the growth of plants, and the flowing rivers in an 'unbroken, uniform course' (UH VIII 17 / 11). To discern this uniform course we must study nature 'in the large,' for otherwise her workings remain apparently chaotic and purposeless. Similarly births, deaths, and marriages, which seem subject to no rule, reveal, in the annual statistical tables that record them, a definite pattern. Even games of chance, viewed over a lengthy sequence of them, exhibit a certain regularity.

Human affairs, then, can be subjected to a kind of interpretation that will give order to them: a sort of natural history. Kant suggested this possibility in the first *Critique* and attempted such a history in his writings on race and in his anthropology. In their statistical tables, the mathematician and social scientist do something quite similar. However, Kant adopted neither this reasonably safe natural history nor the coherence of the statistical approach as the guiding-thread for his philosophical history. In their place he offered a daring and clearly counter-intuitive hypothesis about history. But here we must note one crucial difference between Kant's Copernican revolution in history (which we shall examine in more detail later in this chapter) and the one in the *Critique of Pure Reason*. There the failure of earlier attempts at developing a science of mathematics, of physics, and of astronomy had led to revolutions in scientific method, signalled by the introduction of a new standpoint, namely that of reason, in the place of mere empirical 'feeling about.'

In the writing of history, however, there seems to be no want of available principles, no manifest failure that needs to be righted. How is it, then, that a Copernican revolution is required here? The theoretical failure of the early natural sciences, caused by their reliance on empirical observation, to show the law-governed order of things demanded a new, Copernican hypothesis. Human affairs, understood as phenomenal events, do share in that law-governed order of things that embraces all phenomena, according to Kant. Therefore, the need for a new hypothesis or guiding-thread here can mean only that the 'inconstancy' of human events (the motive, presumably, for seeking a new explanatory principle) reflects the absence not of all order (since they participate in the law-governed domain of phenomena, and since they show a mathematical or statistical regularity) but rather of a certain kind of order – just and, perhaps, consoling. The key to this new Copernican revolution is to be found in the introduction to the *Idea for a Universal History*.

'One cannot suppress a certain indignation,' Kant writes, when one looks at human affairs (UH VIII: 17 / 12). Here on the great 'world stage' what do we see but childish vanity, evil, and destructiveness. In the end, we do not know what to make of mankind, which so rarely exhibits wisdom in its deeds. The empirical view of history, its facts, present us with an unappealing image of man: 'Falsehood, ingratitude, injustice, the childishness of the purposes regarded by ourselves as important ... in the pursuit of which men inflict upon one another all imaginable evils, are so contradictory to the idea of what men might be ... that, in order that we may not hate them we withdraw from all contact with them' (c3 v: 276 / 117).

This same problem appears again in the final section of Kant's essay *On the Old Saw*, where he says that to watch men taking steps upward toward virtue only to be thrown back into vice and misery is a sight unfit for God or man: 'To watch this tragedy for a while may perhaps be touching and instructive, but eventually the curtain has to fall. For in the long run the tragedy becomes a farce, and though the actors, fools that they are, do not tire of it, the spectator will' (TP VIII: 308 / 76). The picture of a stagnant history, a labour of Sisyphus, is again said by Kant to turn the world into a farce, a scandal, which threatens to compel us to avert our eyes lest we become misanthropes (UH VIII: 30 / 25 and RWL VI: 33–4 / 29). The love of man depends on a belief in his progress in history, and thus Kant explicitly connects the wish for a cosmopolitan constitution with a philanthropic view of man (TP VIII: 307 and note / 75 and note). *Respect* (*Achtung*) for humanity, however, needs no interpretation of man's history but only the recognition of his moral worth.

And this tragedy turned farce is a reproach not only to mankind but also to God, his wisdom and justice: what are we to think of his creation, if among the lowliest things of nature, the snowflake for example, we see displayed a wonderful order and beauty, yet among his most noble creatures, only chaos and injustice reign? Thus Rousseau's Savoyard Vicar: 'The picture of nature had presented me with only harmony and proportion; that of mankind presents me with only confusion and disorder! Concert reigns among the elements, and men are in chaos! The animals are happy; their king alone is miserable! O wisdom, where are your laws? O providence, is it thus that you rule the world?'[1]

Love of man and love of God both compel us to abandon the empirical view of history. Just as Spinoza, had he chosen to do so, could have seen the world, for practical (moral) purposes, as a justly ordered whole, so too can we interpret history with a cosmopolitan (philanthropic) intent. Such a history would be a source of hope, of love for humanity, and a theodicy. 'Take a man,' Kant writes, 'who, honoring the moral law, allows the thought to occur to him ... of what sort of world he would create' (RWL VI: 5 / 5). Kant's historical essays begin with the suggestion of a similar imaginary or artistic creation – but with this one crucial difference: that hope and thus love of humanity, not the honouring of the moral law, are what leads us to attempt this philosophical history.

History, Kant often remarks, is a 'theatre' (*Schauplatz*), a 'world-stage,' a 'drama' (UH VIII: 17 / 12 and END VIII: 331 / 73), in which all of mankind are actors. The script for this play is not, as we have seen, a plan consciously adopted by the actors as if they were wholly rational beings. The point, then, is to find a clue to such a history; to paint the bare facts of history, not in the bronze or even duller colours of its empirical existence, but as golden – to represent humanity and nature in a more flattering fashion.

PHILANTHROPY, HOPE, AND HISTORY

Kant's major work on history, the *Idea for a Universal History*, contains nine theses. The first proclaims not the freedom of the will or the dignity of the moral law but rather the teleological organization of nature. All natural capacities, it says, are destined to evolve to their proper ends. Observation of animals, both in their internal constitution and in the system in which each species forms a link, confirms this teleological theory of nature, Kant argues. That nature is a teleological, or purposive, arrangement of things is an idea that stands at the centre of Kant's philosophy of history. And his essays abound in descriptions of nature intended to provide physical evidence of such a purposiveness. In the mechanism of nature, Kant writes, we see exhibited a form that is basic to its (nature's) existence, a form that we cannot conceive of save on the premise of an author of the world (PP VIII: 361 note / 106 note).

We do not directly infer the workings of Providence from the 'cunning contrivances' of nature, but we supply such a wisdom from our own minds (*hinzudenken*) in order to think its possibility 'by analogy to actions of human art' (PP VIII: 362 / 107). By placing reindeer in Lapland, the desert camels in arid regions, and fur and oil-bearing animals and wood in the Arctic, nature has provided for mankind, and these provisions are indirect evidence of the presence of wisdom in nature (PP VIII: 363 / 108–9; but compare with VVR II: 240). It is quite possible, Kant concedes (and perhaps more plausible as well), to interpret these phenomena in the ordinary 'physico-mechanical' manner –

for instance, that the Gulf Stream carries driftwood from temperate to frigid lands. Yet, 'we must not overlook the teleological cause, which intimates the foresight of a wisdom commanding over nature' (PP VIII: 361 note / 107 note).

One might be left with the impression, on reading this first thesis, that Kant is suggesting a science of history, a sort of biology of human society that would reveal the growth of that society as a process similar to that of the generation of a flower from a seed. We remember that in the third *Critique*, Kant said that certain kinds of beings, namely 'organized beings,' seem to demand teleological explanation. Having rejected mechanical-causal and statistical accounts of human life, Kant is perhaps offering here an analogy between the society of men, viewed as an organism that tends, without a conscious plan, to move in a certain direction, and the patterns of development that we find in nature. In this interpretation, the distinction between natural and human history would dissolve into one grand teleological theory of the world, embracing both humans and other creatures. And, indeed, Kant states that the principal question in the philosophy of history amounts to this: are we to conceive of nature as a 'concourse of efficient causes' (in which whatever is good is the result of a fortunate accident), or as following a lawful (teleological) course, or, finally, as mere blind chance (UH VIII: 25 / 19– 20)? These three questions, he concludes, can be reduced to one: is it reasonable to assume a purposiveness in the parts of nature, but to 'deny it to the whole' (UH VIII: 25 / 20, and see C3 V: 378–9 / 225)?

Two related and provisional remarks need to be made here. First, the notion that nature is purposive, not chaotic, can be taken in two senses: as the pre-condition for explaining certain types of phenomena, or as suggesting a designer. The latter sense, when coupled with practical faith or interest, gives physical evidence of a moral (wise, not merely artistic) cause at work in the world. For a coherent, law-like description of the world (human or natural) only the former sense is required. The idea that, in addition to order in nature, a moral designer, or wisdom, must also be postulated has its origins not in the requirements of theoretical explanation but in the needs of religious beings (or, more simply, beings of finite power) who desire a harmony of nature with mankind. Second (an application of the above to philosophical history), Kant, to be sure, adopts as the fundamental premise of history a priori the idea of the 'systematic structure of the cosmos.' He takes up this guiding-thread not with the intention of offering a systematic, lawful account of human affairs, but with a practical interest.

These two tentative remarks can be reformulated. The essence of Kant's Copernican revolution consists in the advancing of a radical, counter-intuitive hypothesis, which puts the spectator (reason) at the centre of its explanation of nature. But this spectator is a knowing, moral, and limited or needy being. Kant's Copernican revolution makes of man, as a knowing being, the legislator of the formal, universal laws of nature. It allows man, as a moral and finite being, to propose a view of the world with a practical purpose. In the present discussion, we are dealing with the same hypothesis, employed now with a theoretical purpose, now with a practical one. Kant's Copernican revolution has to do above all with guiding-threads; but those threads or hypotheses out of which our account (our portrayal of the world, our artistry) of nature is woven are themselves guided by our interests, and those interests are both speculative and practical. Only by grasping this crucial idea can we understand Kant's Copernican revolution in history.

Now if, as the first thesis stated, nature is designed and purposive, what in man is to be furthered by nature? What is nature's intention with regard to us? Kant begins his answer: man is the only rational creature on earth (UH VIII: 18 / 13). Reason is here defined simply as the capacity for having purposes beyond those dictated by instinct – it is practical reason in the broad sense. And if we ask after the ultimate purpose of nature, what it is in man that can be advanced by nature, we discover that it can be either his happiness (assuming a beneficent nature) or his aptitude for using nature, his culture (C3 V: 429–30 / 279).

A mere glance around us teaches that it cannot be man's happiness that is nature's ultimate purpose. Man has the power of imagination and of comparison and is therefore restless and perpetually unsatisfied with what he has – his happiness is not dictated to him by instinct but arises out of an idea which, with his feeble vision, man is ill-prepared to bring into reality. Had nature wished simple happiness for man, it would have done far better to equip him with instinct alone and to take for itself both the ends that its favoured creature was to pursue and the means to those ends (GMM IV: 395 / 63).

And on the other side, we see that nature, in its own operations, has hardly treated man as its darling – in its 'destructive operations,' floods, plagues, and so forth, nature 'has spared him as little as any other animal.' Nor, finally, in the disposition with which it has endowed us in our relations to one another do we see any sign of its beneficence: our self-imposed misery, the 'oppressions of lordship,' and the barbarism of war leave one with the unmistakable impression that we were not intended for happiness.

The 'matter,' as Kant says, of all man's earthly purposes, grouped under the generic term 'happiness,' would have been better achieved by instinct than by reason. It is not in the 'matter' of these purposes that we find what is unique to man, in whose promotion nature might be said to have co-operated, but rather in the mere subjective (formal) condition, the 'aptitude of setting purposes in general' (c3 v: 431 / 281) or culture. Culture, the capacity for placing ends before oneself, implies a liberation from instinct and thus a way out of the pacific, but stagnant, Arcadia of a shepherd's or savage's existence. And it also requires, in the long term, a controlled freedom, since the anarchy of lawless competition constantly threatens to turn the advance of culture into a Sisyphean labour. Strife, or war, is at the heart of both these currents: the release from Arcadia and the establishing of a controlled freedom, a civic constitution.

The true purpose of Providence or nature, then, is not the 'shadow of happiness' that 'each forms for himself,' but the endless progress of culture. Were mere happiness and pleasure nature's end, it would have been just as well, Kant writes, that this world be populated by contented sheep and cattle (RH VIII: 65 / 50–1). Nature's lack of beneficence is, therefore, only apparent. Nature has willed that man himself should 'produce everything that goes beyond the mechanical ordering of his animal existence' and that he shall enjoy only what he 'has created by his own reason' (UH VIII: 19 / 13). What seems on the surface to be evidence of Nature's parsimony appears, in another light, as a mark of the greatest generosity. We have been allowed 'rational self-esteem' instead of the dumb happiness of the sheep. To have granted man the happiness that he so craves would have been to deprive him of that capacity which is, at one and the same time, the cause of his misery and the source of his true worth: reason. The niggardliness of nature, properly viewed, is its real beneficence. We ought to be thankful that nature gave us reason, not instinct, and strife, not happiness.

Nature wills the progress of culture, the advancement of reason. It wishes, therefore, the liberation of reason from the slumber of an Arcadian existence. Nature needs to provide a spur to this progress and also an order among human beings where that separation from the swaddling clothes of instinct will not lead to a collapse into anarchy, a condition that would surely put an end to all advancement in culture. Nature's means to these ends is man's 'unsocial sociability.' It is the opposition between men – their vainglory, lust, and avarice – that awakens all their powers. Without that antagonism and competition they would lead the life of that Arcadian shepherd, content perhaps, but little different from the sheep they tend.

Man, Kant writes, was originally placed in a garden by God, guided by instinct (the 'voice of God') alone. 'But soon reason began to stir' – man chose foods beyond those to which nature pointed him, and he found that he was able to choose a way of life, whereas other animals could not (CB VIII: 112 / 56). By making its first free choice, reason did violence to the voice of instinct. The history of reason is the history of the separation from instinct – of the rejection of the sensual in favour of the spiritual, the expectation of the future and the recognition that we are the true end of nature (CB VIII: 113–14 / 57–8). This progress away from the garden, away from the 'voice of God,' and toward the free use of reason has, however, another side: man left the 'harmless state of childhood – a garden, as it were' for a 'wide world, where so many cares, troubles, and unforeseen ills awaited him.' (CB VIII: 114 / 59).

Seeing the strife that has followed upon this liberation, we long for a return to that childish paradise, the supposed golden age (CB VIII:114–15, 122–3 / 59, 67–8). 'Es ist so bequem, unmündig zu sein' – 'It is so comfortable to be child-like' (WIE VIII: 35 / 3; translation slightly altered). Our love of tutelage, our flocking to that restful state where we will not have to exercise our freedom, and the desire for a return to a golden age expressed by the poets have one and the same source. Nature knows better, though, than to satisfy this craving for the tranquil stupidity of the garden: it has willed discord, and we, who want nothing more than the eternal peace of a life without freedom, unjustly criticize nature.

Nature has made us antagonistic to each other in order that we might progress beyond the idle play of the child's garden. The discord that we see about us, the war and violence at the centre of human history, compels us to advance. This same violence is also the root of man's political association with his fellows, the pre-condition of culture (UH VIII: 22 / 16). Nature, then, wills peace as well as strife – and for the former purpose, it employs our 'evil nature,' our war-like drives (PP VIII: 366 / 112). A harmony is thereby produced among us against our will (PP VIII: 360 / 106).

Theses 5 through 7 of the *Idea for a Universal History* present those problems that must be solved if nature is to achieve its designs. The first of these problems, to the solution of which nature directs man, is the creation of a 'universal civic society': a society of opposition, of individual external freedom, but governed by laws in which the freedom of each is made consistent with that of others. War and conflict are here again the means with which nature comes to man's aid by creating a good constitution through his corrupt nature. This solution does not depend upon moral improvement; it is, on the contrary, possible for a 'race of devils, if only they are intelligent,' namely, able to calculate what is in their interest. The just civic constitution and the good citizen are created by need, under nature's indirect but violent tutelage; and the good citizen by no means has to be a morally good person. We submit ourselves to this restraint because war compels us to seek a commonly recognized and all-powerful force. The boundless freedom that in the non-political situation is the wellspring of all violence and turmoil is not done away with but put to good use: 'All culture, art which adorns mankind, and the finest social order are fruits of unsociableness' (UH VIII: 22 / 17).

Thesis 5 showed us the need that compels us to seek sanctuary in civic society. This Kant termed the 'greatest' (grösste) problem for the human species. Thesis 6 sets out the 'hardest' (schwerste) problem, which will be solved last, if at all. Our needs may force us to establish a civic union, but the same drives that cause those needs suggest to us that we should exempt ourselves from the law. A master is required to break our will, to educate us in the need to obey. But this master is also human – the highest master, like Rousseau's Legislator, must be 'just in himself, and yet a man' (UH VIII: 23 / 17). 'This task is therefore the hardest of all; indeed, its complete solution is impossible, for from such crooked wood as man is made of, nothing perfectly straight can be built' (UH VIII: 23 / 17–18). This person, who is to be just and a master, would have to have a 'correct conception' of a possible constitution, much 'experience' of the world, and, above all else, a 'good will.' The person who is to educate all others would thus have to possess in the highest degree theoretical insight, worldly wisdom, and moral rectitude. He would have to be a philosopher, a prince, and a saint. Such a concurrence is, Kant remarks, very rare, if indeed it is ever to be found (UH VIII: 23 / 18 and PP VIII: 371 / 118).

There is still a third obstacle to be overcome if nature's design with regard to man is to be brought into being. The problem of creating a perfect civic constitution depends upon the establishment of peaceful and law-governed relations between states. For what would it profit man to erect a civic constitution only to have his regime forced to engage others in war? The tranquility and freedom for the sake of which he submitted to law in the first place disappear in the conflict between states. Moreover, war threatens to alter the internal form of the regime (its justice) by making military concerns – war and the preparation for it – paramount over the ideas of freedom, equality, and uniform justice that are the proper foundation of the constitution. War, in other words, tends to make sovereigns view their subjects not as persons having rights and intrinsic worth but as 'trifles' to be expended in foreign adventures.

But just as man's unsociability was both the predicament and the solution, so too is war between nations a problem that points to its own solution. Out of war, from its terror and pain and from the perpetual burden, of both physical suffering and financial cost, that it imposes on citizens, we will be led by our needs to seek that condition that reason (here meaning the recognition of right) 'could have told them at the beginning and with far less sad experience' (UH VIII: 24 / 18–19). That condition is a league of nations, a cosmopolitan constitution (UH VIII: 26 / 20). War, then, as well as our commercial interests, forces us to create a just international order in spite, or rather precisely because, of our hostile inclinations. The solution to this third problem, Kant says, will be 'laughed at as fantastical.' Indeed, he writes that it will be scorned even by Rousseau, whom he elsewhere describes as a 'good-natured' (*gutmütige*) moralist and optimist (UH VIII: 24 / 19 and RWL VI: 20 / 16). Even the naïve optimists will find this third proposal outlandish, it seems.

Kant's three problems, set out in theses 5 through 7 – developing a perfectly just civil constitution, finding a master who will oversee the political education necessary for it, and creating from chaos a league of states without which it (the constitution) cannot prosper – remind us of the 'three waves' of Plato's *Republic*. They suggest a certain fictional, romance-like quality about the whole proposal. And Kant's historical essays abound in such references: the language of drama and theatres, and of romances and fiction (UH VIII: 17–18 / 12; END VIII: 331 / 73; OQ VII: 82 / 141). The centre-piece of Kant's philosophy of history is the idea of war and how it can be seen not as the cause of misery but as the mark of Providence's generosity, as the means to an eternal peace and a just constitution. Peace and justice, internally and internationally, are the promise held out by nature interpreted in this way, and all progress is tied to war or strife, in one way or another. The 'sweet dream,' as Kant calls it (OQ VII: 92 note / 152 note), of progress, the curious fictional quality of its account of war, coupled with the 'three waves' of the *Idea for a Universal History*, lead naturally to two related questions. How is a philosophic history, a history a priori, possible (theoretically legitimate and of practical interest to us)? What is the relation of theory to practice, of an idea to the way in which we orient ourselves in the world? Both of these questions are already present in Kant's description of the Dutch innkeeper's sign. What status does the phrase 'perpetual peace' have, particularly above a picture that seems to contradict it? How can that short phrase, *Zum ewigen Frieden*, serve to guide us – as a comforting dream, or a moral command, or a denial of the possibility of a good life, which then invites us to seek worldly rather than moral wisdom? It comes as no surprise to us that the final two theses of Kant's major work on history should take up the first of these questions: how is a philosophical history possible?

Philosophy too, Kant says, can have its chiliastic beliefs. But its chiliasm is not 'fantastic,' since it 'can help, though only from afar, to bring the millennium to pass' (UH VIII: 27 / 22). How it can bring the millennium to pass Kant does not tell us, except to suggest at the end of the essay that it may direct sovereigns' ambitions by having them consider the way in which they will be judged by future historians: will they be viewed as friends or opponents of peace and justice? This motive Kant calls a '*small* one' for writing a philosophical history (UH VIII: 31 / 26). To this '*kleinen Bewegungsgrund*' Kant contrasts a '*kein unwichtiger Bewegungsgrund*,' a 'not unimportant motive' (UH VIII: 30 / 25). The motive that Kant is speaking of here is suggested to us by the remark that we cannot be indifferent to the fate of our race, even if the ultimate course that fate will take extends far beyond our lifetimes and beyond our 'vision.' Human nature is so constituted that even 'faint indications' of this path are important to us. They give us 'hope' that man will eventually find himself in a condition that will permit him to develop all his capacities. We shall return to this question of the motive for writing history a priori, but for the moment it would be best to turn to the most basic question: how is it possible in a narrow sense?

In the introduction to the *Idea for a Universal History*, Kant states that he wishes only to find a 'clue' to history and that perhaps someone will follow him who will compose a history using that clue. Thus Kepler, in an 'unexpected,' or revolutionary, way subjected the 'eccentric paths' of the planets to law, leaving it to Newton to explain those laws (UH VIII: 18 / 12). Kant seems to be drawing an analogy between himself and a Kepler or Copernicus, and we might infer from this that, like the great hypotheses of the astronomers, Kant's proposal is meant simply to set the foundation for an empirical study of history. However, the accuracy of this inference is called into question by Kant's remark near the end of the essay that experience reveals little of the path that nature follows (UH VIII: 27 / 22). If nature offers little support for the hypotheses advanced by the philosophic historian, how can one write a history 'of how the course of the world must be if it is to lead to certain rational ends'?

'How is history a priori possible?' Kant asks, repeating, in an altered form, his first Copernican question (OQ VII: 79–80 / 137).[2] His initial answer is playful: if the prophet himself creates and contrives to bring into existence the events he himself forecasts. Kant provides three examples of this sort of prophetic historian: prophets, statesmen, and ecclesiastics. The prophets of Israel foresaw the dissolution of their state and created a constitution that brought about just that end. Statesmen complain that people are not good and that if their reins are loosened only anarchy will result. But who is it that, through the unjust treatment of his subjects, has made a liberal obedience to law impossible? And lastly, ecclesiastics foresee the appeareance of the Antichrist – a prophecy that they help to come to pass by failing to teach moral principles from their pulpits. Clearly this is not what Kant intends by his own philosophical history.

Now we cannot solve the problem of history – whether to expect progress, retrogression, or the Sisyphean rise and fall of man's condition – directly through experience (OQ VII: 83 / 141). Here Kant reiterates the idea that experience provides us with little evidence of nature's plan. We are 'too blind,' too theoretically blind, to see nature's secret workings (UH VIII: 29 / 24) – these notions of the wisdom of Providence and of a moral plan for mankind are transcendent from a theoretical point of view and so can be given no philosophical (speculative) support (END VIII: 332 / 75–6). And not only is Providence inaccessible to us, but so too are human actions, insofar as they are strictly free. Only to the extent that man is considered as natural, as a species and 'class of animal' (Tierklasse), can his history have coherence (PP VIII: 365 / 111). Thus the freedom that Kant speaks about in the historical essays is not moral freedom but rather a purposiveness that has its origins in human nature, namely, in the lust for power, in envy and unsociability.

Given our blindness in a theoretical sense, the course of human affairs must seem to us, from an empirical perspective, as a planless conglomeration of actions subject only to the dismal reign of chance. We would have to conclude, with the abbé Coyer, that the only constant thing about man is his inconstancy (oq vii: 83 / 141). Perhaps, Kant suggests, the apparently senseless quality that the course of human events exhibits results from having chosen a poor vantage point from which to observe it. This line of argument recalls Kant's theory of revolutions in science in the first *Critique*: there the natural sciences were said 'to grope' about, relying on experience alone and hence failing to discern the laws of nature. This brought about a radical experiment, placing reason at the centre of scientific activity and making nature conform to the laws prescribed it. Kant's Copernican revolution began with just such a radical hypothesis: 'Hitherto it has been assumed that all our knowledge must conform to objects,' but what if we make an experiment and assume instead that objects must conform to our reason?

Experience and empirical knowledge have failed us in history as well. Because they have failed us in that special sense mentioned earlier, we now look for a better standpoint. We should, Kant writes, adopt the standpoint of the sun, of reason, and attempt a Copernican experiment in history (oq vii: 83 / 141). This will not, to be sure, enable us to foresee free actions, but it will serve other purposes. Thus Kant argues that even though we are blind theoretically we can, from a practical point of view, conjecture or offer a guiding-thread for presenting this otherwise senseless aggregate of human affairs according to a plan (uh viii: 30 / 25 and mej vi: 354 / 127). Here we see the point of view of reason in its practical employment, a conjecture or interpretive strand that we insert into a seemingly chaotic series of events.

The events themselves do not require, either for the bare possibility of incorporating them into experience or for a scientific account of them (as we have shown earlier), such a guiding-thread. Nor do they provide us with much evidence of the plausibility of the hypotheses of history a priori. Our theoretical blindness about the principal problems of history means that these daring hypotheses will find no Newton to give them empirical backing. In short, no transcendental deduction (having to do with the possibility of experience) and no empirical confirmation is available here. Thus we cannot be compelled to suppose the theoretical feasibility of this conjecture (its realism). It is a belief, and there can be no obligation to believe (mej vi: 354 / 127–8). The idea that our vision is too weak to see the wisdom of Providence leads us to a Copernican revolution of a different kind, to the 'modest language' of rational faith.

A philosophical history is possible, then, in the same sense that rational belief is. But why would one wish such a history? The project seems silly, since all that can be expected from it is a fiction, a mere romance. It seems to hold out no promise for an advance of empirical historical science, and Kant is quite emphatic in stating that history a priori is not to displace the work of empirical historians. And such modesty is only fitting for a history that proclaims the slim confirmation that it can hope to receive from the course of things given in experience. Thus the importance of the question: what interest do we have in history, what do we want to know about history (oq vii: 79 / 137)? We do not so much want to clarify the course of human affairs (history a priori certainly cannot provide any scientific clarity) or to further the 'political art of prophecy.' The latter, Kant says, has already been achieved, even without submitting human deeds to a law-like description (Kant, no doubt, had Thucydides – the first 'true' historian – in mind here). Rather, what we wish is to provide a 'consoling view of the future.' This consolation depends on there being a natural plan, for otherwise the future would offer us no hope – it would be a repetition of the bloody past or, worse still, a further decline. Kant's philosophical history, then, rests on hope (tp viii: 309 / 77–8).

The idea of hope is too general and amorphous for our purposes. It needs to be further divided into a theodicy, a justification of Providence, and a philanthropic component. We are now in a position to analyse in greater detail these ideas, which were first suggested near the end of the first section of this chapter. We feel a certain discontent, Kant argues, with the Providence that governs the world when we see ourselves surrounded by so much evil. A good man asks himself what sort of world he would fashion, were he the creator. The just would create a world that would be a mirror for their justice; if the world, as it is, is a 'hell of evils,' what does this say of its maker? Such a thought, aroused by the 'toilsome road' assigned here on earth, teaches us discontent with Providence (cb viii: 120–1 / 66). A justification of nature or Providence is therefore necessary, and with that theodicy come contentment and hope (cb viii: 123 / 68). Kant's philosophical history is a theodicy because it displays before us a nature governed by the justice and wisdom that we attribute to Providence – a new sort of clarity for a nature invisible from a purely empirical standpoint.

This same falsehood, injustice, and violence that conflict with our notion of what a moral God would create also conflict with our 'lively wish' for what we might be, the wish to see ourselves better than we currently are (c3 v: 276 / 117). We are then driven to misanthropy, or a withdrawal from society altogether. In order to love man, one has to believe in his progress from worse to better (TP VIII: 307 / 75). If there is to be no hope for a progress of this kind, then man would become a contemptible plaything – and his history a farce from which the spectators would have to turn their eyes. The inclination that we feel to sympathize with our fellow humans, even those in the most distant epochs, leads us to hope for progress in history.

Philanthropy and the love of God (the latter being the condition of the former insofar as Providence is needed so that we may believe in human progress – a revealing reversal of Kant's teaching that true religion is founded on morality) are at the source of hope: they provide, on the one side, the 'wisdom' required for hope (TP VIII: 310 / 78) and, on the other side, the sympathy and love of man that cause us to feel revulsion at the world seen empirically. In the one, we have the guiding-thread that we introduce into the facts given us in our experience of the world, and in the other we have the interest that leads us in the first place (together with a love of God) to look for that leading principle. Philosophical history is consoling, and it teaches us contentment with God and with our fellow humans.

Philosophical history represents the world as beautiful. It presents to its spectators the events of the world, its human events, not as they are given to us immediately but as they are re-created by an artist. And just as the artist, as Kant writes in the third *Critique*, can take the merely average human form and render it beautiful, so too can the philosophical historian take the bloody facts of history, with the condition of war as its central feature, and show us how, seen from the right perspective, history reveals the generosity and justice of our Creator. We are thus given a basis for hope, that as philanthropists we must have, in human progress. All the elements of the aesthetic sense are to be found here: the ugly made beautiful, the beautiful seen as evidence of Providence, and the sympathy and contentment that are bound up with the beautiful. But Kant's question – how is a history a priori possible? – and its answer, suggested in the phrase, 'the beautiful representation of the world,' reveal the weaknesses of that standpoint. These weaknesses are of two related kinds: in its conception of man and in its representation of the world.

THE MORAL FAILURE OF PHILOSOPHICAL HISTORY

Let us begin with the first weakness, that of the conception of man contained in this philosophical history. We recall, from our discussion of the *Critique of Judgment*, that the 'ideal' of human beauty is not merely an average or composite of human features but an exemplary image of those features. Nevertheless, to the extent that a statue of Venus, say, or of David is an ideal of human beauty, it must in a fundamental sense conform to the nature of that shape. It must begin with the physical character of the species, what is universal to man – his nature in the most literal meaning – and proceed from there to its idealized portrait. Kant saw that if history were to provide consolation by showing the progress of the whole of mankind, it would also have to begin from what is most common, not virtue, for example, but man's disposition, man considered as a 'class of animal.' Not a history of great individuals, such as we find in Thucydides, not even a more homely catechism of small yet moral deeds, but an account of the laws of the species' progress is what is needed for a consoling view of the world.

Man-in-general is thus the starting point for this history; and because only individuals (not the species) have wills and can form plans, the laws that determine this progress are to be sought not in man, but in nature, or, if wisdom is attributed to nature, in Providence. Man as a 'class of animal' guided, though indirectly, by nature is what the beautiful portrayal of history requires. We may appear now as more lovable – since the evil conditions in which we currently find ourselves are not our eternal lot – but also as more diminutive. Gone is the language of sublimity and of the autonomy of man's will: here we read only of need, hope, and consolation. Kant, I think, recognized this and would have agreed with Tocqueville when the latter wrote that such a history, emphasizing as it does necessity and general laws, appeals to an age that doubts the free will and fears what is exceptional. Tocqueville suggested that the great object of our age should be 'to raise men's souls, not to complete their prostration.'[3] Kant, in pointing to the limits of a hopeful history, did just that, though he would have had little interest in aristocratic history, with its emphasis on those few men who excel, above all, in the political arts.

A history with a philanthropic (cosmopolitan), not a pragmatic or moral, purpose – and Kant's principal work on history is entitled *Idea for a Universal History from a Cosmopolitan Point of View* – portrays man as lovable, but to do so it has to pass over that quality in him that most demands respect. History views man not as a being with a free will, the only truly good thing in the world (GMM IV: 393 / 61), but as a species under the tutelage of nature. The inferiority of the historical view of human affairs is to be seen in Kant's statement in the essay 'What Is Enlightenment?' that enlightenment is man's release from 'self-incurred tutelage' (WIE VIII: 35 / 3). Tutelage is the inability 'to make use of his understanding without direction from another.' Kant mentions the lack of courage that causes men to give over the direction of their lives to pastors and statesmen. But philosophical history shows mankind an even greater tutor, who directs us all to an end at once unknown and unwilled. Men flock to what can give consolation, to a story that relieves them of the necessity to act according to the hard standard of duty.

That too is self-incurred tutelage. And as tutelage is comfortable in a childish sort of way, so too is this grand tutelage under which the whole species stands. The 'sweet dream' of a perpetual peace is the promise made us by this most powerful of all tutors. Indeed it is 'guaranteed' to us, as Kant says in the title of the First Supplement of *Perpetual Peace*. It may tell us something of what Kant thought of this 'sweet dream' that he at least twice used virtually identical phrases – 'perpetual peace': *beständigen Frieden* and *immerwährender Friede* – in order to describe the poets' childish longing for a 'golden age' (CB VIII: 114–15,122 / 59,67), an age past or one to come.[4]

The comparison with Kant's doctrine of the *summum bonum* is illuminating. The highest good is the promise (which we add to the moral law) of happiness in proportion to virtue, in this world or in the one to come. We need the *summum bonum*, in the words of the second *Critique*, as 'matter,' as an object for our wills. Or, as Kant writes in the *Critique of Judgment*, we need the idea of a *summum bonum* because we cannot be indifferent to the issue of the sort of life we lead here. The pure moral law commands respect, but to inspire our 'moral feelings' we must love it as well (RWL VI: 6–8 note / 6–7 note). The moral law does not present the love of itself as a duty – only respect for the law is an unconditional duty – but it nevertheless allows it. So that we may love a law that in itself is simply a universal imperative, we are permitted to attribute to it a promise of happiness.

But Kant distinguishes between genuine and sham love: genuine love, for the law or for man, must be based on respect. Love, of whatever sort, is only a conditional good – there can be respect without love, but no genuine love without respect (END VIII: 337 / 82). The love for the moral law is just such a genuine love, since it demands, first, respect for the law as the necessary foundation for the *summum bonum*. This order, of respect first and love only afterward, is reflected in the worthiness that is demanded by the highest good. An object of sham love would hold its charms, its promises, first and win affection on that basis. The *summum bonum* commands respect for the moral law as the condition of its promise.

Philosophical history, however, does not demand worthiness on the part of man; its philanthropy is based not on respect, but on mere love, and its promise, its 'sweet dream,' does not require any effort by us. Quite the contrary, it rests its philanthropy on a progress that neither depends upon nor points to morality.

Both Christianity, in the form of the *summum bonum*, and philosophical history inspire man's moral and philanthropic feelings by beautifying the world. The former shows the Creator's wisdom in the beauty of nature, and offers the hope of a reward for a life well lived, and the latter presents a consoling account of human nature. They speak in the language of need and hope – of the need to see a world different than the one we are given immediately in experience, and of the hope for a just ordering of our fate.

Christianity and philosophical history teach love, for God and man. And Kant calls Christ a 'friend of man,' a *Menschenfreunde* (END VIII: 338 / 82), but in the *Groundwork of the Metaphysic of Morals* he attacks the 'friends of man,' using exactly the same word (GMM IV: 398 / 66). This attack, which is aimed at conduct directed solely by sympathy and philanthropy, applies to Christianity, but even more so to history a priori. The former, if it understands what true religion is (a Kantian-Stoic 'religion of good behaviour,' hardly distinguishable from a simple moral life; cf. chapter 3), seeks the origin of love in respect, while the latter, so as to make man lovable, shows him as the plaything of nature – a plaything even if that nature is well meaning in the course it chooses for man. Both the *summum bonum* and philosophical history turn our attention to nature, to the world, and to God, rather than exclusively to our moral wills. They seek evidence in the world that their promises are not mere illusions.

As a moral education, and that Kant says is the intention of the 'good-natured' philosophical optimists (RWL VI: 19–20 / 15–16), both fail, though Christianity less radically so than history a priori. The Christian teaching can be transformed into the imperative to be worthy, into Kantian morality in other words – and that is precisely what Kant does in one of his short moral catechisms (DV VI: 480–2 / 153–6). In his two principal works on moral philosophy, Kant sketches for us what such education in virtue should properly contain. The premise of that education is not to be found in the pastor's turning of the moral law into the commands of an all-powerful God, or in his terrifying portrayal of hell or his sweet picture of heaven (fear and hope as the incentives to good deeds). Nor is it to be found in the philanthropic view of progress held by many 'moralists.' Rather, the true foundation of a moral education is to be sought in the pure concept of duty (c2 v: 152–3, 156 / 156–7, 160). To the extent that young minds need illustrations, those must be taken from examples of good deeds, great and small. When Kant, in a passage referred to above, criticized prophets, statesmen, and ecclesiastics for bringing about the doom that they foresaw, what he was saying was that none knew how to educate men in respect for the law (moral, political, or religious). Perhaps philosophic historians, these new prophets, commit the same error. History, to conclude, is a vulgarized Christianity:[5] both share much in common, including an inferiority to the sublime point of view, the pure moral perspective of a Spinoza.

## THE THEORETICAL FAILURE OF PHILOSOPHICAL HISTORY

Philosophic history directs our attention to nature: with this observation we see the origin of both of the weaknesses of history a priori. Having discussed the weakness in its conception of man, we must now turn to its second failing. Philosophic history is, as we have remarked, a source of hope, a consoling view of the future, and a theodicy. Now the question 'what may I hope for?' is a problem at once theoretical and practical. Unlike the moral question 'what ought I to do?,' which is answered by stating the laws of pure practical reason, and the problem 'what can I know?,' the answer to which consists in a purely theoretical statement of the conditions of possible experience, the idea of hope takes as its guiding-thread man's practical interests, but in order to interpret nature in the light of those interests (c1 A805 / B833). And a theodicy, because it attempts to explain the coexistence of evil in the world and a moral Creator, must also, Kant says, give an account of nature (FPT VIII: 264 / 29).

Philosophic history, if it is to offer hope and justify Providence in our eyes, must interpret nature at once consolingly and believably. It must be credible: a story written about the world that is centred around the fact of war and injustice and that seeks to show why we ought to be grateful to nature for overseeing our affairs in such a generous manner. And we also need to raise the more theoretical question concerning the limits of what can be said about Providence.

There can be little dispute: history a priori is, to a large extent, implausible as a description of the world, and thus it is frequently the subject of derisive mockery from the cynical and worldly wise (TP VIII: 277 / 43; c1 A316 / B372; PP VIII: 343 / 85), and sometimes even from such good-natured moralists and optimists as Rousseau. It is quite possible, however, that this sort of story appeals to the common understanding. That Kant thought so is indicated both by the popular flavour of these essays and, more important, by the fact that their central premise – that nature does nothing in vain, that she works purposefully – is also the initial premise in the first chapter of the *Groundwork*, concerned with the ordinary, or common conception of morality. The thesis of a teleologically organized nature is a more convincing pedagogical device in the *Groundwork*, since there it is used to make a rather abstract point about why nature has given us reason and not instinct. The historical essays, however, require that we read that thesis back into an aggregate of facts, and it is then that difficulties with it emerge.

The question of the story's plausibility can be pushed to a still deeper level. Kant, in the third *Critique*, wrote that beautiful works of art, though designed by man, 'must not seem to be designed, i.e. beautiful art must *look* like nature' (c3 v: 307 / 149). Art must, of course, agree with the rules that govern painting or sculpture, for example, yet the artist must not allow his presence, his conformity to those rules, or his personal intentions to become '*painfully* apparent' (c3 v: 307 / 150). The rules and the purposes of philosophical history are indeed painfully apparent and reveal the work of art immediately as artful and not as a mirror held up before nature. When the artist is seen to be the historian, and not the Creator himself, where is there consolation in that?

We come, then, to the more theoretical question concerning the grounding of philosophic history in the idea of the 'systematic structure of the cosmos.' It is this idea, curiously enough, that is intended to suggest the plausibility of a history a priori rather than any direct evidence of progress as such. The crucial premise of a systematic (designed) world is a key ingredient in giving hope a foundation in nature (UH VIII: 27 / 22; PP VIII: 360–8 / 106–14). We recall from our analysis of the sections on teleology in the third *Critique* that nature does provide abundant evidence of design and hence of a designer. The attributes (and intentions) of that designer cannot, however, be discerned in his works. We see only the manifestation of his artistic powers. For that reason, the move from physical teleology to theology is illicit, according to Kant; illicit, because through experience we can detect only his artistic, not his moral wisdom. Yet in a philosophic history, the premise of natural teleology is used to support the argument for

Providence. It is not sufficient, given the purposes of a history a priori, to show merely a designer of nature. What is sought is to demonstrate the goodness, justice, and holiness of the Creator as revealed in his handiwork (FPT VIII: 257 / 285). This cannot be done.

Hence Kant's references to the need to see justice in the world are characteristically phrased in terms of desire and wish. In short, design in nature is readily discernible, but moral purposiveness lies beyond our ability to see it. And Kant quite consistently applies this restriction to his remarks in the historical essays themselves: the standpoint of Providence and of its justification is 'too high' for us – it cannot be supported with theoretical arguments about the constitution of nature (OQ VII: 83–4 / 142–3 and END VIII: 332 / 75–6). We can indeed conjecture or adopt the viewpoint of practical faith (PP VIII: 362, 380 / 108, 128), but this can have no basis in the study of nature. Though no proof from nature can be provided for it, the practical point of view, here embodied in historical faith, has the charm of all faith, that of being irrefutable.

## KANT'S CRITIQUE OF THEODICY

All philosophical theodicies fail to fulfil their promise: they fail to justify God and evil in the world, not because belief is impossible, but rather because they overreach themselves in their efforts to interpret nature. To succeed they must give an account of nature, just as the related question of hope has to offer some sort of theory of nature in order to find that for which it is searching. In both cases, we approach nature with practical interests; but here, unlike Kant's first Copernican experiment in the theory of knowledge, nature is reluctant to yield, for she already has laws, necessary laws, and an order of her own – this order having been defended on transcendental grounds before the 'tribunal of reason.' And that order is not a moral one. Doubts arising from experience are by no means simply the voice of cynicism, but seem to reflect the failure of theodicy to justify its claims about nature before that same tribunal (FPT VIII: 255, 263 / 283, 290).

In his essay 'On the Failure of All Attempted Philosophical Theodicies,' Kant shows the justification of God in the world incapable of defence. We acquire something useful from this failure, though – a sort of 'negative wisdom' about our limits: all attempts to fathom the workings of God must be given up as necessarily fruitless. This type of argument is simply a repetition of the attack on ideas to which no possible experience can correspond that Kant made throughout his critical period. It leads, as it did in the *Critique of Pure Reason*, to a recognition of the boundaries of knowledge and of the fact that belief is possible, if unsupportable. Here, however, we find a different conclusion: the theoretical critique defines limits and then allows a practical sphere, an 'empty space' for faith beyond those limits – a sphere to which it is indifferent. In the essay that we are considering, Kant rejects all philosophical theodicies, all the theodicies that rest on an interpretation of God's intention as revealed in the world (and thus far, we are still in the realm of the first *Critique*) but then offers a new, Kantian theodicy (FPT VIII: 264 / 291). And this new 'theodicy' does not need an interpretation of nature. In order to see the weaknesses of philosophical theodicy and history, we must pause to examine this peculiar Kantian version.

The world is a closed book, Kant writes, if one looks to it so as to read God's intentions out of the objects of experience. There is another sort of theodicy, though: this is the 'voice of God' or, as Kant says, the voice of our reason (FPT VIII: 264 / 291). This voice tells us simply to reject all reproaches to divine wisdom. Kant refers to this as an 'interpretation' of God's intentions in creation, but one set forth by practical, not speculative reason – that is, concerned with morality rather than nature. While Kant calls it an interpretation of creation, it is not, as becomes clear in his account of such a theodicy, creation understood as the world (nature), but, on the contrary, the crown of creation, the good will itself that is the object of interpretation here. This authentic theodicy Kant finds expressed in the biblical parable of Job. Job, Kant writes, was deprived of all his blessings save his good conscience. Job complained of his ill-fate, and friends gathered 'to comfort' him, each offering a theodicy, a moral explanation of his fate. Job insisted that he had done no evil that would warrant divine punishment. ' "God is unique" ,' he concluded, ' "and does what he wills" ' (FPT VIII: 265 / 292).

Kant calls the arguments of both Job and Job's friends for divine justice 'speculation or overly subtle speculation' (*vernünfteln oder überverünfteln*) (FPT VIII: 265 / 292). Neither is worthy of note, he says, but Job's honesty and outspokenness do merit respect, and for this God rewarded him. The conclusion that Kant draws from the story of Job is this: Job confessed 'that he had spoken unwisely about things that were too high for him and which he did not understand' (FPT VIII: 266 / 293). God forgave Job and revealed to him the wise ordering of the whole: proof that such insight is above human reason and depends rather on a miracle. Job's friends, for all their seeming piety, were punished, showing that the 'uprightness of the heart, not the merit of one's insights' (FPT VIII: 266 / 293) is what is most important. Job based his faith on morality and on the truth – this faith may be 'weak,' Kant says, but it is also purer, for it is a religion of 'good behaviour,' not of 'self-interest.'

Kant transforms Job into a Kantian moral man and then holds up his steadfast goodness, coupled with his insistence on the truth rather on consolation, as a reproach to those who seek such satisfying explanations. This new 'theodicy' is really no theodicy at all, or at least not one that meets the intentions of earlier attempts: its interpretation of creation is the same as that presented in the first pages of the *Groundwork* – the moral will is the only truly good thing in the universe, good, that is, without qualification. It is an account not of nature, but of the place occupied by the good will in creation. It can thus ignore nature, of whose purposes, if any, we are to remain forever ignorant. Job's theodicy consists in adopting a pure moral attitude to a world that is, for man, a closed book, at least as to how it may co-operate with his moral purposes.

The lesson of Job is that one must not seek comfort or consolation in the world, for that can end only with falsehood and pretense, but rather one should strive for the uprightness of the heart. And one should live well, not so as to be rewarded with revelation or paradise – for that would be a 'religion of self-interest' – but because morality has a priority over consolation, and ultimately over faith itself. We are reminded here of the sublime view of the world, of the rectitude without hope that Spinoza displayed. That this is possible is the authentic justification of creation.

## HISTORY, ORIENTATION, AND MORAL JUDGMENT

Philosophical history, then, is one way in which the philanthropist, this 'friend of man' as Kant calls him, can make sense of a world that gives no direct evidence or justification for hope and consolation. It is a way of representing what is given immediately in our experience of the human world, and it is written for spectators who are also, unavoidably, actors as well, and so its composition has a practical purpose. Philosophical history introduces a guiding-thread into those events, and in that sense it is a priori. However, it must be connected to some experience, Kant says (OQ VII: 84 / 142). This experience will serve as a 'historical sign,' evidence of the progress of the human race. Thus just as we take the presence of reindeer in Lapland as pointing to a designer, so too in the course of human affairs we have to find some sign that shows an advance toward the better.

The 'historical sign' that Kant offers has to do with the French Revolution, perhaps the greatest historical event of his lifetime. Kant is frequently presented as an admirer of that revolution, despite his clear and quite unequivocal arguments against all revolutions. That presentation of Kant's views is based, in no small part, on his comments in 'The Old Question Raised Again ... ,' on his essay on enlightenment, and on his pronouncement that the present age is the 'age of criticism.' Kant's feelings are difficult, perhaps impossible, to determine, and in any event they would not be as interesting to us as his analysis. That analysis can be divided into two sorts of judgment about the revolution in France: the one, which we shall consider here, centred around a philosophical history of those events, and the other, discussed in the next chapter, taking as its standard the idea of political justice.

What is this experience, Kant asks, that acts as a historical sign, a mark of progress? – not great deeds or ancient constitutions which, however splendid, all disappear. It is rather the attitude of the spectator 'which reveals itself publicly in this game of great revolutions' (OQ VII: 85 / 143). A 'universal' and 'disinterested' (uneigennützige) 'sympathy' is displayed in this mode of thinking of the spectator. It is universal and therefore not merely subjective or particular, and it is moral because it is disinterested (OQ VII: 85 / 144). And what is that moral mode of thinking (Denkungsart)? It is a universal, disinterested sympathy. This should immediately call to mind Kant's parallel between the formal properties of moral and of aesthetic judgment – both are free, universal, and disinterested. But this parallel Kant called merely 'symbolic' (having a similar mode of judging), for aesthetic judgment, though free, was playful or liberal and not a law-bound freedom — the freedom of a child. And now we see the historical spectators, standing before a new spectacle, showing a disinterested, free, and philanthropic sympathy with events in France. There is no strictly moral judgment here, only a formal parallel with it.

These spectators have only a 'wishful participation' in what Kant calls the 'game' being played out in France. This sympathy is to be found in their 'good-naturedness,' not in their reason or moral judgment. The observers, looking from afar, have no intention of participating. And well they should not![6] A wise man, Kant says, would not want to repeat this experiment, filled as it is with misery and atrocities (OQ VII: 85 / 144). 'It is the formal execution of a monarch that fills the soul, conscious of the Ideas of human justice, with horror, and *this horror returns whenever one thinks of scenes like those in which the fate of Charles I or Louis XVI was sealed*' (MEJ VI: 321 note / 87 note; emphasis added). This last remark, taken from Kant's principal work on justice (not history), says that one is filled with horror at the remembrance of such deeds – the just memory should be contrasted with the remembrance spoken of in the *Contest of the Faculties* (OQ VII: 88 / 147). There it is a glorious memory, whereas when we are 'conscious of the Ideas of human justice,' these events fill us with disgust.

The glorious or beautiful portrayal, and the recollection that will ultimately take that portrayal as its compass, depend upon representing affairs not in their true colours – those of misery and injustice – but as 'the *evolution* of a constitution in accordance with natural law' (OQ VII: 87 / 146; emphasis added). The uninvolved spectators, the friends of man, watching this 'game' see it as the 'evolution,' the natural growth of history, in short, progress toward the better. Their standard is sympathy and hope for the future, not morality or justice – they may love justice, but to respect it is to submit to its laws, which are unconditional and have priority over sympathy. And since they are spectators, primitive philosophical historians as it were, they have the luxury of a playful interpretation of events in France.

Their disinterested sympathy and philanthropy show a certain moral character, but their fellow-feeling leads them to ignore the principles of morality and justice. For those principles, they substitute a picture of the evolution of justice – as the rain falls so that the flowers will bloom in spring, so too the revolution and its misdeeds are but a moment in the emergence of justice on the world-stage. Events in France have, to be sure, filled a part of that graveyard depicted on the Dutch innkeeper's sign. But seen from the standpoint of the philosophical historian, the philanthropic spectator, this can be interpreted as a step in the natural unfolding of a 'constitution in accordance with natural law.' The ugly is here made beautiful, and future generations will recollect it as such.[7]

The philosophical historian looks at events as part of the emergence, the unfolding, across time, of justice and peace – a toilsome road, to be sure, and one in which the suffering and injustices of earlier generations are seen as setting the foundation for future progress (UH VIII: 20 / 14). Man is here made into a means not for the purposes of others – the species has no conscious plan of its own – but for those of nature or Providence. History a priori shows us how we can at once hope to secure for ourselves the benefits of the violations of the moral injunction never to use others simply as instruments but always as ends, and yet not have to accept any culpability for it. Questions of justice and right are given less importance than the teleological problem of evolution. But there is another way of viewing a constitution: not according to the laws of progress, of natural generation, in which we are means serving a distant *telos* but judged by the standard of the '*respublica noumenon*,' an 'eternal norm' or 'Platonic Ideal' (OQ VII: 91 / 150). Both the future state – the perpetual peace of the historians – and the eternal standard of what is simply right are ideal, Kant suggests. One directs us, however, to nature and so allows us hope and sympathy for our fellows; the other introduces the standard of justice and right. The former requires a playful, even childish (because irresponsible, in the literal sense) re-creation of human affairs; the latter calls on us to exercise our faculty of moral judgment in accordance with its ideal. One is beautiful, the other is sublime.

Philosophical history and the eternal norm of a *respublica noumenon* are ideal representations of the human form, much as sculpture represents the ideal individual form. We recall, from the third *Critique*, that only man can be given an ideal form, and that only as the external expression of a moral idea. Philosophic history, the beautiful representation of human affairs, has only a surface beauty. Like the consoling portrayal of war, philosophical history takes what is ugly in itself and shows it as beautiful. It charms us, perhaps, but the shallowness of its beauty is revealed by the corruption of which it is the idealized form. The Platonic Ideal, however, has nothing to conceal, no 'repulsive irregularity,' natural or human, to right. It points to the sublimity of justice and the moral law, ideas to which no experience can object (C1 A317 / B373–4). Perhaps the beautiful representation of the world is ultimately impossible, or if not impossible, then based on falsehood, a sham beauty, a lovely portrait of human evil. We are then left with the sublime point of view, a surer 'compass' (GMM IV: 404 / 71) with which to orient ourselves.[8] Both the beautiful and sublime views of the world are answers to the questions of our place in creation and of what we are to do to fulfil that place. They are, in short, attempts to determine what 'one must be in order to be a man' – to provide that 'practical science' for which, as Kant said, we have so great a need. We have seen the shortcomings of the historical account of man's position; we must now turn to the standpoint of law or autonomy.

# 7

# Justice and the sublime

There is, we say, justice of one man; and there is, surely, justice of a whole city too?

Plato, *The Republic*

Philosophical history, as we saw in the preceding chapter, is concerned with the narration of the external affairs of humanity. It is an account of those affairs that takes man as a species whose evolution is governed by a nature or Providence which, though at first sight niggardly, nevertheless emerges at the end of this tale as a generous and beneficent tutor. According to this view of man, he is a being guided by nature against his will to the realization of that condition – a free and secure internal regime and an international peace – in which his faculties will be able to develop freely. This condition, Kant argued in the third *Critique*, is nature's ultimate purpose, and the philosophy of history is taken up with a description of how that purpose is achieved. This viewpoint, we said, is at once too high and too low. It is too high because the theoretical claims (concerning nature) that it has to make in order to provide hope and a theodicy are unsupportable and implausible. And it is too low because it portrays man as a plaything of nature, of a generous nature to be sure, but a plaything none the less, not a moral being. It sets a good heart, sympathy, and hope above moral judgment and indulges the irresponsibility of the mere observer, as is clearly shown in the philosophic historian's account of the French Revolution.

Politics, too, considered as a practical science, an a priori system of justice, and hence as one branch of morality, is concerned with men's external affairs. But rather than seeing a just political order as the result of historical evolution or as the means for achieving some further purpose of nature, politics begins with the concept of personality, moral and legal – with freedom, in other words, under self-given law, not with laws supplied by nature, as in the philosophy of history. And it proceeds from there to the ideas of duty and rights and thence to a republican constitution. Here the constitution is seen not as the goal of history, as the outcome of nature's intentions working through the agency of man's evil designs, but rather as the phenomenal reflection of the moral worth and dignity of man. As such it offers what Kant calls a 'higher point of view' – higher, certainly, than that of the worldly wise statesmen who know 'men' but not 'man,' and superior also to that historical anthropology which, though noble in origin, is yet implausible theoretically and weak from a moral perspective.

The practical science of politics is the science of the law-determined relations between free beings, of their duties and rights – in general, of their obligations to one another in their external relations (VZR XXIII: 344). Juridical relations among persons consist of their reciprocal duties and rights, and thus only those creatures capable of obliging and of being legally bound are the proper participants in a legal order. People can have no juridical relation to beings who have neither rights nor duties (non-rational beings 'who do not bind us, nor could we be bound by them' [MEJ VI: 241 / 47]) or with those – slaves, for instance – who have duties but no rights. The idea of personality, in a juridical sense, has its foundation in the concept of autonomy and moral personality to which we shall now turn.

What elevates man above the world of sense is his personality, that is, his freedom and independence from the mechanism of nature (C2 V: 86–7 / 89). Now a person is a subject whose actions are capable of imputation, someone who can be regarded as the originator of an action (MEJ VI: 223, 227 / 24, 29). A thing or an animal may indeed be the cause of something; and animals certainly do act, though they do not perform 'deeds.' We do not consider them as the authors, in any strong sense, of their actions, and hence they are not, properly speaking, susceptible of imputation. The crucial question here becomes: what is meant by authorship? Certainly a marionette, for example, is in no sense the originator of its motions. But why are the actions of an animal not its own? – no outside hand directs it, but only its appetites and instincts.

Kant is employing the idea of authorship in a rich or full sense – the freedom of a rational being under moral (self-given) laws (MEJ VI: 223 / 24). It is the autonomy of the will that is the foundation of personality, the property of the will by which it gives the law to itself. Not simply freedom, in the negative sense of independence from external forces, but, as the word 'autonomy' itself suggests, self-rule or freedom under laws legislated by oneself is what stands at the centre of Kant's conception of freedom. Autonomy, or intelligible personality, not man's empirical person, is what gives him that unique dignity that is his alone to enjoy, and it marks him as an end in himself. (GMM IV: 428–9 / 96). The demand for respect for his person, the ultimate meaning of all arguments for rights, is based, in Kant's account, on man's 'humanity' (the capacity for autonomy) residing in his person. This same fact is also the basis of obligation, the duty to treat others always as ends, never simply as a means.

Autonomy is the ground of the dignity of human nature (GMM IV: 436 / 103). It is what separates us from things, the latter having a merely relative worth, the former being an end worthy of respect. This intrinsic worth of humanity, its holiness, however persons may in fact act, leads Kant, in the second formulation of the categorical imperative, to conclude that autonomy is the 'supreme limiting condition' of the person's freedom of action: it demands of us that we act in such a way as is consistent with the autonomy of others, and thus never to treat them as playthings or mere instruments (GMM IV: 428, 430–1 / 96, 98). In the 'Conjectural Beginnings,' Kant gave a historical gloss to this move from rational nature (humanity) residing within oneself to a condition limiting man's treatment of his fellows. There Kant writes that the 'fourth and final step' in man's exit from the garden happened when he contrasted himself with those animals around him and 'came to understand, however obscurely, that he is the true end of nature' (CB VIII: 114 / 58). This idea raised him above all other creatures, and insofar as it revealed his fellow human beings as sharing in the same 'gifts of nature,' it caused him to restrain his behaviour in relation to them. The principle of autonomy, in contrast, is taken neither from history nor from experience (GMM IV: 430–1 / 98). But it does lead, not via comparison with animals or with other members of one's own species – rather, simply a priori – to the thought of an intelligible world, a kingdom of ends founded on this principle of autonomy.

A kingdom, Kant writes, is a 'systematic union' of rational beings under common laws. Positive law may vary from regime to regime, but there is one law under which all stand: to treat other humans as autonomous beings, as ends in themselves. This *mundus intelligiblis*, the Kingdom of Ends, is a law-governed community that (as is appropriate to the concept of law and the universality and necessity that that concept implies) abstracts from all empirical differences between humans and considers only the moral personality inherent in each. From this point of view, all are equal and independent because free and self-legislating. All therefore are bound equally by the law. But a union of free (in the sense of autonomy) and equal people in such a kingdom would violate the dignity required by their autonomy were it to enact law for subjects who were never themselves legislators. In other words, the self-legislation that is the key ingredient in moral life must also be carried over into this Kingdom of Ends.

This Kingdom is rational or moral nature 'writ large.' Like Plato's *Republic*, it is an image of an internal order, of justice, or, in Kant's case, of humanity, painted on a broad canvas in order 'to bring an Idea of reason nearer to intuition (in accordance with a certain analogy' (GMM IV: 436 / 103).[1] And also like Plato's *Republic*, it may be found nowhere in its perfection save within us[2] – which means, for Kant, that it is a standard, an imperative obliging us to act as if we were citizens of that Kingdom. Now as an image of the rational nature of man, the Kingdom of Ends must consist of citizens, members who obey no laws other than those they enact (GMM IV: 435 / 103). The members of this community, then, are at once subjects and sovereigns bound by the laws that they freely enact. In short, they are autonomous. Their kingdom is one of equal, free, and independent citizens whose laws mirror the moral nature of man by making him legislator and subject both.

The Kingdom of Ends reveals one side of the idea of personality. It shows that the union of such personalities or autonomous beings would (so as to be consistent with their rational nature) have to be one that treated them with the respect merited by the humanity inhering in them, that is as equal and free co-legislators. Benevolence and happiness do not figure in this account, only freedom and the respect demanded by it. Personality, then, leads to the idea of rights (rights to equality and dignity and to a part in making those laws that are to govern one) and, at the same time, to a necessary limitation of one's own freedom in order to make it harmonious with the autonomy of others. The autonomy of the moral agent, the rational nature in which all people share, however few may exercise it, thus has direct consequences for relations between people.

Those consequences can be stated in two words: 'rights' and 'duties.' Three central political concepts, right, duty, and law (obligation), all have their origin in the idea of personality: the first two in the respect demanded by autonomy, the last (taken in its narrow signification and apart from the notion of self-given law) because law requires the possibility of imputation, of culpability and innocence, and imputation of a deed makes sense only where there is a subject who is the author of his actions. To say that much of Kant's political thought is grounded in his concept of personality is not to suggest that morality and political justice are identical for him. The doctrine of right is certainly a branch of practical philosophy and the theory of justice is a part of the theory of morals, because both have to do with freedom and law. Yet there are crucial differences, and having set out the common foundations of morality and right or justice in the concept of personality, I must at least sketch those features that render the theory of justice a separate branch of the metaphysics of morals.

The laws of freedom are one and all called moral, as opposed to natural laws (MEJ VI: 214 / 13). When these laws are directed to external actions alone, they are called juridical, and compliance with them is termed legality. However, when they also demand that the law itself be the incentive for obedience, they are called ethical. All legislation (moral or legal) consists of two elements: a law commanding certain actions and an incentive that subjectively links the will with the law. The law presents an action as a duty, and this is common to both branches. What distinguishes them is the incentive they provide – the moral deed requires respect for the law as its sole incentive, whereas external legislation or justice must be indifferent to the quality of the will. The difference between incentives, respect in the one case and ultimately coercion in the other, points to the different sources of legislation as well. Respect for the law as the incentive for obedience to it can never be the object of external legislation, for it (respect) is an 'act of the mind' (MEJ VI: 239 / 45), and though external actions may be commanded, an internal state can neither be called into being nor banished at the wish of a legislator, however great his power.

Ethical legislation, therefore, can never be external (MEJ VI: 219 / 20). Nor, by the same token, can justice concern itself with the will's incentive. Strict justice, Kant says, is 'founded on the consciousness of each person's obligation under the law; but, if it is to remain pure, this consciousness may not and cannot be invoked as an incentive in order to determine the will to act in accordance with it. For this reason, strict justice relies instead on the principle of the possibility of external coercion' (MEJ VI: 232 / 36–7). Thus, for example, the law that one ought to keep one's promises imposes a duty common to both ethics and justice: the former combines this duty with no incentive other than respect, the latter transforms it into a contract the performance of which (in a juridical condition) is guaranteed by a public coercive force.

The distinction between the two branches of morality can be reformulated as follows: the different types of incentive are linked to the different sources of legislation. Respect as an incentive cannot be commanded from without, and so no strictly ethical imperative can ever emerge from an act of external legislation. An ethical imperative immediately loses its ethical quality upon being made the subject of external legislation; and justice, since it speaks to nothing other than legality – the conformity of deeds to the law – and not the quality of the will, misunderstands itself if it seeks to legislate internal states as well. Thus while the Kingdom of Ends mirrors central characteristics of both justice in the soul, or morality, and political justice, it more closely parallels the former – and this can be seen in the absence of any mention of public coercion as an incentive in Kant's discussion of it.

The 'systematic union' of rational beings as presented in the Idea of the Kingdom of Ends is unattainable, then, not because of any necessary evil in human nature (though Kant was far from denying that there is such evil) but rather because of what external justice is. And ultimately its attainability is not a question, since its purpose is to serve as a maxim by which we are to govern our behaviour (GMM IV: 438–9 / 106), moral and political. Its laws are obeyed out of duty, and no other incentive is allowed in this Kingdom. The Kingdom of Ends is an intelligible world, all the features of which are contained in the idea of a morally legislative reason. The just regime exists in the phenomenal world, and it reproduces there the equality, freedom, respect, and the nature of law given expression in the Kingdom of Ends. But it reproduces them in a form compatible with external justice between individuals: the juridical condition is the aggregate of those circumstances 'under which the will of one person can be conjoined with the will of another in accordance with a universal law of freedom' (MEJ VI: 230 / 34). Justice, then, governs the external and practical (having to do with the exercise of freedom) relations of humans to one another, so as to allow the freedom of each to coexist with that of all. Properly understood, justice has nothing whatsoever to do with the content of these particular wills, their desires, needs, or incentives, but only with the law-determined relations between wills under the universal law of the greatest possible freedom of the will.

## STATE OF NATURE AND SOCIAL CONTRACT

This juridical condition is not natural to man; rather, it has to be created or established (PP VIII: 348–9 / 92). It does not follow, however, from the fact that this condition (freedom under coercive laws) is created that its principles are equally the work of artifice or caprice. Laws must be established, but their foundation is given a priori and is eternal. Those principles are contained in the concept of personality (or 'innate rights' as Kant calls them in the *Metaphysical Elements of Justice*), which is given its political expression in the theory of an original contract. The Kingdom of Ends, which is centred around the idea of personality and autonomy, points to all the crucial elements of political justice, including the original contract – but, by preserving the distinction between duty and external coercion as incentives, it shows the difference between ethics and justice. In short, the metaphor of this Kingdom is particularly useful, because it both illuminates the basis of justice in the concept of a person and marks out the juridical relations between persons as a special case of morality in general.

Kant's state of nature is not meant to provide a sort of anthropology or psychology upon which a political theory can be erected. Rousseau performed this thought-experiment in order to know the 'nature of man' and to proceed from there to the 'true definition of natural right.'[3] Hobbes began, like Rousseau, with the Delphic maxim to 'read thyself' – which for Hobbes meant especially to see the 'similitude of passions.'[4] Kant uses the idea of a state of nature solely to distinguish between a juridical and a non-juridical condition. Or, to be more exact, the question of man's nature, at least insofar as it bears on the problem of an a priori science of right, is already settled in the concept of a person.

No historical or pseudo-historical experiment in which man is stripped of his present attributes is required here. It is the idea of law (particularly external law) and the relation of external law to innate rights that occupy Kant, not a psychology or a description of the generation of political order from that original condition. Thus when Kant first mentions the state of nature, he has already concluded his answer to the Delphic imperative, and what he then wants to do is to introduce the distinction between private and public law, between the different duties of justice (MEJ VI: 242 / 48). By contrast, Rousseau's *Second Discourse* begins with the words, 'It is of man that I am to speak ... '[5]

In the philosophy of history, in contrast, the natural condition is indeed employed in the more common manner. Man's 'unsocial sociability' is cited as the cause that, despite his intentions, forces him to enter civil society. But there, as we noted in the preceding chapter, the question is not of morality or right, but rather of evolution. This type of explanation requires an anthropology to provide it with a 'motor force,' as it were, a mechanism by which to explain the organic growth of human society that will, in turn, yield hope and a theodicy. At the heart of this historical account of men's affairs is men's predicament and the solution to which nature points the way. The idea that politics can best be understood as an answer to a predicament is a major theme in state-of-nature and contractarian writings, but it is not to be found in Kant's political thought. Viewed from the perspective of the 'practical science' of morality, of the set of rights that must be the supreme limiting condition of all political life, the state of nature loses its historical sense as well as its anthropological purpose. There may well be historical explanations for why we seek the safety of society, but these do not provide an adequate guide for how we ought to behave, any more than they reveal human nature. They do not touch that central characteristic of political society – its law-governed quality – except in a contingent, empirical manner. If there is a sense in which law is a necessary feature of human society, it is not to be found here. Whether man is innocent or evil, compassionate or murderous in a non-political condition is not the problem that Kant has in mind when he speaks of a state of nature (MEJ VI: 312 / 76; PP VIII: 381 / 129).

The point of Kant's theory of the state of nature can best be seen in the distinction between intelligible and sensible possession. Intelligible possession may be defined as possession without detention, whereas empirical possession is the actual, physical securing of an object (MEJ VI: 245–6 / 51–2). Now physical possession or detention contains a right, and in removing the apple that I hold in my hand someone does me a wrong, regardless of whether or not a juridical state exists. My 'internal freedom,' my right with respect to myself, is violated when the apple is taken without my consent (MEJ VI: 249–50 / 57). A part of me is taken, so to speak, and thus Kant concludes that all propositions about empirical possession are analytic – which means that they can be derived directly from the right of a person to himself.

But to say that a thing is mine is a different matter altogether. Here what ties an object to me is not a physical connection, holding the apple for example, but a noumenal or intelligible bond by which, even if the object is separate from me, I can nevertheless be injured by an unauthorized use of it. 'If there is to be anything externally yours or mine, we must assume that intelligible possession (*possessio noumenon*) is possible' (MEJ VI: 249 / 56). What this possibility amounts to is that a pure *de jure* connection of the will with the object exists, independent of actual retention. And that in turn is founded on the 'juridical postulate': 'to act toward others so that external objects ... can also become someone's' (MEJ VI: 252 / 60). The act of claiming something as mine (property in the full sense) places an obligation on others to respect a non-physical connection between myself and an object, and at the same time I acknowledge a similar duty by which I am bound to all others. It is a universal and reciprocal obligation, a systematic union of rational beings according to external, juridical principles. It is a civil society (MEJ VI: 255–6 / 64–5).

*De jure* possession Kant entitles a synthetic proposition a priori – synthetic because it begins from the concept of a person, his freedom, and the obligation that that personality imposes on others, and extends this concept by adding to it a claim to objects in the public realm – to things not directly part of one's own person. The difference between the state of nature and a juridical condition is that while property is certainly possible in the non-political situation, it is merely provisional there (MEJ VI: 264 / not translated). It is provisional because that public realm is in fact an empty space, a 'no man's land' from the point of view of justice, until it is bound down by rules or law – that is, until it is recognized as public and not simply empty. Where there is no systematic union of reciprocal obligations, expressed in a universal will (law), these rights are provisional. The right of intelligible possession thus antedates civil society, but it is a right the exercise of which is precarious as long as it is not embedded in a system of mutually recognized (public) obligations. And the term 'precarious' here does not refer to a psychological fact, to a desire for felicity at whatever cost to one's neighbour, for instance, but rather to the distinction between a mere 'empty space' between persons, and that same 'space' made public and juridical by law. Whether the non-political condition is violent or not is beside the point: it is a situation in which 'justice is absent' (MEJ VI: 312 / 76).

The command to quit that condition is an extension of the idea of an intelligible personality in oneself, here in the guise of provisional *de jure* possession, so that it now includes other persons, coupled with the only incentive adequate to an imperative that is to govern external deeds (the public realm), namely, universally recognized (lawful) coercive force. We recall that in the Kingdom of Ends man is led from the consciousness of his own autonomy, of humanity residing in his person, to the thought of a community in which all people, as moral beings, participate in a public order founded on the mutual recognition of autonomy (respect). Similarly here: the obligating power of all rights, Kant says, is to be found not in what is peculiar to the person but in the right of mankind, or humanity, that inheres in him (RZR XIX: 538, No. 7862). All people have the obligation to extend the respect that they demand for themselves as free, autonomous beings to other individuals. Political justice (right and duty in the creation of a public sphere) gives a phenomenal form to the principle already contained in the concept of a person: it gives voice to man's freedom according to law, to the respect he demands for himself and owes to others, and to his essential equality – it is empirical man governed by '*homo noumenon*' (MEJ VI: 335 / 105 and PP VIII: 374 / 121).

It is not experience that tells us that public lawful coercion is necessary, then, and the latter's origins must not be sought in history, which can, at best, provide only a contingent and not a necessary ground for law. Rather, the idea of right draws us to the distinction between a juridical and a non-juridical condition and commands the former together with the public legal justice that is its pre-condition. Now a state is a multitude of people under such laws. These laws vary, as we noted before, but the principles that are their foundation exist in pure reason alone, in the idea of a state – the norm for every actual union (MEJ VI: 230, 313 / 34, 77). This idea of the state is itself grounded in the theory of an original contract, which takes its bearings, again, not from psychology or history but from the concept of personality. Its key ingredients are derived not from an imagined bargaining situation in which calculative actors consider their future utility (in a context in which they are blind as to what particular advantages they may have) but from a conception of the moral person. Just as intelligible, *de jure* possession emerges synthetically from man's right in himself (freedom) by the addition of a type of property (together with the conditions that would permit it to exist) not possessed immediately but reciprocally recognized in public law, so here moral personality is extended synthetically to civil personality. That extension demands a government, which will transform an empty into a public space, the person into a public person – and it is that mixture (synthetic) of the rights of a person and universal coercive force that stands at the centre of the original contract.

## RIGHTS AND OBLIGATIONS

There is only one innate right, Kant says, and that is the freedom that belongs 'to every human being by virtue of his humanity' (MEJ VI: 237 / 43–4) or personality. And contained within this common property of freedom are the further rights of equality and independence. The fundamental fact of freedom, of moral personality, together with its derivative rights is the basis for civil personality, and indeed the idea of a constitution in harmony with that personality is the source of all just political forms (OQ VII: 90–1 / 150). Now the act by which a state is established or, to speak more exactly, the 'Idea' of that act is what alone allows us to conceive of the legitimacy of the political form in general (MEJ VĪ: 315 / 80). There are two parts to this notion of legitimacy: one is the essential fact of freedom and the personality of the contracting agents, and the other is the concept of external law, the use of coercive laws to regulate the behaviour of people toward one another.

The problem here is somewhat similar to Rousseau's: how can freedom and government be combined? How can man find himself enmeshed in a public order and yet remain free? The dilemma may be somewhat less trying for Kant than for Rousseau, however, because for Kant there is no (practically) interesting sense in which freedom can be distinguished from law-governed action. To be sure, Kant did speak of a 'negative' freedom – but then only briefly, for there is little to be said about it except that it is at least thinkable from a critical standpoint. The practically important question is not whether we can act but how we should act (RSV VIII: 13 and C1 A803–4 / 831–2), and that implies the submission of the will to law. Freedom attains its dignity and commands respect for its sole possessor (man) not by its mere independence from nature but by its capacity for autonomy, for self-given law. Law is not the antithesis of freedom but precisely its foundation. Thus, in Kant's political thought there is no parallel to Rousseau's remark that 'man's constitution' is 'mutilated' in entering civil society.[6] Personality, what is truly and uniquely human, is not simple independence but the ability to give law to ourselves, and the political order can reflect that faculty – not perfectly, perhaps, but certainly not in a mutilated fashion either.

The idea of external law is derived completely from the concept of freedom in the relation of individuals, and that in its turn from the idea of personality. The middle term between external law and freedom (a middle term is required here because external, unlike moral, law is not immediate self-legislation by the subject) is the original contract. It is the idea of this contract that unites the innate rights common to all (freedom, equality, and independence) with a public or civil freedom, freedom brought under external law so as to have the liberty of each coexist with that of all others. The original contract is one way of expressing the thought of a network (public realm) consisting of reciprocal obligations. The essence of political law, to which it provides the standard, is thus obligation, the mutual recognition of the bounds of freedom or, what amounts to much the same thing, reciprocal right (RZR XIX: 548 No. 7897).

Three points, which are at the heart of Kant's theory of the original contract, need to be discussed here: the elements of civil personality, the nature and purpose of law, and the activity of legislating itself. They are, as we shall see, directly tied to the idea of freedom and autonomy extended to a public union of autonomous beings. Let us begin with the elements of civil personality, which can be enumerated as follows: freedom, equality, and independence. All are familiar to us from the analysis of personality presented in the *Groundwork* – freedom as moral freedom; equality in virtue of moral freedom, the capacity for which is the principal defining characteristic of humanity; and independence, because that is the minimal condition for the exercise of freedom (GMM IV: 434, 435–6 / 101, 103). Civil or external freedom can be further subdivided: the freedom of man qua man living in political society and the freedom of the citizen.

The freedom of the human being is the right he has, limited only by the need to make his freedom consistent with that of others, to choose his own sources of happiness and well-being (TP VIII: 290 / 58). Because law is a reciprocal obligation, presided over by a universal will, to respect the external freedom of others and oneself, its function can only be strictly to regulate that freedom. It may not, therefore, pretend to preside over the happiness, thoughts, or moral judgments of the persons who are subject to it. This conception of freedom corresponds to mere independence (transferred now into a public setting, and hence bounded by the reciprocal nature of that public sphere), to freedom in the negative sense.

The freedom of the citizen, in contrast, mirrors the autonomy of the moral agent, the positive freedom that consists in submission to self-given law. Here the juridical freedom of the citizen is understood to refer to the right to obey only those laws to which consent could have been given (MEJ VI: 314 / 78). The consent that is given or could rationally be expected to have been given to this public order is the political (external) equivalent of moral (self, internal) legislation. We shall later return to the issue of consent, but for the moment it need be said only that the freedom of the citizen consists in being a co-legislator, a participant in the making of those laws that bind him – the empirical form of the self-legislation of the Kingdom of Ends.

Citizens are free in the double sense defined above. This fundamental fact – freedom – means that they are not naturally divided into superior and inferior: all are equal, and not simply trivially equal, in virtue of their shared capacity for freedom. And it follows that the basic obligations they have to one another, as well as the right to bind their fellows to those obligations, are also equal. Nobody stands above obligation, and, by the same token, nobody has obligations alone and no rights against others. Their equality as free beings and as civil personalities leads to the full reciprocity of their obligations and to the rejection of any kind of hereditary authority (TP VIII: 292–3 / 60–1). They share, consequently, an equality as subjects – equality under the law. Once again, as in the Kingdom of Ends, duty applies 'to every member and to all members in equal measure.'

And lastly, civil independence is the condition under which the citizen owes his livelihood to his own powers and not to the 'arbitrary will of another person' (MEJ VI: 314 / 79). Independence is a necessary qualification for an entitlement to participate actively as a co-legislator, both in the Kingdom of Ends and in political society. In the Kingdom of Ends, independence is meant in the sense of freedom both from the mechanism of nature and, more important, from one's own desires and interests. To be a legislator in that Kingdom, then, one must be radically free of the particularity and finitude that make us mortals, not gods. Civil independence, however, as a prerequisite for enacting law excludes from that activity those who are 'naturally' dependent (women and children) (TP VIII: 295 / 63) and those who, by their occupation, are servants or, in any event, directly dependent upon another person for their subsistence. These cannot be counted upon to be autonomous political legislators, and so they enjoy only the rights of passive citizenship: equality before the law and the right to just law, namely, law consistent with respect for their persons, and law to which they could have consented (MEJ VI: 315 / 79–80 and RZR XIX: 568, No. 7974), these last two conditions being at bottom one and the same.

The one form of independence, then, is to be achieved only by the overcoming of the base nature within oneself; the other form is an independence in the public realm, the independence from the control of other people. Both forms set conditions as to who may legislate in their respective realms, and it may just be that the servitude that must be abolished in order to take one's seat among the legislators of the moral kingdom is far less easily vanquished than that which, by making one person the servant of a fellow, deprives that person of the right to active citizenship. Thus, Kant concludes, all men are equal under the law (passively and as worthy of respect) but not in the right to enact it (TP VIII: 294 / 62). It is worth remarking, in advance of our more detailed discussion of it, that Kant's theory of consent is such as to make actual participation in law-making a rather secondary concern.

We do not intend to speak of virtue here, Kant writes in the *Rechtslehre*, but only to 'give an account of what is just' (MEJ VI: 231 / 35). Justice, for reasons previously mentioned, is not identical with virtue, nor could it be, since it consists of external laws that neither can nor should speak to the quality of the will. Law is essentially coercion. It is the voice of right, and right as between individuals, if it is to be more than provisional, must be reciprocal in the obligations that it imposes. Thus right implies the limiting of the freedom of each to the condition of its being consistent with the freedom of all. Law limits freedom, in both moral and political life. But in the latter, there is an external, public dimension to this limitation. Boundaries are set for the relations between individuals. Obligations and rights that have an undoubted existence a priori are now also given a concrete existence by transforming the empty, non-juridical 'space' between persons into a public, law-governed one.

Right, as an idea or standard by which we determine our conduct, has what Aristotle called a 'logical priority' over all political forms – it is the latter's supreme limiting principle. By a 'synthetic' step, namely, the establishment of a public order, the idea of right, its universally compelling (a priori) set of obligations and freedoms are taken up and given a concrete shape. To have a right in this created public domain is to have it universally recognized and made necessary by the political equivalent of a categorical imperative, namely, public coercive force. Coercion is a part of all right, the just use of force to secure one's freedom: the political order takes this elementary right and weaves it into a public lawful order – its a priori universality and necessity are thereby transformed into the closest possible (empirical) approximation to the moral law. Hobbes's Leviathan was an artificial, a created man and mortal god that reflected in its principles what its maker had discovered as he carried out the oracle's dictum to 'know thyself.' Kant's public, lawful order is also artificial, and it too mirrors what we find in ourselves – only not what we find in our history or in our desires, but what we discover in our rational nature.

Now since this coercion must be universal, if it is to be law at all and not mere force or violence, it cannot, Kant says, be the work of a 'unilateral will.' To be subject to a unilateral will, whether in a non-political condition or in society, is to find oneself in a literally lawless situation. It makes no difference how benevolent that private will may be, its operations do not attain the status of law until they overcome their particularity and achieve the universality that is the central feature of all law. It is universal because it is tied to no sort of particularity; no individual interest or desire shapes it. It is rather the expression of a fully reciprocal relation between the freedoms of each.

We are now in a better position to understand Kant's argument that right or justice means the authorization to use coercion (MEJ VI: 232 / 36–7). 'Authorization' clearly has two senses here. One is the bare sense of an entitlement, even in the non-political condition, to use force so as to secure one's person and freedom (MEJ VI: 312 / 76–7). The other, and related, sense is political: the authority 'given' to the public sphere, in whatever form that sphere is embodied or represented, to use the coercive force needed to win universal recognition for rights. The creation of a public sphere, where that realm has as its leading principle the freedom, equality, and independence of its occupants bound to those principles by a universal coercive force, is the idea at the core of the original contract. We see in this brief account the meaning of civil personality, the nature and purpose of law, and the critical elements of legislation (universality and authorization).

Viewed as a class of animals, namely, seen from the standpoint of philosophical history, men's external relations to each other originate in war, need, and violence. Society here begins with a 'master,' and perhaps with something like Rousseau's 'mutilation' of man (PP VIII: 371 / 118 and UH VIII: 23 / 17–18). Kant was far too clear-eyed to deny that the political order has its empirical or historical beginnings in need and force. And interpreted in one way, these very origins become the source of consolation, of a perpetual peace created out of fear. But those who depict society in this manner, even if they see standing over its birth not a Machiavellian prince but Rousseau's benevolent legislator, reduce man's worth in his own eyes. They reduce man's worth not by the nastiness they may attribute to him but by turning his attention to need and to his lower nature rather than to law and freedom: 'They deserve no hearing, particularly as *such a pernicious theory* [of the 'natural mechanism of a mass of men forming a society ...'] *may occasion the evil which it prophesies,* throwing human beings into one class with all other living machines, differing from them only in their consciousness that they are not free' (PP VIII: 378 / 126).

Kant adds that the principle, 'Let justice reign ... cuts asunder the whole tissue of artifice or force' (PP VIII: 378–9 / 126). This reminds us of his playful remarks in the *Contest of the Faculties,* where prophets produce through their own teachings the very results that they have foreseen. (OQ VII: 79–80 / 137–8). And there, we recall, Kant suggested a better vantage point than that of the empiricist or the worldly-wise. Here, too, Kant offers a different, Copernican, view of the origins of society: as a 'teacher of law,' he will 'set aside everything empirical in the concept of civil or international law (such as the wickedness in human nature which necessitates coercion)' and present in its place a 'transcendental formula' of public law. (PP VIII: 381 / 129).

From the perspective of a true political science, the science of right, an account of the 'origins' of the external relations among people is set forth that is neither derived from a set of empirical facts, nor confirmable or refutable by them (RZR XIX: 504, No. 7738). It is not necessary to prove its historical accuracy, nor is its conformity to the facts of psychology an issue: it depends on a theory of rights alone (TP VIII: 302 / 70). Plainly, Kant's discussion of the original contract cannot have as its purpose either historical or psychological description, both of which might be said to belong to empirical anthropology. And it is not meant to be a source of consolation, of optimism, or, for that matter, of pessimism – it is neither philanthropic nor misanthropic. Rather, the idea of an original or social contract is a measure, a compass that contains the ideal of legislation, of ruling and public justice (RZR XIX: 503, No. 7734). The social contract, in short, has to do not with the founding or building of the state (*Errichtungsgrund*) but only with its order, its law-governed character (*Verwaltungsgrund*) (RZR XIX: 503, No. 7734); 564, No. 7956). It is the sum of the rules of conduct, the guiding principle (*Richtschnur*) for law and justice.

As a guiding principle the social contract serves to orient citizens and legislators alike. To the former it says that the ruling power is holy and inviolable and that inquiry into its actual origins is both pointless and dangerous. Such inquiries are dangerous because they suggest that law and legitimacy have their foundation in historical, contingent fact; and they are pointless since even if these origins should prove, on close inspection, to be violent rather than consensual, the person who takes this as an invitation to rebellion is nevertheless outside the law, a criminal. Kant argues that the maxim that all ruling power comes from God is useful not as a result of its historical accuracy or its source in revelation, but rather because it expresses the 'practical principle' that the origin of legislative authority is not a question when obedience is at issue (MEJ VI: 319 / 84–5). And to legislators the idea of a contract gives a rule according to which every lawmaker ought to act in framing laws – this rule is the principle of right, of civil personality, freedom, equality, and authorization before which all politics must bow if it is to be rightful (TP VIII: 297 / 65). The detail of this argument we shall discuss when we come to consider the theory of a republican constitution.

## DIGRESSION: KANT AND HOBBES

But we should now step back briefly and review the essential features of Kant's politics. Like his moral philosophy, Kant's writings on politics are open to the charge of formalism.[7] In the former case, Kant answered that having discovered a principle, even a formal one, that would at last set morality on a solid foundation was perhaps no small achievement. Kant's central purpose in the moral works was not an exhaustive description of moral behaviour – that, he thought, would require a practical anthropology (GMM IV: 388 / 56), something along the lines of Aristotle's *Nicomachean Ethics* – but to display those conditions without which no act could properly be called moral. His political philosophy sets out to provide a similar collection of fundamental principles: those of the *Rechtsstaat*, the lawful, juridical condition. The crucial elements of a public life bound by right are contained in that theory, and specific political consequences can be deduced from them. Yet these essays are not works destined for pragmatic statesmen in search of advice about the machinery of government. They contain a practical science which, as in the case of Kant's moral philosophy, means that they have a two-fold task: to provide a principle, a rational foundation, or account, for justice (to the extent that that is possible), and, in so doing, to be practical – that is, to offer a compass or guide to rulers and citizens by which they may know better what it is to be just (GMM IV: 404–5 / 72–3).

The foundation of political justice, we noted, is the idea of personality. Personality is the freedom of man as a rational being, and it distinguishes him as the sole bearer of rights and duties. From the equality, freedom, and independence at the heart of personality, Kant, in both the *Groundwork* and the *Metaphysic of Morals*, Part I, moves to rights and duties toward others, both in the Kingdom of Ends and in the *respublica phaenomenon*. The principal innate right is freedom; other rights are only derived from it. Now freedom in the external relations between people, reciprocal freedom where the liberty of each is restricted to the extent needed to render it consistent with the freedom of all, requires the creation of a mesh, a public space, in which those relations do in fact become fully reciprocal. The law gives concrete universality to the idea of reciprocity implied in the concept of a person (his freedom and equality) by establishing this public order. Right limits, and public law is the agency of that limitation, its imperative. If men were perfectly holy, Kant wrote in the *Groundwork*, they would have no need of a moral imperative, for they would will the good immediately, without a command – and similarly in politics. And to repeat, Kant's distinction between holy beings and humans is not a psychological observation implying varying degrees of virtue and evil, but a remark on the fundamental finitude of the human will, and the character that its operations acquire from that finitude (c2 v: 32 / 32–3).

The relation between right and law tells us that coercion, the power to limit, is only justly used to guarantee right – the essential political right of reciprocal freedom. Since coercion is an inseparable part of political law, it follows that law has no other purpose than to give expression to this idea of consistent freedom between people. When it sets itself ends other than that, it loses sight of its nature, of its origin in the idea of right and personality. Governments and sovereigns have one standard that they are to consult in their activity: not the happiness of their subjects, or the quality of the wills of the citizenry, or their material equality, but only their freedom (private and public – as possible co-legislators), their equality as civil persons, and the respect due to that personality.

This argument appears on the surface to be a version of Hobbes's assertion that government has no other end than the preservation and contentment of citizens[8] in their several private trades and callings. And in an age where it is doubted whether liberalism has any foundation other than ambition or avarice or any purpose more noble than that of a night watchman, Kant's political philosophy would seem to fall victim to similar attacks. Indeed, Kant himself almost appears to encourage critiques of that sort – for instance, in his well-known statement about a 'race of devils', that is, the notion that the political problem depends for its solution not on the moral improvement of mankind but only on knowing 'the mechanism of nature in order to use it on men' (PP VIII: 366 / 112). This infamous passage is to be found in that section of *Perpetual Peace* concerned with nature's 'guarantee,' namely, with the philosophical historian's perspective. We have seen that from that standpoint, man is a species of animal, and just as the taming of animals requires some knowledge of the mechanism of nature at work in them, so too is that same knowledge indispensable if men are viewed as animals, even freely acting ones. Seen from the higher standpoint of personality, however, government without a foundation in the pure doctrine of right is a 'mere mechanical concoction' (*ein blos mechanisches Machwerk*) (OP XXI: 178 note), with no objective basis in law but only a subjective origin in the arbitrary (not universal) will of the holder of power.

The difference between Kant and, for example, Hobbes can be schematized in the following manner. Hobbes's state of nature portrays man as free, equal, and independent: but his freedom is lawless, the mere absence of external impediment, where 'he finds no stop, in doing what he has the will, desire, or inclination to do.'[9] His equality is that of physical strength, of common experience, and of passions.[10] And his independence is that of war, of the want of an authority to protect him against his neighbours. When there is added to this the 'synthetic' step by which man finds himself necessarily in the company of others, man's nature becomes, in Oakeshott's felicitous phrase, 'the predicament of mankind'.[11] The conception of the person and his worth that emerges from this account is that he has a 'price' that is never absolute – 'it is no more than it is esteemed by others.'[12] It is difficult to imagine that Kant did not have Hobbes in mind when he distinguished between price and dignity and said that the personality of man entitles him to the latter (GMM IV: 434–5 / 102). Between Hobbes's commercial conception of worth and Kant's moral idea of dignity there is a considerable distance, and this is reflected in the fact that the horizon of Kant's political philosophy is defined by public right or justice as the phenomenal analogue to moral self-legislation, while Hobbes's politics never loses sight of the predicament that gave birth to it.[13]

The crucial point here, which the comparison between Kant and

Hobbes illustrates, is that Kant's liberalism rests on an understanding of moral personality, especially the freedom that is taken to be what gives personality its worth. The respect that is owed to such a being is central to the law-governed state and to the idea of an original contract that underlies it. It has not only a foundation other than mere avarice, but also a conception of the best life hardly distinguishable from the foundation itself. To say that liberalism is empty because it fails to educate citizens as to how they ought to live is not accurate, at least as it applies to Kant's variety of liberal thought. The *respublica phaenomenon* is the external construction of the noumenal republic, of the Kingdom of Ends. It teaches us the exercise of our liberty, and that freedom and law are not merely consistent with each other but virtually identical. And that, Kant thought, was no small lesson to learn, either politically or in one's own life. As Socrates says to Glaucon at the end of Book IX of the *Republic*, we can build that city within us. Politics governed by right can never, for reasons already mentioned, command the only truly moral incentive – simple respect for the law – as its incentive; but in its principle of a law-bound freedom, of equality and universality, it can educate us as to how we ought to live. Granted, this education is not its purpose, but insofar as it demands a self-legislating, lawful freedom its existence is its pedagogy – it brings before our eyes the sense of human freedom writ large.

CONSTITUTIONS AND CONSENT

To return to our analysis, then, there are three issues that need to be looked at: the relation between the original contract and the various constitutional forms, the right to revolution, and international relations, particularly as they concern the problem of war and peace. The first two, namely, the questions about the types of regime and about revolution, deal respectively with the duties of sovereigns and of subjects; and the third concerns the relation between states considered as moral persons. This list contains the three principal forms of public juridical relations between persons. Now we have said that the idea of an original contract in harmony with man's rational nature (personality) is the basis of the justice of all political forms and is the 'touchstone' of legitimacy. This Kant terms the 'spirit' of the original contract, and the specific types of state are only the 'letter' of that contract (MEJ VI: 340 / 112). In 'Perpetual Peace,' Kant again makes this crucial distinction between the forms of government and the forms of sovereignty (or state). The latter concerns the 'substance' of the state, the number of persons who are endowed with the power of government – one, few, or the many. Accordingly, there are three forms of sovereignty: monarchy, aristocracy, and democracy. The forms of government are of only two kinds – either republican or despotic.

The difference between the two forms is not to be found in the number of those who hold power but in the mode of administration of power – and that may be either in accord with the idea of an original contract or the merely capricious exercise of power by a private (unilateral) will, in which case it is not legitimate but despotic (PP VIII: 352 / 96). A democracy may, for example, be despotic if, as was the case in Athens, it makes and changes laws and punishes citizens according to the shifting fancies of the majority. Which of these two standards Kant thought more important should be plain: the centrepiece of the law-governed state is universal reciprocal law, which preserves the freedom of all. The particular claims made by the many or the few as to their entitlement to rule are not significant when the foundation and purpose of the state are taken into account. And those, as we have said, are not benevolence, or happiness, but the well-being of the state itself, which means its conformity to the principles of justice (MEJ VI: 318 / 83–4) embodied in the idea of an original contract. A regime that does not, or does not seek to, meet those principles thereby renders itself unjust in a very literal way, a state with no foundation in the fundamental elements of law. However tolerable it may be, and Kant thought that statesmen were often quite ready to act benevolently even while they violated basic rights (PP VIII: 385–6 / 134), it is less than just if it cannot be seen as the product of a social contract. The heart of the distinction can be formulated in this manner: if legislation is attached (not in its actual exercise but in its form) to a specific person or persons, whatever their number may be, it does not have the status of law, while if it is universal (which does not signify unanimous but rather that in its enactment it was subjected to the test of universalization and thus did not have its form determined by any particular will) then it can properly be called law.

A republican constitution is the only one in which 'the law is autonomous (*selbstherrschend*) and is not annexed to any particular person. It is the ultimate end of all public law and the only condition under which each person receives his due peremptorily' (MEJ VI: 341 / 112–13). The idea of the 'autonomy' of the law, is self-rule, brings to mind Kant's moral theory. Autonomy or self-governance means in

both instances to have the universal principle as the source of legislation over the will (of the person or of the regime), or more exactly
to have the universal as the form of the maxim or law. If the form of
the dictum is not universal, then it cannot be law and must therefore
subject the will to the commands of what is particular: in the case of
politics, a particular person or persons, and in that of morality, a particular subjective inclination or desire that renders the will's maxims
merely conditional or hypothetical. In short, what is particular is by
definition not universalizable and therefore also not law-like. For that
reason, as well as from the fact that it alone (in conformity with the
idea of an original contract) recognizes civil personality as the basis of
political life, Kant says that the republican constitution is the sole
legitimate child of the concept of law and that it is the duty of every
state to approach that ideal (PP VIII: 349–50 / 93–4).

From this, two further points follow. First, every true republic is
representative (MEJ VI: 341 / 113). Whether this is taken to mean representation in an institutional sense – a procedure for electing deputies,
for example – or in a broader sense will be discussed shortly. The latter
possibility is justified by Kant's statement that all three forms of sovereignty can be republican and hence representative (VZEF XXIII: 159).
The truly republican regime is representative for one very clear reason:
a non-representative regime, whether the one, the few, or the many
shape the law according to their particular need, has no distinction
between the legislative will (and through this the form of the law) and
the will or wills of particular persons. Only a representative legislative
will separates law-making from the wills of private persons, of whatever number. Of course, representation is also a characteristic of a just
or republican regime because it unites legislation with the idea of
universal consent implied by the original contract; but more of this
when we discuss Kant's concepts of consent and publicity.

The second and related point is that the universality of the law leads
not only to representation but also to the separation of powers into
legislative, executive, and judicial branches. That the principal purpose
of such an arrangement is to secure the universality that is central to
law can be seen in Kant's comparison of the division of powers with
the three terms of a syllogism: the major and minor premises and the
conclusion (MEJ VI: 313 / 78). The conclusion of a syllogism has its
authority because it shares in the universal premise. To collapse that
universal or first premise into the particulars that ought to be subsumed
under it is therefore to void the conclusion, to deprive it of its character
as an instance of the universal. Similarly, the universality of legislation

must be preserved by keeping it sharply distinct from those instruments of government by which it is 'mixed' with particulars and made into the day-to-day administration of justice. If it loses its universal character, either by failing to be representative or by involving itself in particular matters, the acts of the legislative will lose their authority by being deprived of the universality that alone gives to those acts their juridical status.

This is the meaning of Kant's rather enigmatic assertion that every sort of government that is not representative and that thus has no separation of powers is *without form* (PP VIII: 352 / 96). It still has 'substance,' persons ruling and an order, perhaps, but just as a syllogism without its unifying universal principle dissolves into a collection of particulars, void of structure, so too without the universality of law (as the form of the law and of the legislative will making it) political society is reduced to an aggregate of private wills, whose order can be itself only a private, contingent act of the will. The move from 'Socrates is a man' to 'Socrates is mortal' (the minor and concluding elements of the syllogism) loses its necessary and lawful quality if the universal premise 'all men are mortal' is absent. Thus it is with political law as well.

I now wish to proceed to another issue directly related to that of representation, namely consent. We recall Kant writing that law that accords with an original contract is the act of a public will. The idea of a general will is thus at the heart of Kant's conception of political justice (PP VIII: 383 / 131). This Kant develops into two notions of consent (and here our account blends in with the remarks on representation made above): one, a direct institutional expression of the public will, and the other, which takes consent less literally and transforms it into the idea of publicity as the measure of all law. The first is quite straightforward: consent and representation there mean the right to vote (for all independent and not merely 'passive' citizens) for deputies who are to protect the citizens' rights (MEJ VI: 341 / 113). The argument that Kant intended representation and consent to be understood in this literal manner is given further confirmation in his comments on the relation between representative institutions and the possibility of peace among nations; the latter goal, he argues, is advanced by direct consent, since the citizens, having to bear the financial and physical costs, will less readily give their nations over to war than will monarchs, who suffer nothing personally.

But Kant uses consent in another fashion, which suggests that actual consent, the real exercise of the will of the citizens in the process of legislation, was of less importance to him than the universality of public law and, related to that, respect for civil personality. This is consent defined as the 'form of publicity': 'Every legal claim must be capable of publicity' (PP VIII: 381 / 129). Publicity provides the 'form of universal lawfulness.' In its 'negative' form it says that any principle that would fail to achieve its end were it to be publicized is unjust and incapable of becoming public law. The 'positive' formulation of this same idea is that a principle that requires publicity in order to achieve its purpose is more than simply not unjust but rather is just in the full sense (PP VIII: 384–5 / 133).

Kant offers a number of examples of the application of this publicity test: in constitutional law (revolution) and in international law (the keeping of treaties and acquisition). In each instance, the illustration is designed to show that candour would defeat the intended purpose – for example, if a great power announced its desire to conquer its smaller neighbours, it would soon cause them to unite or to seek outside support. Kant's illustrations here are no more compelling than those he provided for the principle of universalization in the *Groundwork*. There is, however, a substantial and revealing parallel between the two arguments: the universalization formula (*Groundwork*), the 'typic' of pure practical reason (in the second *Critique*), and the 'transcendental principle' of publicity are meant to secure the universality of the law, moral or political – to guarantee that it will have the necessity and universality that constitute the form of the law (PP VIII: 381 / 129). 'For laws as such are all equivalent regardless of whence they derive their determining grounds' (c2 v: 70 / 73) – they are equivalent in their formal properties, especially that of universality.

Now the principle of publicity, applied to law, ensures its formal universality. In other words, the question is: could the citizens have agreed to such a law, is it capable of publicity (MEJ VI: 329 / 97)? What 'could consent to' means Kant does not say in so many words, yet its import is obvious – citizens are, first and foremost, civil and moral persons whose personality demands that their autonomy (freedom, equality, and independence) be respected. They could not be expected to consent to acts that violate their 'juridical honour' (MEJ VI: 236 / 42), the humanity residing in their person. The measure of the possibility of consent, then, is not whether citizens might be happier or more prosperous as a result of the law, but whether the law being considered could be consistent with their worth as civil and moral persons. Actual or substantial consent would require that citizens, through their deputies, be the real authors of all law. Contrasted with this, formal universality does not demand that the imaginary universalization schema (law of nature, legislation for a Kingdom of Ends, or publicity) become real – its demands are satisfied if the law could be submitted to the public for its approval. If it *'might'* have come from a general will – whether or not the people now would actually agree to it – then it has the character of law. Actual consent is not needed (TP VIII: 297, 299 / 65, 67). And that is because nothing is lost from the point of view of lawfulness if the test is met.

This suggests to us the conclusion that Kant, unlike other contractarians, including Hobbes, was largely indifferent to the issue of actual authorization. For Hobbes, Locke, and Rousseau, the idea of a real act of consent (leaving aside their different accounts of what could be included as real consent) at one or more of the stages of political life is a crucial feature and the foundation of law itself. Not so for Kant. The original contract is an ideal compelling legislators to respect civil personality; and representation, by however many persons, is meant to preserve the universality of the law. Finally, the idea of consent is transformed into the transcendental principle of publicity; again as a standard to guarantee universality and respect for the personality of citizens.

When Kant wrote that all three forms of sovereignty (monarchy, aristocracy, and democracy) could be republican, he meant that as long as legislative authority is distinct from the executive and the judiciary, and while the original contract (extended to the principle of publicity) governs legislation, there exists a condition of public justice that acknowledges the civil personality of the citizenry. Kant's concern is with the *Rechtsstaat*, with law and universality, not with the actual consent or authorization of the contractarian tradition. The notions of contract, consent, and publicity are just so many ways of formulating the centrality of law (and its qualities) to a juridical order, and, in turn, the centrality of that order to any political life that is worthy of man. Kant may well have favoured one institutional arrangement over another – the real representation of a parliament, for example – but the ease with which the ideas of actual consent slip into those of 'probable consent' tells us that he was not a full-blooded contractarian. Legitimacy, for Kant, does not rest on an original act of authorization (Hobbes), or on direct participation in law-making (Rousseau), or, lastly, on actual representation (Locke). Rather it is based on the presence of a law-governed condition in which civil personality is respected; which amounts to the universality of legislation, and (hence) its equal application to citizens who could have consented to it (WIE VIII: 39 / 7).

## REVOLUTION AND POLITICAL JUDGMENT

We have now examined the sovereign's obligations toward citizens. We come, then, to the citizens' duties to their sovereign, which we shall consider in the form of a discussion of the supposed right to revolution. This alleged right to revolution is asserted by its proponents to hold under three distinct conditions: the illegitimacy of the origins of the regime, wrongs done to subjects, and where revolution would bring about greater well-being for the members of the society. The illegitimacy of the origins of a government provides no such right, Kant states. There may perhaps be, indeed there almost certainly are, regimes (maybe most) with unjust beginnings – the 'master' that Kant speaks of in the 'Idea for a Universal History' hints at that – but the historical or empirical origins of legislative authority in no way touch the foundations of that authority. Juridical authority rests on an a priori idea of legislation contained in the metaphor of an original contract. Like all types of law, those of natural phenomena as well as those that guide human actions, political law cannot be based on experience or history: experience, broadly understood, can provide only contingent, not necessary principles, the particular, not the universal. The authority with which law speaks is in no sense dependent upon the historical origins or evolution of the institutions that make it, but only upon its conformity to those standards described above (MEJ VI: 319, 323 / 84–5, 89).

It does not follow from that, however, that subjects can never be wronged by their sovereign. They have inalienable rights in their own person, rights over which they alone preside and that can indeed by injured by the sovereign. Yet these rights against the ruler cannot be coercive rights, which entitle the citizen to use force or extra-legal means against the sovereign (TP VIII: 303–4 / 71). For a citizen to claim a coercive right in a situation already strictly just, namely, governed by law, amounts to the assertion of the superiority of violent particularity over law. By a claim of this sort, 'they would be supposing that they had a right to put violence as the supreme prescriptive act of legislation in the place of every right and law' (MEJ VI: 372 / 140). In making a revolution on such a foundation they violate the form of justice, the universality of its laws, and substitute in its place the 'arbitrary wills' of individuals or of sects. Far from being the protectors of right, revolutionaries are its mortal enemies. Citizens must, Kant concludes, treat legislation that does them wrong as an error in prudence on the part of the representative of the general will (TP VIII: 299, 305 / 66, 73), not his true intention. To inform the sovereign of their grievances is thus the citizen's right and duty, and so too is it the obligation of the sovereign to allow that freedom of speech that would permit him to bring specific acts of legislation in line with his true intention. The latter, since the sovereign is the legislator only in virtue of being the representative of the people's (universal) will, cannot be different than a juridical condition in harmony with moral and civil personality.

The final ground for revolution is the claim to improve mankind's condition thereby – where that condition is taken not in the sense described above (the condition of respect for citizens' rights) but rather as its lot in this world, its material and spiritual comforts (MEJ VI: 353 / 126–7 and RZR XIX: 591, No. 8045). That man's happiness, however benevolent the wish for it may be, can provide no justification for overriding the moral or political claims of law is an argument already clearly stated in Kant's moral works, where such a view is termed 'heteronomy.' The termination of a lawful order, even for the best and most noble of reasons, is a gross injustice, for it destroys the framework that is the external expression of right and respect among people – public law. Moreover, it is evidence of a deep misunderstanding both of political life and of man: it subordinates the centre-piece of civil society (justice and law) to happiness, and it considers happiness his most important end, more important even than the rational nature, the personality, which makes man unique among the beings of this world.

While revolution based on the assertion of a wrong done to the inalienable rights of citizens and revolution that proceeds from the wish for a 'better world' may be equally disastrous in their practical consequences for a *Rechtsstaat*, the latter sort is perhaps the more evil. It is more corrosive of the spirit of law because it opposes not right (human or civil) to coercive right (public justice) but happiness or well-being, the non-lawful, to law. The former sort at least has the merit of leaving the idea of right and its theoretical (if not practical) priority intact. The latter attacks law-governed society at its roots by offering the standard of well-being in place of that of law. The society that emerges from this kind of revolutionary doctrine is certain to have a very shaky respect for law or right.

To understand the common theme that unites Kant's objections to all three purported rights to revolution, we should consider again the maxim of publicity, now applied to revolution. The essence of this application can be stated succinctly: the people must ask itself, when contemplating revolution, whether a clause allowing such an exception to the constitution could have been publicly inserted in the original contract. By so doing, the people would have established themselves as a power over the chief magistrate, in which event he is no longer the chief magistrate at all. Or, 'if both are made the condition of the establishment of the state, no state would be possible' (PP VIII: 382 / 130). Under circumstances of this kind, there is no longer a general will to which the citizens are subject, and hence no juridical condition, but only competing factions, a popular one and a ruling group.

Kant's point here is that the supposed right to revolution is anti-juridical in the extreme, and not just in its immediate practical results. This is so because it seeks to deny 'in advance' – in the original contract (the foundation of political life) – the basis of legislative authority as a representative of the general will. Somewhat more abstractly, it undermines the universality claimed by law, by reserving an authority over the law for the mass of individual citizens. Law is thereby made inferior to the (by definition) non-representative actions of the discontented citizenry. Every revolution, however it may choose to justify itself, is the lawless assertion by the particular (considered even as the aggregate of all particular wills) of its superiority over the universal, over the sovereign as the representative of the general will. For that general will, it substitutes a particular will – of ambitious individuals (for example, Alcibiades), of oligarchs, or of the insurrectionary mob – and from the particular will no law can arise (TP VIII: 295 / 63).

Thus the same standard that required of sovereigns that their legislation conform to the maxim of publicity, that it be cast as if it had come from the general will, also binds subjects – that they (no more than their governors) may not place a particular will over the law. Subjects and sovereigns are equally bound by the form of the law and by the public order in which they both share. The preservation of the law and of the order of respect and obligation that it creates between men – especially the protection of its universality, without which it ceases to be law – is the first duty of all men.

To obey the law is 'a categorical imperative' obligating all subjects, just as conformity to the idea of an original contract obligates all legislators. For reasons previously suggested, revolution is a far worse crime than the misdeeds of the sovereign. This would not be so were, for example, the people's welfare to be the principal measure of a state's well-being. It is because the health of the regime consists in the presence at its centre (as its leading principle) of public justice or law that revolution is such a radical evil. Revolution destroys the 'entire lawful constitution,' whereas the sovereign's errors remain, to continue with the analogy of a syllogism, misunderstandings of the universal premise. They leave the idea of law intact.

To explain further the severity of his judgment upon revolutions, we should refer to Kant's parallel between degrees of criminality, in moral life and in politics. All violations of the law, he writes, 'must be explained only as arising from the maxim of the criminal' (MEJ VI: 321 note / 87 note). But in adopting that unlawful maxim, this individual may make it into a 'presumed objective rule (supposed to be universally valid),' or he may claim it as an exception to the law the authority of which he otherwise recognizes. In the first example, that authority itself is denied, and the maxim is not 'merely deficient (*negative*) with respect to the law,' but is contrary to it. The second case shows a situation in which the law is acknowledged but an exemption from it is claimed. Both are crimes and fully culpable deeds, but the former is perverse – in its principle it would destroy all law. Similarly in revolution: the execution of a reigning monarch, Charles I, for instance, is a more heinous crime even than the murder that it involves. It kills not only the man, but law: it is 'a complete subversion of the principles governing the relationship between a sovereign and his people ... a crime that is incapable of being expiated' (MEJ VI: 322 note / 88 note).

## REVOLUTION: THE STANDARDS OF JUSTICE AND PHILANTHROPIC HISTORY

The clarity and sharpness of this condemnation of revolution should be contrasted with the account of the French Revolution given from the point of view of philosophical history. There, we remember, affairs in France were used as a 'historical sign' pointing to a tendency in mankind to progress from a worse to a better condition. In that interpretation, the constitution as well as mankind itself was viewed not from the juridical perspective, the standpoint of right, but each as a mere moment in a process of evolution (OQ VII: 87–8 / 146–7). As stages in this process, their intrinsic worth (law and personality) is not what is important – justice and injustice, the overturning of a constitution, and the execution of a sovereign are not the criteria for an evolutionary account of man's external affairs.

Rather, the philosophical historian, the benevolent 'friend of man,' asks only whether these events are 'signposts' pointing to a better future. If violence and crimes are the necessary midwives of this world to come, if that world emerges from the womb, as Marx wrote, bloody and imperfect, then philosophical history sees this in the light of evolution and hope. The issue of right is put to one side. In doing this, the philosophical historian shows philanthropy, a love of mankind, but not respect: he ignores the sole possible foundation for a claim to respect, namely the personal dignity of an autonomous being, together with its corollary, public justice. Good wishes and the hope for happiness are offered in place of respect, evolution in the place of the a priori standard of right, beauty in place of the sublimity of justice.

The juridical point of view can represent events in France only according to the principles of morality, not from an 'aesthetic' standpoint, as Kant calls it (MEJ VI: 321 note / 87 note), in which 'compassion' is awakened by 'imagining oneself in the place of the sufferer.'[14] The aesthetic standpoint of sympathy and compassion, whether for the struggles of the revolutionaries or for the miserable fate of the old rulers, is rejected here. A crime has been committed, and a great one: people have been treated as mere trifles, and law, which is or ought to be everything between people, has been cast aside, to be replaced by the cries of the mob for blood. It is not that one should, or even could, view those events with an olympian disdain: Kant's argument is rather that sympathy must yield to respect, hope and edification to the sublime dignity of justice and law.

INTERNATIONAL LAW

International law, Kant writes, is the end or ultimate extension of all other forms of public law (MEJ VI: 355 / 128–9). This is the case because the 'surface of the earth is not unlimited in extent.' What this rather elliptical statement means is that since we find ourselves in contact with one another, not only within the commonwealth but with citizens of other nations as well, the same principles that demand the creation of a juridical condition – the public, external recognition of rights and reciprocal obligations – lead to the imperative to establish such a state among nations too. Particular systems of justice vary, of course, but the underlying principles of justice are universal and demand, insofar as is possible, universal application. Their a priori universality requires a phenomenal or worldly universality, since we are all one in point of autonomy and dignity. It is also the end of all law because its opposite condition, namely international violence or the threat thereof, makes the furthering of internal or constitutional justice more pragmatically difficult, though certainly no less imperative. Why that is can be said briefly: a barracks society is not conducive to freedom, equality, or the treating of individuals as ends. And a military camp is what societies become, for the sake of bare survival, in a lawless international situation.

Now international law can be divided into the law of nations (including the idea of perpetual peace) and the law of world citizenship or cosmopolitan law. Kant explicitly states, and this is crucial for understanding the distinction between philosophical history and the pure moral (juridical) standpoint, that perpetual peace and a cosmopolitan condition are being discussed here not with a philanthropic intent but solely from the point of view of law and right (MEJ VI: 352 / 125 and PP VIII: 357 / 102). This repeated insistence on the non-philanthropic character of the just viewpoint on international relations stands in marked contrast both to the *Idea for a Universal History* and to the philosophical historian's interpretation of international affairs set out in the concluding chapter of Kant's theory and praxis essay, which is subtitled 'with a philanthropic intent.'

Under the law of nations, Kant argues, a state is regarded as a 'moral person': not as a civil person, but rather as an individual in a condition of natural (lawless) freedom. This state is unjust – without public justice – and the idea of rights, both of individuals and of states as moral persons, commands them to quit this condition and to establish a public order (MEJ VI: 344 / 116). The law of nations contains two parts: one that attempts to impose a legal framework on the prosecution of war so as to facilitate the realization of a league of nations, and, ultimately, the laws of peace themselves.

The rights of war can be dealt with quickly. There are those that apply internally to the citizens who must conduct the war, rights in the initiation of war and during and after hostilities. Citizens are not mere implements to be used by the sovereign for the purposes of state; they are autonomous beings, and to treat them differently, under any circumstances but especially when their lives are at stake, is to reduce them to the status of tongs, used to pull hot coals from the fire (PP VIII: 354 note / 98–9 note). 'For in the face of the omnipotence of nature ... the human being is, in his turn, but a trifle. But for the sovereigns of his own species also to consider and treat him as such ... exposing him in their conflicts with one another in order to have him massacred – that is no trifle, but a subversion of the ultimate purpose of creation itself' (OQ VII: 89 / 148).

The ruler must have the consent of the people for war, and in consulting this standard he both recognizes their rights and advances the cause of peace by making the declaration of war dependent on the consent of that group most likely to oppose it. (The previously noted ambiguity in the idea of consent should be kept in mind here.) The right to initiate war, considered now not in relation to the citizenry but as an affair between states, is the right to secure redress where there is no public authority, no common judge, to whom one may appeal. The desire to acquire, however natural it may be (as Machiavelli claimed), does not make a war just, for that would be to treat another state (a moral person) as a mere thing to be seized (MEJ VI: 346 / 118–19). The notion of rights during a war is difficult to grasp, since war is lawlessness carried to its most extreme point. Kant, in his *Rechtslehre* and in 'Perpetual Peace,' provides a similar list of restrictions on the conduct of war – for example, no war of extermination, of subjugation, or of a punitive kind. All these restrictions are derived from the principle that nothing must be done during a war that would make an exit from that condition impossible. And finally, the set of rights that come into effect immediately after the cessation of war are grouped around the limits of what may be done to a conquered people and state – there can be no slavery and no loss of civil freedom (for the state or its population), and no punitive damages can be levied against the vanquished.

The rights of war are only a small part of what interests Kant in the theory of international law. Apart from the citizens' rights in regard to war, which are properly speaking an element of constitutional law, the other rights between warring states are provisional and must be ultimately superseded by an enduring peace, not a mere treaty ending war for the time being. One might expect, on a parallel with the transition from moral to civil personality, that these individual states would dissolve themselves into a world state in order to secure peace and a just international order. But this would have to be a state composed of nations that would then, Kant says, become in fact one nation. And this, as desirable as such an extension of civil order might be, is not practically feasible. It is impossible, not only because of the unmanageable size of a world state but also, more important, because a nation that has given itself a juridical condition is in a very ambiguous position when the question arises of laying down its self-legislation so as to permit a universal government.

The individual in a non-juridical condition has only provisional external rights, which can become actual only when they have been given a public, political form. Now between states, where no recognized order or authority exists, rights are also provisional; but internally these same states, through the idea of an original contract and by the 'consent' of their citizens, have established a lawful condition. Thus the notion of a world government, which implies the relation between a commanding and an obeying part, introduces the possibility of infringements upon an already existing legislative power.

The core of this argument is the idea of a conflict between two public authorities, between rights that are provisional and need to be guaranteed (international) and rights that are currently actual (internal justice). Kant's conclusion is that perpetual peace, understood as world civil order, is not possible (MEJ VI: 350 / 124). Yet there remains a duty to approximate it to the extent within one's power. And this is to be accomplished by a 'league of nations,' a confederation of states that will act as a surrogate for a government among nations (PP VIII: 356 / 101).

We have finally to say something about cosmopolitan law, which need be mentioned only briefly here. It consists in universal hospitality, which people have a right to expect as they travel. It is the right of a temporary sojourn and, as well, the right to free commerce across international boundaries. In both cases, these rights are founded on the original common possession of the world, when 'no one had more right than another to a particular part of the earth' (PP VIII: 358 / 103).

WAR: THE STANDARDS OF JUSTICE AND PHILANTHROPIC HISTORY

Here again it is useful to compare the treatment of war from the perspective of right and from the point of view of the philosophical historian. For the latter, war is, as we have seen, the driving force behind progress in history – strife is the source of all the fruit of civilization

(UH VIII: 22 / 16–17). War supplies the mechanical-causal principle required for an evolutionary interpretation of external human affairs. History a priori required that principle in order to be able to read progress into events, to demonstrate that that seemingly perennial feature of human society – war – which gives to empirical history its resemblance to the myth of Sisyphus is not evidence of stagnation or decline but is rather the instrument of mankind's betterment. This we called the beautiful portrayal of war, the source of consolation and hope.

But from our new standpoint, we see war not as the driving force of the improvement of man's lot but as the direct antithesis of a juridical condition, as the overturning of all notions of worth and respect between people. It is the violent assertion of one particular will against another (states being considered as moral persons), which is the 'sad recourse' where a public, lawful domain has not been created. The rights of individuals and of states call for the termination of that condition and for the establishing of peace. And they call for peace not on the basis of experience, of hope, or of sympathy but rather as an a priori practical command of reason.

The theoretical question of the feasibility of the project of perpetual peace is a matter for belief – it cannot be known with certainty, and sceptical attacks against it cannot be refuted on theoretical grounds, on the basis of an analysis of human or physical nature. But belief and scepticism both dwindle in importance when contrasted with moral duty. Neither belief nor scepticism can provide what they claim – a supportable affirmation or denial or purposiveness in human events, and they are also, as was suggested in the preceding chapter, inferior as guides for our conduct in the world. Duty, however, speaks with a clear and unequivocal voice: from its 'throne of supreme moral legislating authority,' it voices its 'irresistible veto: *There shall be no war ...* ' (MEJ VI: 354 / 128). The issues of feasibility, belief, and scepticism disappear here: *'wir müssen so handeln, als ob ...* ' ('we must act as if ... ') (MEJ VI: 354 / 128) a condition of perpetual peace existed.

We must act, morally and politically; however great our uncertainty about the purpose of the world or about God's existence, we are left as worldly beings who have to make their way through the world, who have to act. What nature intends as the result of those actions, what will come of them over the course of history or in the life that Christianity promises us after this one we cannot know. Nature and God are not adequate to guide us here and now, since our vision is too weak to see them with sufficient clarity. What we can know, however, is the law that we give to ourselves – with it we can orient ourselves, act as we must, and this without fear of losing our way.

Everything passes by us as if in a river, Kant wrote. Where can one find a firm point that can never be lost sight of and that will tell us to what shore we must hold (BZB xx: 46)? The question suggests its own answer. As if in a river, 'everything passes *before us'* – nature, inanimate and human (*die verschiedenen Gestalten des Menschen*), is a flux with no visible landmarks. But it flows 'before us'; we seem to stand outside it, as self-legislating beings it is we who are the fixed points by which our direction may be determined. The seeming clarity of daylight, of beauty and order in nature and history, and of a just God illuminates apparently firm markers. They dissolve as one approaches them more closely, and they can easily come to offer false and misleading directions. The apparent emptiness of night, of the sublime, reveals to us the surest reference point we have – our moral reason. Nature, to be sure, remains shrouded in the deepest blackness – seemingly formless and without purpose – but in all that darkness the light of our moral nature remains as a guide. By its light we shall never come to know nature's design, but we shall learn how we are to act.

# Conclusion

# 8

# Kant on theory and praxis

Here is now what Archimedes needed, but did not find: a firm point upon which reason can rest its fulcrum, in order to move man's will, by means of its own fundamental laws, against the resistance of the whole of nature – and this indeed, with reason relying neither on the present world nor on a future world, but rather only on its inner idea of freedom, an idea which, through the unshakeable moral law, is revealed as a solid foundation.

Kant

Reason's peculiar fate is that it is burdened by questions that it can neither ignore nor answer. These questions occupy a central position in all traditional metaphysics – in the form of the problems of freedom, God, and the soul. And those issues have their ultimate origin not in a theoretical need to understand nature but in our practical interests (c1 A797 / B825). How am I to make my way through the world? What ought I to do? What may I hope for?. Metaphysics has its source in our practical need to find a guiding principle – a moral law, revelation, a just and coherent nature. Experience, the world as it is given to us directly, seems inadequate to our needs. Like that 'light dove' to which Kant compares both reason as such and Plato as the greatest metaphysician, we find the limits of the world too narrow, and so, when the empirical domain fails us, we seek certain knowledge of an intelligible world. The science (knowledge) of nature, even if it were possible to attain a science of the whole of nature, leaves (as Wittgenstein wrote) these, our most important questions, unresolved.

It is the cruel fate of human reason that that which is bound up with its 'highest interests' is placed beyond our reach (c1 A743–4 /

B771–2). Outside of possible experience, nothing can be known, and claims to knowledge about such 'objects' are empty: the world, its objects, its events, and the fundamental laws that govern it are all that is the case. That is the 'negative' conclusion of the *Critique of Pure Reason*. Reason's ascent is thus a flight into an 'empty space,' a dialectic of illusion, an adventure that is bound to be fruitless as long as the vain hope is entertained of being able to secure knowledge of God, freedom, or the soul. Yet the practical necessity of the questions remains, and so too the need for a guiding principle or thread by which we may find our direction in a world that itself offers no immediate guidance. How are we to orient ourselves if metaphysical knowledge, as traditionally understood, is impossible? If we cannot know of God, of a future life, or of a divine plan for human affairs in this world, are we then reduced to the status of animals, having no other law than that given by nature? Or worse, are we creatures condemned to the 'abyss of the purposeless chaos of matter,' conscious of our fate but lacking even that instinct that directs the other beings of this world?

Nature is all that is the case, at least from the theoretical point of view. The mind is the source of order in the world, but those basic laws that make possible the combination of intuitions in a single consciousness and the dependence of the mind on what is given to it in intuition mean that reason's proprietorship is extended over a very small domain indeed. Beyond those limits there is, to be sure, only emptiness, but that very emptiness allows the spontaneity of reason an activity that is not bound down by the confines of possible experience. Here, no supportable claims to knowledge can be made, but for precisely that reason, the mind is left free, completely unhindered, and artistic or legislative in its powers. From that standpoint, reason's most pressing needs, its practical concerns, can be satisfied not by a futile and ultimately dialectical struggle to win knowledge of an intelligible world but rather by reason setting out its own guiding-threads. Nature and science can tell us nothing about how we ought to live, but self-legislating reason can, that is, reason in its practical employment.

This is Kant's revolution in metaphysics: he reveals its practical foundation and the emptiness of its pretensions to knowledge. And then he takes the central concepts of that tradition – God, freedom, and the soul – frees them from their claim to speak about the nature of things, and gives them a new status, as guides (c1 A569 / B597; A828–9 / B856–7) by which we may orient ourselves here and now. That is the sense of the famous passage in the *Groundwork* where Kant writes that a philosophy that 'presses forward in its principles to the very limits of human reason' can show only the (theoretical) 'incomprehensibility' of the idea of a moral imperative, but that nevertheless the viewpoint of freedom, provided by reason in its pure spontaneity, is 'sufficient' for our practical purposes (GMM IV: 463 / 131). We can, as Kant said, build a tower high enough to oversee the world and to serve our purposes here, though not, as we had originally hoped, of such a height as to reach the heavens.

From the standpoint of freedom, this theoretically empty and un-bounded 'space,' we can read a sense back into the world, legislate for it (with laws other than the categories – laws of purposiveness and of beauty) and for ourselves according to our practical interests. This is the aesthetic element in Kant's Copernican revolution. We are at liberty to choose a viewpoint, to 'think into' the world that of which it does not provide us direct evidence. The world, with its pale colours that seem to offer man no support or comfort, can be taken up, and re-presented now as golden and beautiful. From this beautiful point of view nature, which seen empirically appears to thwart man at every turn, is portrayed as ordered, as if in harmony with man's aesthetic sense and practical interests. The order of nature shows the work of a wise designer, and it teaches man contentment and allows him hope.

Similarly, human nature (the external phenomena of human affairs), which at first sight seems little more than a chaotic collection of events subject only to the dismal rule of chance, can be transformed by another sort of artist – the philosophical historian – so that it too reveals an order, a designer, and a source of hope or consolation. Nature, physical and human, is here represented as a thing of beauty, for practical purposes – a theodicy and a support for our moral life. A guiding-thread is woven back into nature, to render it purposefully beautiful, and man himself, in his history, is represented as lovable, since that history displays a gradual advance toward a better condition. We have seen the weaknesses of the latter way of portraying man – it must give a plausible and consoling account of nature and (in order to provide a historical foundation for the love of man) must treat him as a plaything of nature, a moment in a process of evolution, not as a moral agent, an autonomous being.

The guiding-thread is something that we choose, and the two great standpoints from which the world can be viewed are the beautiful and the sublime. The beautiful portrayal turns our attention to nature, its order and designer. The sublime leaves untouched the dissonance of nature, whether the 'storm-tossed waves' or the dismal chaos of human phenomena. It begins from the fact that nature seems to serve no purpose, that it is formless, giving no evidence of a wise architect and offering no support for man and his hopes. Here man's gaze is turned inward, to his capacity for resisting nature, his moral faculty. This Kant calls the pure moral standpoint. Nature is ignored, except insofar as our own nature must be overcome by self-given law. And human affairs are not treated teleologically or historically, as an evolutionary process in which past injustices are mere steps on the way to a brighter future, but rather as the phenomenal expression of moral personality embodied in law. Justice, not progress, and respect for man, not philanthropy, are the hallmarks of the sublime portrayal of man. There is a common starting point for the Christian and the philosophic historian, who represent man from a hopeful and consoling perspective; for those who adopt the sublime standpoint, ignoring nature (and thus hope) in favour of man's moral agency; and for the worldly wise, who do not reinterpret nature but use it as an excuse for their own actions. All three approaches begin from the same point: the lack of any direct evidence of a purposeful harmony (a moral or just order) in physical or human nature. The first re-creates nature by reading into it the purpose it lacks in its empirical form, the second leaves it as it is and turns to man's moral agency, and the third turns to the 'effectual truth,' the 'imaginary one' having been shown to lead to one's undoing.

Kant's Copernican revolution placed the self, the knowing *Ich*, at the centre of experience and made of it the law-giver of nature. But the known world, nature given to us in intuition and ordered according to the categories, does not answer the demands of the practical, willing self. Nature and our knowledge of it do not provide us with the means to orient ourselves. We are rather in the position of that traveller wondering about the picture of the graveyard displayed above the door of the Dutch inn. We recall that the question there was how we were to understand the artist's intention. We are like that traveller, except in this one crucial respect: for him the problem of the artist's meaning is an aesthetic issue, a question of interpretation. For us, however, the problem is of immediate practical importance. Since it was discovered that that intention could not in fact be discerned (the negative side of Kant's Copernican revolution), we were left with the problem of how we could make sense of it. Here we found that we are, to some extent, at liberty to interpret this work, to read into it a guiding-thread or to find a compass within ourselves (the positive aesthetic, or law-giving element of the Copernican revolution).

The sense that we choose to give to the world is not a mere product of the free-floating, playful imagination. Rather, its origins are practical, having to do with the free exercise of the will. The Copernican revolution demonstrates that in order for there to be coherent experience, the synthetic activity of the mind is necessary in addition to intuition. It has shown also that nature or experience does not give the acting self the orientation that this self requires, but that we must ourselves mark out the path we are to follow. Just as Kant's first Copernican revolution demonstrated the role of legislative reason in making experience possible, this second revolution points to the relation between theory (reason) and praxis. This relation is reflected in the Dutch innkeeper's sign: in the words (the theory, legislative reason) 'perpetual peace' and in the image of the graveyard, human affairs as they are given directly in experience. We turn, then, by way of conclusion and summary to Kant's essay on theory and praxis (*On the Old Saw: That May Be Right in Theory But It Won't Work in Practice*).

Theory, Kant writes, is a set of rules, of principles of a certain order of generality. But theory in that definition no longer refers to the underlying order of nature and experience – rather, it is a practical theory, rules of conduct and not of nature. Thus whereas the first *Critique* began with the teaching that the mind must introduce an order into intuitions, so here ideas are meant to infuse human deeds with an order. Praxis is activity that follows 'generally conceived principles of procedure' (TP VIII: 275 / 41), and it is to be distinguished from mere 'practices,' deeds that possess a contingent or shifting foundation in experience (PP VIII: 373 / 121) alone. Praxis requires a practical science, and Kant cites examples from medicine, agriculture and economics. No one would now be so foolish as to disdain theory in such sciences, and where the practical ends of these sciences are not met, the fault is not with too much theory but rather with the insufficiency of the rules governing the particular cases. More or better theory is needed – and that is Kant's answer to those 'ignorant' men who hold that science can be advanced by the mere 'groping about' (*herumtappen*) of experimentation. This sort of language and argument is already familiar to us from Kant's discussion of science in the *Critique of Pure Reason* (C1 Bxiv–xv).

Now, as we noted, Kant begins his essay by mentioning such practical sciences as medicine, agriculture, and economics, to which he subsequently adds ballistics and mechanics. But it is not in sciences of this kind that Kant wishes to bring about his second Copernican revolution. Let us consider for a moment what these sciences have in common. They all have an end external to themselves – health, food, business, or war – and their success as science is measured against the external ends that they are intended to realize. In practical sciences of this sort, Aristotle writes, the 'products are essentially superior to the activities' (the practice of the sciences themselves).[1] This type of science is inferior to its products and to those sciences that control its products – in Aristotle's argument, the art of politics.

Kant's interest is not in dependent sciences, which do indeed stand to be corrected by experience (though requiring theory as well), but in what he terms 'self-existing theory' (TP VIII: 277 / 43). A self-existing theory is one that does not allow of correction by experience; on the contrary, the practice attached to this theory can be measured only by its conformity to that theory and not by an external end, by the results that it may achieve. Duty, considered as a collection of practical rules, is such a theory. And because the value of all moral praxis depends on its adherence to the moral law, it is there that the attempt to correct theory by experience works the most harm. 'All is lost' if empirical considerations are made to serve as the foundation for duty and moral judgment – the autonomy, or 'self-existence,' of both the law (theory) and the praxis is thereby lost. 'This pretense,' Kant writes, 'is advanced in a tone of lofty disdain full of presumption to have reason itself reformed by experience in the area which reason deems its highest honour, and with the sapient conceit to see farther and more clearly with the eyes of a mole, fixed upon experience, than with the eyes of a being that was made to stand erect and to behold the heavens' (TP VIII: 277 / 43).

The relation of theory or duty to praxis is discussed in three parts – the strictly moral, the political, and the historical (or the cosmopolitan point of view, as Kant calls it). The first concerns the maxims that the person adopts for his own actions; the latter two take up the public relations between persons. The first chapter of the essay considers duty as a rule and contrasts it both to the *summum bonum* and to happiness. Though it is not stated quite so baldly, the issue in the first chapter might be said to be the Kantian or Stoic conception of morality as against the Christian one. The final two chapters, on politics and history, differ as do the sublime and the beautiful – one looks at political right and duty; the other at what Providence can do to guarantee progress, an advance that may make man more lovable. These three perspectives – of man as man, man as citizen, and man as historical being

– are exactly the three standpoints that Kant mentions in describing the Dutch innkeeper's sign.[2]

The opening chapter of Kant's essay on theory and praxis is taken up with an answer to the charge that Kant sought to deny happiness as an end for man, leaving duty as the only force inspiring the will. Kant's response reveals the general direction of all his arguments against the claims of experience over reason. Kant states that he suggested not that we should renounce our desires, but only that we should abstract from them when considering what we ought to do (TP VIII: 280 / 47). As a 'finite' being, man could not renounce these urges in any case – they are part of his 'subjective constitution,' of the fact that he is not a perfect moral being. We recall that Kant's criticism of the Stoics was just this – that they tried to make of man a holy being, above all the limitations inherent in his nature. It was Christianity's principal service to mankind to show him the distance between his condition and moral perfection.

Kant adds that he did not dismiss the notion of an end for moral actions – an end which, not determining the good will, nevertheless arises out of it, accompanied by the 'beliefs of reason' needed to support it. Quite the contrary, the idea of the highest good is precisely such an end. But, and this is crucial, Kant's critics have misunderstood the *summum bonum*: they took Kant to mean that morality needs the highest good as a support and source of strength. Kant's answer is unequivocal, and it reflects the weight that he attached to the sublime viewpoint over that of the faithful: he says that, so far as the '*principle* of morals' is concerned, 'the doctrine of the *highest good* as the ultimate end of a will that is in conformity to its laws, can ... be wholly ignored and put aside as an episodic ... Where the real issue is at stake, no attention is paid at all to this doctrine, only to the universal moral standpoint' (TP VIII: 280 / 47). Duty, then, always has a priority over what emerges from the subjective limitation of our will, here the wish to see virtue rewarded.

There is still another objection that Kant wants to meet: that though the critic can allow, in thought, a distinction between how one can be happy and how one can be worthy of happiness, he cannot find this distinction in 'his heart.' Such subtle distinctions between different kinds of motivation collapse, it is said, when we come to act. Again, Kant's response is intriguing. He answers that the moral law in its clarity and simplicity is superior to happiness as a guide for action.

Happiness contains only what nature, broadly understood, can give us (TP VIII: 283 note / 50 note). When we come to act, happiness is at best an obscure marker by which to orient ourselves: to pursue it with any certainty of success, we would have to know a long series of causes and effects; and our reason is not sufficiently far-seeing to permit us to predict with confidence such a future course of events (TP VIII: 287 / 54 and GMM IV: 418 / 85–6). We cannot be certain that the 'Kingdom of Nature' will act in harmony with our desire to be happy (GMM IV: 438–9 / 106). Happiness, then, is too varied a notion, and the pragmatic calculations required for its attainment are too imprecise for it to be useful as a guide. Virtue, in contrast, contains only what the person can give to himself or herself (TP VIII: 283 note / 50 note). Here I can be completely inexperienced in the affairs of the world; I have no need to study nature, human or otherwise, in order to know what duty commands (GMM IV: 403 / 71). The moral law is both clear and self-sufficient (PP VIII: 370 / 118); it is autonomous in the full sense of that term.

Yet the usefulness of the moral law cannot recommend it, though it may be a simpler and surer guide than the psychological principles of happiness. Morality is self-sufficient, and usefulness can add no worth to what exists of itself – the way it might add value to a practical science such as ballistics, for example. Kant seems to acknowledge this indirectly by conceding, after a fashion, his critic's point that the history of maxims does not contradict the thesis that the desire for happiness is never in fact abstracted from in action. But this thesis does contradict 'inner experience': it offends the absolutely clear injunction that some actions are simply evil, others simply good, and that we are commanded to shun the former and pursue the latter. 'Even if there have never been actions springing from such pure sources, the question at issue here is not whether this or that has happened; ... on the contrary, reason by itself and independently of all appearances commands what ought to happen' (GMM IV: 407–8 / 75). Here we recognize the sublime view of morality, and so it comes as no surprise to hear Kant once more speaking in that kind of language: 'no idea does more to lift [erhebt] the human spirit and to fan its enthusiasm than the very idea of a pure moral character ... This is the revelation of divine tendencies within himself deep enough to fill him with sacred awe, as it were, at the magnitude and sublimity of his true destiny' (TP VIII: 287–8 / 54). Man needs to be reminded of the sublimity (autonomy) of his nature, not of the failures of history, nor for that matter its successes, in presenting evidence of good deeds.

The sum of Kant's answer to his critics can be stated thus: experience may contradict morality in the sense that it gives us only instances of the flouting of duty. But it does not, for that reason, touch the heart of duty, its imperative quality, the demands and nobility of which in no way depend upon experience. Theory, which in this context means duty, is self-sufficient and autonomous, and everything is lost if it is made to bow before experience. How we have acted is ultimately of less importance than how we ought to have acted. The 'consciousness of duty' – *Pflichtbewusstsein* – is far superior to the 'mole's' view, which finds in the evils of the world an excuse for its own misdeeds. It is also superior to the standpoint of the faithful, who think a moral sense into the world, who wish for the *summum bonum*. The consciousness of duty stands above the latter because its majesty resides in nothing other than duty, the pure moral faculty. It is absolutely self-sufficient in a way that faith can never be; and indeed the first sentence in Kant's *Religion within the Limits of Reason Alone* proclaims the complete independence of the moral law from religion (RWL VI: 3 / 3).

The second chapter of the essay on theory and praxis is taken up with a consideration of external, political law. The problem here is to demonstrate the a priori character of right and its superiority to the practical wisdom of the worldly wise statesman who seeks to dismiss any concern with right by appealing to a Thrasymachus-like position that power is its own justification or to the seemingly more benign emphasis on benevolence over right and law. Again, my intention is not to offer a detailed analysis of Kant's contract theory (that has been done elsewhere in this book) but rather to go directly to the issue of theory and praxis.

Now the structure of the argument that we are considering, and that found above in chapter 1, are virtually identical. Kant advances the claim that principles a priori, far from being of little use to practice, in fact provide a much clearer guide to political life than do empirically conditioned principles. In other words, political or moral duty speaks with a voice incomparably simpler and more certain than happiness or any other subjective end (TP VIII: 290 / 58). The reasoning here is similar to that invoked on behalf of the moral law – happiness can provide us with no fixed principles, its content is subject to the changing whims of the age, and, in any event, securing it demands an insight into the future effects of policies that is quite beyond our abilities.

However, that this is not Kant's central argument can be seen from the following considerations. Granted, the notion of an a priori duty (taken here in its political form, as the idea of an original contract) is simpler than other competing standards and certainly requires less experience in order to be mastered. Clarity, however, is not the only or even the principal measure of a theory's practicality – its efficacy must surely be taken into account as well. And that is the measure, as we saw, of other practical sciences – economics or ballistics, for instance. The moral law and political right may well not meet that crucial test of usefulness. But a truly 'self-existing,' autonomous theory is not to be judged in the light of its efficacy or usefulness – that would be to make it a dependent and not a controlling theory. This idea can be seen in Kant's distinction between the two sayings 'honesty is the best policy' and 'honesty is better than any policy' (PP VIII: 370 / 117). The former, Kant writes, is all too often refuted by experience; the latter is 'beyond refutation.'

The nominal target of this chapter is Hobbes, though he makes only a single appearance in the text. Kant's major interest, as is evident in the above remarks, is in the mischief done by the notion of happiness when it is made to serve as the basis of political conduct: it makes sovereigns despots and subjects rebels (TP VIII: 302 / 70). It encourages rulers to become despots (lawless wielders of power) by holding out, as a rule for the exercise of their power, not respect for the civil personality of the subjects but benevolence, the maximizing of happiness. The benevolent and the savage despot share one essential trait: the rejection of the idea of right as the foundation of legislation (cf PP VIII: 385–6 / 134). The decency or brutality of the despot depends on contingent circumstances, his disposition or the current state of affairs, not on an abiding principle. Similarly, the citizen whose political conduct is guided by a desire for well-being or happiness (the only true well-being of a citizen, according to Kant, is that of membership in a law-governed state) undermines right and law and clouds political judgment. To judge a political act in the light of present conditions, of, for example, the happiness that has resulted from certain deeds, is to render politics the plaything of the vagaries of shifting fortune. Successful revolutions are praised and the new masters applauded: these same new leaders, had their enterprises failed, would have been judged common criminals. Success and well-being are precarious standards, and though they may masquerade as the basis of a clear-eyed practical science, they subject human affairs to the caprice of mere chance (TP VIII: 301 / 69).

The practical science of right, in contrast, begins with the concept of freedom, not happiness. The original contract, which is to guide subjects and sovereigns alike, proceeds from this innate freedom and its corollaries (equality and independence) and gives them a political, public expression. The strength of the original contract and the reason that it obliges all legislators to enact only such legislation as would be compatible with it have nothing to do with its efficacy or simplicity – rather, the original contract is an idea of reason and a duty (TP VIII: 289 / 57). And for Kant, it is important to speak of politics in this way not because of the empirical accuracy of its account of the origins of society – Kant knew very well the role of coercion in politics – but because it reminds us that what is central to this created public order is duty and freedom in balance. Those who portray the beginnings of society in some natural mechanism reduce man's value in his own eyes. The fiction of an original contract, unlike the romance of philosophical history, is meant to be a guide to duty, not a source of consolation.

The philosophical historian seeks a theodicy and hope and must give an account of nature that is both plausible and comforting. He has to make sense of, or find an order (a just order) in, the empirical facts. The purpose of philosophical history demands that it explain nature. The pure political science of right is not bound by the same requirement to explain nature; the ideal state is an archetype, justice 'writ large,' and its rightfulness is in no way diminished for its not having come into being (C1 A317 / B373–4). Whereas the philosophical historian takes as a model the success of statisticians and meteorologists in discovering patterns in what had previously seemed random, the science of right turns away from nature or history to duty (TP VIII: 297 / 65). We recall that one difference between the beautiful and the sublime was that while the former perceived art in nature, the latter left nature in all its unruliness. A similar distinction might be said to hold between the standpoints of the philosophical historian and that of duty. The teleological approach to history relies on a certain balance between the empirical facts and the idea, and so it cannot afford to ignore altogether the central facts of human affairs but must rather reinterpret these empirical data, reading into them the guiding-thread of a just order in the world. The respublica noumenon, in contrast, can afford to disregard nature and history, its emphasis being on duty, not consolation.

The concluding chapter of Kant's essay on theory and praxis is perhaps the most unusual in the whole text. And this distinctiveness is signalled in its very title: the first two chapters dealt with moral and political law respectively, and their titles said just that. Chapter 3 purports to speak of international law, but from a 'general-philanthropic' point of view: not law simply, but law and philanthropy – and it will be recalled that Kant, in his *Rechtslehre* and in 'Perpetual Peace,' explicitly separates the idea of international law from philanthropy. Kant, in a footnote appended to the chapter title here, tells us that the connection between law and the love of man will become clear in the conclusion (TP VIII: 307 note / 75 note). The implication is that the body of the chapter will present philanthropy in another light – and that is indeed the case: the standpoint adopted is that of the philosophical historian, not the 'teacher of law.'

The chapter begins with the question not of how man is to be worthy of love or respect but of love simply. The answer to this question is to be found in the solution to a further problem – is man progressing? And that question is the principal concern of history a priori. Now some portray history as a Sisyphean labour in which progress is always illusory. Moses Mendelssohn, one of these critics, argues that one should forge 'no hypotheses' about Providence's intentions, but rather look to the empirical facts. These show that man's misery 'must have been approved or at least included in the plans of wisdom' (TP VIII: 308 / 76). Mendelssohn's claim is that any propositions concerning God's intention are nothing other than 'hypotheses,' unless they are arrived at from a study of the facts of history as it is given to us empirically. In short, he attacks the possibility of history a priori. Kant's counterargument, as we shall see, is twofold: on the one side, he maintains that such 'hypotheses' ('theory' is used to describe moral and political law) are possible because experience can neither confirm nor deny the belief in a divine purpose. On the other side, however, Kant (like Job, in Kant's essay on the failure of all philosophical theodicies) puts aside all attempts to speak of a moral purposiveness at work in the world, and turns instead to the principle of right.

'*Ich bin anderer Meinung*' – 'I am of a different opinion,' Kant begins (TP VIII: 308 / 76), and he then moves directly to the language of plays and theatre, and of the repugnant view of history contained in the Sisyphean account. This, he says, is a sight unfit for God and man. We are therefore allowed 'to assume' that the species is progressing. And the burden of proof is on those who deny this assumption. This is a hypothesis that is the expression of a wish, attached to the duty we have to benefit posterity. The argument of the sceptics is also hypothetical (TP VIII: 309 / 77), since the futility of these hopes can never be proved, any more than can other beliefs in the suprasensible be shown as false.

The choice, then, is between two sorts of hypotheses – the one warms the heart, Kant writes, with its hope for a better future, represents man as lovable, and cheers the mind (TP VIII: 309 / 77); the other shows a world from which all good-willed people must avert their eyes. As hypotheses they both stand in marked contrast to the moral law, which would remain even if all hope were to be lost (as is shown in the example of Spinoza in the *Critique of Judgment*) as long as its practical impossibility has not been demonstrated. All that is needed for the principle of right to apply is that the demands it makes of us not be shown to be impossible. We cannot be commanded to do the impossible, nor can we be held accountable for failure to do what cannot be done. But this condition, inherent in any moral principle, is entirely different from hope or optimism – it is more of a formal or logical principle than an attempt to explain nature and history. Kant's famous *'als ob'* ('as if') formulation is intended precisely to detach duty from the problem of empirical possibility: we must act as if a condition of perpetual peace existed (MEJ VI: 354 / 128, and see also EVT VIII: 397 note) – we have to act according to the moral law, and respect the moral and civil personalities of our fellows, regardless of the present state of affairs.

We are free to choose belief, to assume progress in history. But the 'whole as such is too large for men,' and they cannot be the authors of their own advance. Success depends not on what we do, on the education we give to youth, for example (TP VIII: 310 / 78) – and this already hints at the moral inferiority of the historical interpretation – but on what human nature will do *'to force us'* onto the correct path. Or, to speak more exactly, Providence must arrange things so that what the species does not intend will nevertheless be its future. The mechanism by which Providence works its plans is already familiar to us: violence and distress compel us to submit to a civil constitution, and violence between states, as well as the enormous cost of maintaining standing armies, forces us to seek the shelter of international law. Thus, it is not out of a duty to attempt to improve the lot of future generations, or even from a benevolent concern for them, but from the *'self-love* of each era' that progress occurs (TP VIII: 311 / 79). Self-love, not duty, is what the philosophical historian relies upon in the hopeful description of the world. This optimistic history is, Kant concludes, 'just an opinion

[*Meinung*] and mere hypothesis' – hypothesis and opinion rather than 'self-existing' theory (the moral law). So ends Kant's presentation of philosophical history.

The cynical, worldly wise observer counters that states '*will* never submit to such coercive laws' and that however attractive the words of an Abbé de St Pierre or a Rousseau may be, they are nothing more than empty ideas (TP VIII: 313 / 81). It comes as no surprise that we find Rousseau, the 'well-intentioned' optimist, referred to at the end of this chapter, which has history and hope as its centre-piece. Rousseau, it seems, is being attacked by the cynics for his vain schemes. But Kant wants to distance himself from both Rousseau and the worldly wise. Thus he says at the beginning of the last paragraph of the theory and praxis essay: '*Ich meinerseits*' – 'I for my part put my trust in the theory that proceeds from the principle of justice [*Rechtsprincip*], concerning how relations between individuals and states *ought to be*' (TP VIII: 313 / 81).

A superficial reading of these lines might lead one to the conclusion that Kant is here defending Rousseau against his worldly critics, just as he had defended Plato against similar attacks in the first *Critique*. Kant's statement belies this interpretation – he does not say that he puts his trust in Rousseau's optimism or indeed in the hope for progress that is at the heart of this chapter. He trust primarily in the *Rechtsprincip*. Rousseau and the pragmatic politician both have hypotheses about the order of things and about whether that order is wisely and justly designed by Providence – the one is hopeful, the other pessimistic. Their emphasis on the nature of things, what will be the case – both of which are beyond our power to control – is to be contrasted with the emphasis on what ought to be. And to act according to the moral law is, as Kant remarked in the first chapter, very much within our power.

Trust in the 'nature of things' (fate or Providence) can only be secondary, and Kant immediately turns from it to 'human nature,' not the self-love spoken of earlier but rather human nature viewed from the perspective of a 'higher' anthropology, as 'respect for right and duty.' To the extent that this respect is still alive in us, we are '*worthy* of love' (TP VIII: 313 / 81). Here we see the true relation between philanthropy and law that Kant promised would be shown in the conclusion. Love based on worthiness (won by the respect for the moral law), not on the hope for progress in which we are dragged along, unwillingly and unknowingly, by fate, is the only true philanthropy. The benevolence and seeming love of man that are a crucial part of philosophical history are based on theoretically implausible premises (hence mere 'hypotheses') and on a conception of man as a being pulled like a slave by his master (self-love) into a better future. As in the chapters on the moral and the political law, Kant concludes this last chapter by insisting on the primacy of right over both the cynical and the optimistic views of the world.

The accuracy of this interpretation is confirmed by our analysis of Kant's portrayal of Job and the new Kantian 'theodicy' that emerges from it (see chapter 4). It is confirmed also by the following reflections on a parallel passage from 'Perpetual Peace.' There the 'political moralist' seeks to justify Providence by claiming that the moral principle in us has never been extinguished entirely and by arguing that with 'advancing civilization reason grows pragmatically in its capacity to realize ideas of law' (PP VIII: 380 / 128). Yet it could also be said that the culpability for transgressions grows and that man 'never will or can be improved' – thus theodicy is unable to justify creation itself. Here we see once more the optimistic and cynical standpoints. But, Kant continues, we cannot 'theoretically support our philosophical concepts of the supreme power, which is inscrutable to us' (PP VIII: 380 / 128). The sense of this remark, as well as the fact that it uses the plural 'concepts' (*Begriffe*), indicates that it applies to both hypotheses about Providence. The conclusion, as in the theory and praxis essay, is that we are led 'to such dubious consequences' if we do not allow the pure 'principles of right' an objective reality.

The Copernican revolution that Kant has brought about in the philosophy of history and politics is more clearly visible now. The facts of history and politics, the violence, deceit, and injustice at their core, are 'givens,' or, in the more modern jargon, they are the incorrigible data with which we are confronted. Kant says that history is like a play, a world-drama to which we are spectators, but in which we are also necessarily actors. And some plays produce no good disposition in us; they make the heart languid or frivolous (C3 v: 271–4 / 112–15). What matters then is how we view (for practical purposes) this spectacle, this seemingly purposeless, bloody chaos – and in this we have a choice. Some acknowledge the facts, seek no consoling explanation for them, and do not resist them. The world rewards the unjust and punishes the good; therefore be unjust and reap your reward – this is their maxim. They never once raise their eyes from the dirt in front of them to the heavens above. From the spectacle of history, this audience takes away only an apology for its own misdeeds.

Then there are those who, seeing the facts, choose to interpret them, to see a moral purpose in the Author's works. They are the faithful, whose 'subjective assent' permits them to believe that, though they may expect no consolation or evidence of moral purpose in their lifetimes, nevertheless, viewing history over the generations, one can 'detect' such a purposiveness. Their morality thus remains unshaken.

The final way of viewing this play is again to allow what is indisputable, that politics and history hardly offer an appealing vista, but instead of resorting to faith, to cling to duty, to be courageous, and in so doing to recognize the sublimity of one's moral nature. Here we see the absolute autonomy of practical reason, which takes its bearings in the world not by means of a romance written about history, but by the certainty that duty speaks with a single and unqualified voice.

All three viewpoints begin with the chaos of nature and history; one bows to those horrendous facts, another supplies mentally, or believes in, a moral purpose in nature so as to support morality, and the third looks unflinchingly into the void and sees in obedience to duty the mark of man's superiority to nature.

After a long and roundabout journey, we now return to that Dutch innkeeper's sign – eternal peace painted above the image of a graveyard: the facts one might say, and an idea. Some will think that sign to be making fun of those who would be bothered to 'raise their eyes,' those impractical people who, instead of settling down to the business of making their way through an admittedly nasty world, think of impossible things. Others may find in that graveyard a path that nature has laid out for us on the way to a future that will be peaceful and in which man will be able to cultivate the talents that nature has given him. And finally, there are those who see in the words 'Perpetual Peace' an injunction, a command to act in a way consistent with being a citizen of such a state. Looking to duty does not mean that one is oblivious of the graveyard; what it means is rather that one has the courage to act as one must despite it, to lead a sublime sort of life. From seeing this void with the vision of the worldly wise statesman to seeing it with the eyes of a Plato, a distance is traversed incomparably greater than that found in the systems of the heavens. That is Kant's Copernican revolution.

# Notes

ABBREVIATIONS

CC  Karl Marx 'Contribution to the Critique of Hegel's Philosophy of Law: Introduction' in MECW III 175–87

EPM  Karl Marx *Economic and Philosophic Manuscripts of 1844* in MECW III 231–346

GI  Karl Marx and Frederick Engels *The German Ideology* in MECW V 19–539

MECW  Karl Marx and Frederick Engels *Collected Works* (New York: International Publishers, 1975–  )

TF  Karl Marx 'Theses on Feuerbach' in MECW V 3–8

TLP  Ludwig Wittgenstein *Tractatus Logico-Philosophicus* trans D.F. Pears and B.F. McGuinness (London: Routledge and Kegal Paul, 1978)

PREFACE

1  G.W.F. Hegel *The Philosophy of History* trans J. Sibree (New York: Dover Publications, 1956) 389–94, 408–11
2  Ibid, 411
3  Cf Karl Marx and Frederick Engels GI in MECW V 51–2
4  Cf Karl Marx *On the Jewish Question* in MECW III 152, 154–5
5  Alexis de Tocqueville *Democracy in America* trans George Lawrence (Garden City, NY: Doubleday Anchor, 1969) 432
6  Ernest Gellner *The Legitimation of Belief* (Cambridge: Cambridge University Press, 1974) 188
7  Compare, for example, Kant's and Marx's treatment of colonialism: in Kant PP VIII: 358–60 / 103–5, and Karl Marx 'The British Rule in India' in

Robert C. Tucker ed. *The Marx-Engels Reader* (New York: W.W. Norton and Company, 1978) 657–8.

8 Marx GI 193. Compare this to Arendt's account of Kant and Marx in Hannah Arendt *Lectures on Kant's Political Philosophy* R. Beiner ed. (Chicago: University of Chicago Press, 1982) 36. This book, which was published after the completion of my manuscript, touches on a number of points that will be of interest to the reader of the present work. I have sought to include those points in the notes.

9 Heinrich Heine *Religion und Philosophie in Deutschland* in *Heinrich Heines Sämtliche Werke* (Leipzig: Insel Verlag, 1910) II 309

10 Dieter Henrich *Identität und Objectivität* (Heidelberg: Universitätsverlag, 1976) 9–10

CHAPTER ONE: THE LIMITS OF KNOWLEDGE

1 Martin Heidegger *Vier Seminare* (Frankfurt: Vittorio Klostermann, 1977) 67

2 Ludwig Wittgenstein TLP Proposition No. 5.641. (Wittgenstein's book consists of a series of numbered propositions, and those numbers, rather than pages, are cited in the references to his TLP.)

3 Ibid, No. 5.641

4 See also P.F. Strawson *The Bounds of Sense* (London: Methuen 1975) 94, Dieter Henrich *Identität und Objectivität* (Heidelberg: Universitätsverlag, 1976) 59, 72.

5 See Strawson *Bounds* 93–4.

6 Wittgenstein TLP No. 5.6

7 Ibid, No. 1

8 I am indebted to Susan M. Shell for drawing this phrase of Kant's to my attention.

CHAPTER TWO: THE MORAL IMPLICATIONS

1 Wittgenstein TLP No. 4

2 Ibid, Nos. 6.41, 6.42, 6.52, 7

3 Ludwig Wittgenstein *Tagebücher, 1914–1916* in L. Wittgenstein *Schriften 1* (Frankfurt am Main: Suhrkamp Verlag, 1969) 142; see also TLP No. 6.45.

4 Aristotle *Metaphysics* trans Richard Hope (Ann Arbor: University of Michigan Press, 1975) 982B. Page numbers refer to the standard marginal pagination.

5 It is with pleasure that I note Yirmiahu Yovel's reference to this parallel between Kant's 'needs of reason' and Platonic eros in his book *Kant and the Philosophy of History* (Princeton: Princeton University Press, 1980). Professor Yovel and I, as will become clear, disagree deeply about the status and meaning of Kant's philosophy of history.

6 Wittgenstein TLP No. 6.41

7 See also Strawson *Bounds* 188ff; Jonathan Bennett *Kant's Analytic* (Cambridge: Cambridge University Press, 1966) 59–60; and George Schrader 'The Thing in Itself in Kantian Philosophy' in R.P. Wolff ed *Kant: A Collection of Critical Essays* (Notre Dame: University of Notre Dame Press, 1967) 173–4.

8 See Jonathan Bennett *Kant's Dialectic* (Cambridge: Cambridge University Press, 1974) 184–5

9 Aristotle *Metaphysics* 994A10–20, 994B20–30, and see L.W. Beck *A Commentary on Kant's Critique of Practical Reason* (Chicago: University of Chicago Press, 1960) 184.

10 Sadik J. Al-Azm *The Origins of Kant's Arguments in the Antinomies* (Oxford: Clarendon Press, 1972) 87, 94–5

CHAPTER THREE: THE NEEDS OF REASON

1 There is an extensive literature on this and related themes, much of it centred around varying interpretations of the second Analogy. Some of the more interesting studies are Gerd Buchdahl *Metaphysics and the Philosophy of Science* (Oxford: Basil Blackwell, 1969) 649–65, and 'Causality, Causal Laws and Scientific Theory in the Philosophy of Kant' in *The British Journal for the Philosophy of Science* XVI (May 1965–February 1966) 187–208; L.W. Beck 'Six Short Pieces on the Second Analogy of Experience' in L.W. Beck *Essays on Kant and Hume* (New Haven: Yale University Press, 1978) 130–64.

2 Wittgenstein TLP No. 6.341

3 To see this point clearly, consider Kant's distinction between pure and applied logic. Pure logic treats only of the universal rules of thought, quite apart from the limitations or circumstances under which they may be applied – the latter being the concern of applied logic. This distinction, Kant writes, parallels that between 'pure morals' and the 'doctrine of virtue' (*Tugendlehre*) (C1 A54–5 / B78–9). Pure moral theory sets out the notion of a law as it bears on free human actions – that is, it analyses the idea of autonomy. The 'doctrine of virtue' discusses the 'matter,' the ends of practical reason (DV VI: 380 / 38). Kant's various 'universalization' formu-

lae are so many attempts to show what principal features a judgment must have if it is to be law-like. And just as the fundamental laws of nature (the categories) are 'empty' if they are not combined with intuitions, so too a full account of moral action requires more than a theory of law – it needs a doctrine of virtue, a practical anthropology.

4 Aristotle *Nicomachean Ethics* trans H. Rackham (Cambridge, Mass: Loeb Classical Library, Harvard University Press, 1975) 1095B30–1096A5. (Page numbers refer to the standard marginal pagination.)

5 Karl Vorländer *Immanuel Kant. Der Mann und das Werk* II (Leipzig: Felix Meiner Verlag, 1924) 325

CHAPTER FOUR: THE ORIGINS OF KANT'S PHILOSOPHY OF HISTORY

1 Karl Marx EPM in MECW III 176. See also Marx GI 31–2.
2 Karl Marx *Das Kapital* I (Berlin: Dietz Verlag, 1968) 193
3 Karl Marx CC in MECW III 175
4 Ibid, 176, emphasis added
5 Marx GI 30
6 Ibid, 30
7 Marx CC 181
8 Karl Marx TF in MECW V 7
9 Ibid, 8
10 Marx CC 182
11 Wittgenstein TLP No. 6.54
12 Ibid, No. 7
13 Marx GI 50
14 Karl Marx *The Leading Article in No. 179 of the Kölnische Zeitung* in MECW I 201
15 For different interpretations of the relation between Kant and Marx see, for example, Lucien Goldmann *Immanuel Kant* (London: New Left Books, 1971) 206, 218ff; William Galston *Kant and the Problem of History* (Chicago: University of Chicago Press, 1975) 5, 26–7; Yirmiahu Yovel *Kant and the Philosophy of History* (Princeton: Princeton University Press, 1980) 32, 237, and, on related issues, 273 (humanizing nature), 23 note, 131 note, 133 (alienation), and 143, 194 (man as producer of his own history).
16 Marx GI 193–5
17 For a valuable discussion of 'practical objectivity' see Susan M. Shell *The Rights of Reason: A Study of Kant's Philosophy and Politics* (Toronto: University of Toronto Press, 1980) 70–1.

18 See also ibid, 84–5.
19 See Goldmann *Kant* 199.

CHAPTER FIVE: NATURE: THE SUBLIME AND THE BEAUTIFUL

1 For an interesting commentary on Kant's aesthetics and on his notion of aesthetic 'disinterest' see Martin Heidegger *Nietzsche* I, trans David F. Krell (New York: Harper and Row, 1979) 107–14.

CHAPTER SIX: PHILOSOPHICAL HISTORY AND THE BEAUTIFUL

1 Jean-Jacques Rousseau *Emile or On Education* trans Allan Bloom (New York: Basic Books, 1979) 278
2 The decision to ignore the question is perhaps the single weakest point in Fritz Medicus's article 'Kants Philosophie der Geschichte' (*Kant-Studien* VII (1902) 1–23, 179–229. Medicus's lack of interest in this question leads him to see contradictions where there are none, and ultimately to advance dubious biographical explanations for the inconsistencies he claims to have found in Kant's historical essays.
3 Alexis de Tocqueville *Democracy in America* trans George Lawrence (Garden City, NY: Doubleday Anchor, 1969) 496
4. For a different interpretation of tutelage and history, see George A. Kelly *Idealism, Politics and History* (Cambridge: Cambridge University Press, 1969) 170ff.
5 Compare to William Galston *Kant and the Problem of History* (Chicago: University of Chicago Press, 1975) 68–9.
6 See Kant's handwritten fragments in 'Ein Reinschriftfragment zu Kants "Streit der Fakultäten",' *Kant-Studien* LI (1959–60) 2–13. 'Why does the French Revolution find such nearly universal approval among those who suffer no injury because of it – [approval] approaching enthusiasm' (p. 10). 'The most dangerous of all experiments is the violent altering or rather overthrow of a state's constitution. Thus a person with a conscience would not want to assume responsibility for the evils which arise out of revolution' (p. 4).
7 Compare this account of spectators and the French Revolution to Hannah Arendt *Lectures on Kant's Political Philosophy* R. Beiner ed (Chicago: University of Chicago Press, 1982) 46, 48, 52–4, 55–6, 65. And also see L.W. Beck 'Kant and the Right of Revolution' in L.W. Beck *Essays on Kant and Hume* (New Haven: Yale University Press, 1978) 181–3; Galston *Kant and the Problem of History* 29.

8 For competing interpretations of Kant's philosophy of history see: Yirmiahu Yovel *Kant and the Philosophy of History* (Chicago: University of Chicago Press, 1980) 222, 292 (Kant as a utopian thinker); Susan M. Shell *The Rights of Reason: A Study of Kant's Philosophy and Politics* (Toronto: University of Toronto Press, 1980) 59–60, 94; Kelly *Idealism* 149ff, 177–8; and Emil L. Fackenheim 'Kant's Concept of History' in *Kant-Studien* XLVIII (1957) 381–98.

CHAPTER SEVEN: JUSTICE AND THE SUBLIME

1 Plato *The Republic* trans Allan Bloom (New York: Basic Books, 1968) 368d–e (Page numbers refer to the marginal pagination.)
2 Ibid, 592b
3 J.-J. Rousseau *Discourse on the Origin and Foundation of Inequality among Men* in J.-J. Rousseau *The First and Second Discourses* ed R.D. Masters and trans R.D. and J.R. Masters (New York: St Martin's Press, 1964) 91, 93
4 Thomas Hobbes *Leviathan* ed Michael Oakeshott (Oxford: Basil Blackwell, n.d.) 6
5 Rousseau *Discourse on the Origin and Foundation ...* 101
6 J.-J. Rousseau *Geneva Manuscript* in J.-J. Rousseau *On the Social Contract* ed R.D. Masters and trans J.R. Masters (New York: St Martin's Press, 1978) 180
7 Cf G.W.F. Hegel *The Philosophy of Right* trans T.M. Knox (Oxford: Oxford University Press, 1945) 33.
8 Hobbes *Leviathan* 109
9 Ibid, 27, 136–7
10 Ibid, 6, 80–1
11 Michael Oakeshott, 'Introduction' to ibid, xxx
12 Ibid, 57
13 For a different account of the relation between Kant and Hobbes, see Susan M. Shell, *The Rights of Reason: A Study of Kant's Philosophy and Politics* (Toronto: University of Toronto Press, 1980) 153, 155–6.
14 Compare the critique of the 'aesthetic' spectator with Hannah Arendt *Lectures on Kant's Political Philosophy* R. Beiner ed (Chicago: University of Chicago Press, 1982) 55–6 (and Beiner's interpretative essay in the same volume, 123–4, 127).

CHAPTER EIGHT: KANT ON THEORY AND PRAXIS

1 Aristotle *Nicomachean Ethics* trans H. Rackham (Cambridge, Mass: Loeb Classical Library, Harvard University Press, 1975) 1094a
2 Compare to Hannah Arendt *Lectures on Kant's Political Philosophy* R. Beiner ed (Chicago: University of Chicago Press, 1982) 26ff.

# Index